TIME AND THE FIELD

TIME AND THE FIELD

Edited by

Steffen Dalsgaard and Morten Nielsen

berghahn
NEW YORK · OXFORD
www.berghahnbooks.com

First published in 2016 by

Berghahn Books

www.berghahnbooks.com

© 2016 Berghahn Books

Originally published as a special issue of *Social Analysis*, volume 57, issue 1.

Library of Congress Cataloging-in-Publication Data

Names: Dalsgaard, Steffen, editor. | Nielsen, Morten, 1971– editor.
Title: Time and the field / edited by Steffen Dalsgaard and Morten Nielsen.
Description: New York : Berghahn Books, [2015] | Includes index.
Identifiers: LCCN 2015027690| ISBN 9781785330872 (pbk. : acid-free paper) |
    ISBN 9781785330889 (ebook)
Subjects: LCSH: Ethnology—Fieldwork. | Ethnology—Research—Methodology.
Classification: LCC GN346 .T55 2015 | DDC 305.80072/3—dc23
LC record available at http://lccn.loc.gov/2015027690

British Library Cataloguing in Publication Data

A catalogue record for this book is available from the British Library.

ISBN 978-1-78533-087-2 (paperback)
ISBN 978-1-78533-088-9 (ebook)

CONTENTS

INTRODUCTION
Time and the Field

Steffen Dalsgaard and Morten Nielsen

The increasing global flows of persons, things, and ideas continue to pose peculiar methodological problems for social scientists doing ethnographic fieldwork. According to several recent studies on the status of ethnographic methodology, the conditions of fieldwork and, implicitly, the constitution of the field itself have been radically transformed by emerging global assemblages that consistently resist being pinned down by spatial scales, such as global-local, urban-rural, center-periphery (Ong and Collier 2005). This transformation is influenced by the emergence of new technologies and intensified processes of exchange and communication that frequently work as a compression of time and space (Harvey 1989) or, conversely, entail their disembedding (Giddens 1990). The gradual expansion of the anthropological discipline has furthermore led to the inclusion of a larger variety of fields (e.g., bureaucratic workplaces, transnational

Notes for this section begin on page 15.

organizations, media-driven networks, diasporas, etc.), which may be constituted by spatio-temporal demarcations differing from those of the small-scale communities (stereo-)typically studied by anthropologists of yore. Faced with the challenge of aligning methodological and analytical perspectives to these shifting milieus, anthropologists have experimented with novel ways of addressing the ethnographic field and its context, for example, as global 'scapes' (Appadurai 1990); through the use of 'multi-sited' fieldwork (Marcus 1995); and by critically examining the particular location of the fieldworker and his or her relationship to the field (Gupta and Ferguson 1997b). Still, whereas the effects of global processes have been documented by privileging spatial changes and consequently discussing fieldwork as a spatialized practice (e.g., by mapping associations between sites that are locatable, both physically and ideationally), there is a need to understand as well the temporal aspects of these processes. Based on the hypothesis that 'the field' might be understood not solely as a spatial concept but equally as a temporal one, the goal of this volume is to explore how particular 'sites' contain and actualize different social times and temporalities while also reflecting on the methodological and analytical perspectives by which they can be approached.

Seeing discrete areas of social life as amalgamations of temporal directions, time-scales, and time-cycles indicates that there might be both analytical and methodological purchase to exploring fields as temporal phenomena. The instantaneous contacts and re-entries to the field made possible through modern media make it apparent that the separation of 'field' and 'home' is being challenged, not just as a spatial configuration, but, equally important, as a temporal one. The new technologies of communication and travel have enforced a form of 'coevalness' (cf. Fabian 1983) onto the relationship between anthropology and the Other, which, on the one hand, gives access to a wider range of knowledge formations and fields, but, on the other, also potentially generates a sense of discomfort because the field is ever-present. For example, the anthropologist can receive text messages from informants now covered by mobile phone networks, while the Internet enables the anthropologist to befriend informants on Facebook, follow them on Twitter, or exchange material with them on YouTube—even as a direct part of the fieldwork process, where researcher and informant engage in reciprocal transactions of granting access to each other's social worlds (see Boellstorff 2008; Wulff 2002).

Considering that fieldwork is fundamentally about identifying spaces *and* times, which will enable the ethnographer to explore in detail the initially posed research questions, it is striking that so little has been written about the field as a temporally defined phenomenon. Our aim is therefore twofold. Firstly, building on a critical examination of recent (postmodern) critiques of fieldwork practice, we wish to explore the temporal properties of the field (understood as both an analytical and ethnographic concept). Secondly, if, as we argue, there is a lack of research on the temporal aspects of what constitutes the field, we need to clarify in greater detail how discrete temporalities can be studied and represented via ethnographic accounts (James and Mills 2005: 1). What scales of comparison may be employed to identify the production of time in various socio-cultural environments? And how do we account for the qualities ascribed to different dimensions of time—its rhythms, durations, episodes, and temporal ruptures? Serendipity, for instance, heralded as a key ingredient in the encounter with the Other, entails the surprise resulting from the breakdown of anticipation and the change of what one had thought to be 'one site'. In the moment of such surprise discovery, otherwise clear-cut distinctions between temporal and spatial dimensions of the field are momentarily dissolved as new insights make hitherto detached elements come together, often in paradoxical or even counterintuitive assemblages of, say, ideas, occurrences, and things. Our argument is consequently that central aspects of doing fieldwork are better accounted for by taking the field to be a processual configuration through which time and space continuously interweave to chart out new analytical terrains.

The Idealized Time of the Field

According to the well-rehearsed Malinowskian canon, fieldwork is a period in a sequence of doing research where the ethnographer is spatially separated from home. Ideally, it is done after formulating a research problem and prior to 'writing up' data in a coherent textual representation (Gupta and Ferguson 1997a: 12). And, as has consistently been emphasized, it takes a lot of time. Since the birth of the discipline, the length of the fieldwork period has constituted a central albeit much contested factor for determining the quality of collected ethnographic data. More than four decades ago, Paul Radin ([1933] 1966: 178–179; see also Gupta and Ferguson 1997a: 45) criticized Margaret Mead for claiming deep cultural understanding based on less than one year spent in the field. Even five years, Radin thought, could give only superficial knowledge. Today, this notion of knowledge based on extensive fieldwork is almost impossible to achieve unless one is an indigenous or 'native' anthropologist having lived a lifetime as a cultural 'insider'. To be sure, long-term and longitudinal qualitative studies that include extensive periods spent in the field were (and still are) regarded as strongly promoting the fieldworker's chances of serendipitous findings or surprises, which will supposedly destabilize the researcher's prior understandings and generate new insights.

Recently, the debate on the appropriate length of fieldwork has also focused on the relationship between ethnographic knowledge production and the increasing number of 'outside' constraints that significantly affect the collection of data. Firstly, research time might be severely constricted due to funding constraints and fewer funding agencies, demands on degree programs and the gradual limitation on students' final fieldwork before writing up their dissertations, increasing pressure to identify 'relevant' (read 'practically useful') data, and growing bureaucratic obligations to account for one's research time (Marcus and Okely 2007). Secondly, anthropologists often find themselves challenged by the time it takes to gather sufficient data to formulate ethnographically valid arguments. In a nutshell, the length of fieldwork appears to be a paradox arising from the tension between demands for the 'timely' relevance of an ethnographically informed anthropological analysis and the necessary 'slowness' and 'belatedness' of its creation (e.g., Rabinow et al. 2008; see also Marcus, this volume).

Still, rather than automatically discounting someone for not having endured a prolonged period of ongoing fieldwork and thus not living up to the tacit standard of the discipline, should we not assess the person's data in relation to the problem that he or she set out to answer (Faubion 2009: 163)? Radin's demand for protracted immersion and a lifetime of study is admirable, but it stipulates a number of requirements that may be impossible to align with the practicalities of fieldwork. Firstly, Radin knew very well that the ideal of a holistic study in itself is problematic. Even if given an infinite amount of time, it is less than likely that all significant data will be collected, let alone perceived as such. Secondly, and this is the cue that we want to pursue, the demand for lifelong immersion only superficially takes into account the discrete temporalities that constitute and are constituted by fieldwork. To take a few examples, analytical insights tend to erupt through a continuous oscillation between (temporal as much as physical) approximation to and distance from one's informants and research sites, so periodic absence from the field is logically as necessary as one's presence (see Whyte, this volume). Conversely, in contrast to Radin's days, when the field was generally a faraway place that was difficult to reach, it is today possible to be continuously in contact with one's informants and thus never to leave entirely (see Wulff 2002). The pressure to deliver 'on time' is not a new thing to researchers. As demonstrated by several of the chapters in this collection (e.g., those by Otto, Sjørslev, and Whyte), negotiating time schedules and lengths of stay as part of one's fieldwork planning is equally crucial to finding out where to go. In addition, not just the possibilities of fieldwork, but also the relationships that define it, change as time passes (see Foster et al. 1979; Howell and Talle 2011; Kemper and Royce 2002).

If ethnographic fieldwork constitutes a recursive temporal oscillation between different sites that are spatial but also inherently conceptual (*pace* Strathern 1990; see also Holbraad 2008), a corollary must be that the field contains similar conceptual properties. What constitutes the field emerges in and through the immediate moments of surprise discovery, when otherwise detached elements come together in discrete assemblages of concepts, persons, things, and sites that seem to chart a relatively coherent configuration through their confluences. Although recent elaborations of the field do take seriously the need to pursue the scales of differentiation of one's interlocutors (cf. Marcus 2006: 115; see also Candea 2007), such endeavors might end up merely as bounding spatial sites rather than considering temporal properties. Paradoxically, the reliance upon spatial tropes in the distantiation of multi-sited ethnographies from the earlier holistic ideals potentially seems to have licensed these as 'thin' rather than 'thick' descriptions, because more sites have had to be fitted into the same conceptual frame (see Hage 2005; Marcus 2006).

Spatial Tropes …

Not least as a methodological after-effect of the 'writing culture' debate in the 1980s, several works have critically examined and elaborated upon the conceptual tropes buttressing the field (Candea 2007; Clifford 1997; Coleman and Collins 2006; Gupta and Ferguson 1997b; Olwig and Hastrup 1997), but it remains that the field has generally been discussed as a spatial configuration, and doing fieldwork has been addressed as a question of choosing between going 'there' or staying 'at home' (Clifford 1997). Consequently, the field is 'somewhere'—a location, a site, a place, or a space where the ethnographer is situated physically.

In the introduction to their edited volume *Anthropological Locations*, Akhil Gupta and James Ferguson (1997a: 2; emphasis added) ask: "But what of 'the field' itself, the *place* where the distinctive work of 'fieldwork' may be done, that taken-for-granted *space* in which an 'Other' culture or society lies waiting to be observed and written? This mysterious space—not the 'what' of anthropology but the *'where'*—has been left to common sense." Gupta and Ferguson express doubts about traditional ethnographic methods and concepts and whether they can address the problems of a constantly shifting globalized and post-colonial world with mobile populations. Considering that the field is closer, with people increasingly able to be interconnected and globalized, Gupta and Ferguson ask about the ways that conceptualizations and ideas of fieldwork and ethnographic methods can be adapted to this interrelatedness (ibid.: 4). Some fields (the exotic and faraway) have long enjoyed a privileged recognition because of their spatial distance to the researcher's (frequently) Euro-American location; however, fieldwork practices and methodologies with less emphasis on distance have more recently gained ground. While distance is no longer (and should no longer be) a prerequisite for doing 'good ethnography', Gupta and Ferguson emphasize that location is still crucial (ibid.: 5). They want to rethink fieldwork praxis accordingly by shifting focus from spatial sites and localities to 'political locations'. What constitutes a field location will depend on the overall objective of one's research and the subsequent political practice and engagement. From Gupta and Ferguson's perspective, then, the field emerges through the 'situated interventions' made necessary by the particular project. Rather than a bounded place with a distinct 'culture', it therefore needs to be understood as a series of shifting (spatial) locations (ibid.: 35, 38). By thus focusing on the interconnections between inherently heterogeneous sites, Gupta and Ferguson have moved toward a deeper understanding of the composite character of social phenomena, while also calling for new methodological approaches to parallel these insights. Strikingly, though, while they acknowledge the importance of time in the structuration of fieldwork practices, they fail to move beyond the primacy of spatiality, evidenced by the predominant usage of space-oriented tropes, such as locations, and by an emphasis on 'somewhere' rather than 'sometime' (ibid.: 35).

In recent years, one of the most significant contributions to the discussion of the field and fieldwork in a globalized environment is the notion of 'multi-sited ethnography' as proposed by George Marcus. Similar to Gupta and Ferguson, Marcus (1995: 95) argues that ethnographic research is moving away "from its conventional single-site location, contextualized by macro-constructions of a larger social order ... to multiple sites of observation and participation that cross-cut dichotomies such as the 'local' and the 'global', the 'lifeworld' and the 'system.'" This shift has been necessitated by the dissolution and fragmentation of the world system, which is paralleled by the emergence of new forms of socio-economic power (ibid.: 98). According to Marcus, ethnography may identify these interweaving and mutually contingent processes by following strategically selected entities (ideas, metaphors, persons, objects, stories, biographies) across multiple settings and thereby outline a unique multi-sited system, which simultaneously operates as 'figure' and 'ground'.

We nevertheless argue that the spatiality of a field remains dominant when associations are made only between analytically separate settings that are exterior to each other. Although a unique social configuration may be discerned by connecting discontinuous sites and settings, this says little about their potential temporal interlinkages, such as when a temporal site also contains traces of other temporalities.[1] Indeed, as argued by Marilyn Strathern (1999: 163), multi-sited ethnography "may reveal the contingency of what began as initial identity—the tracing both defines and queries the chain of associations." It is consequently by emphasizing a spatial connectivity that a multi-sited approach may come to predetermine what is held together through the different sites. In contrast, Strathern reasons that "what the locations ... have in common has not necessarily happened yet" (ibid.). As demonstrated by Pedersen and Nielsen's contribution to this volume, what is shared by an assemblage of sites may be a reserve of potentialities that have not yet been realized as aims or intentionalities. By focusing on a momentary 'hunch' about what was at stake in a given situation during a field trip, Pedersen and Nielsen examine how different moments and analytical ideas interlink without the ethnographer knowing exactly what those connections might be. What stitched past, present, and future together in that particular situation was nothing other than the almost imperceptible sensation that something significant was taking place. Hence, the advantages of multi-sited ethnography notwithstanding, unstable associations between potentialities in the present and their (possible) future realizations, such as those crystallized through a momentary hunch, remain analytically invisible unless attention is given to the temporal oscillations and modulations constituting the field. What is suggested by Strathern and elaborated upon in several of the contributions to this book is that the sum of information that is produced by connecting different sites, things, and ideas cannot be understood merely as a quantifiable aggregation of entities. The kinds of connectivities that might not 'have happened yet', such as hunches or surprise discoveries, assert their effects by charting momentary conceptual and spatial grounds upon which to figure ethnographic analyses.

In contrast to dominant spatial conceptualizations in anthropology—such as those suggested by multi-sited ethnography, where social life seems to be played out in and through a network of identifiable sites—we suggest that the field, as a confluence of different times and temporalities, emerges rather as a dynamic force of becoming that shifts in intensity and clarity, depending on the ethnographer's immediate position and immersion. An exemplar of multi-sited research often referred to by Marcus (2006; see also this volume) is Kim Fortun's (2001) study of the long aftermath of disasters in Bhopal. Interestingly, although Fortun explicitly attempts to break with the single-site location, the ethnography requires a constant reference to the singular moment of the disaster invoked by informants as a constant 'presence' through its effects. Although not locatable as a single spatial entity, the Bhopal disaster clearly operates as a dominant temporal site that orientates both informants and ethnographer.

... and Ethnographic Temporalities

Despite the lack of anthropological attention to the temporal aspects of delimiting the field, time has been an important aspect of a wide range of anthropological studies, from the Manchester School's specific focus on process and transformation (Gluckman [1940] 1958; Mitchell 1956; Turner 1957) to the praxis studies a few decades later (Bourdieu 1977; de Certeau 1984) and the more recent historical emphasis on traditions and historicity (Hirsch and Stewart 2005; Hobsbawm and Ranger 1983; Keesing and Tonkinson 1982; Otto and Pedersen 2005). In this regard, it is worth considering the recognition of the temporal contextualization of the Other (e.g., Fabian 1983). To take but one example, the gradual move from a structuralist approach toward increased attention to praxis and change is accompanied by a general recognition of the temporal dimensions of social life. Based on the latter perspective, any social configuration emerges from a series of overlapping, reciprocal exchanges and encounters and from associations of varying durability. These erupt and appear both over and in time, and whether they are delineated as objects of study or as 'context' (i.e., as figure or ground), such processes and connections are intimately related to people's orientations toward pasts or futures, for instance, as inscribed in ideologies of modernism or traditionalism (Otto, this volume), or when felt as hope or despair (A. Dalsgaard and Frederiksen, this volume).

A series of important contributions has documented the emergence of subjective temporal understandings from agents' positioned practices (Bourdieu 2000; Jackson 2002), ritual and cosmological times (Evans-Pritchard 1940; Geertz 1973; Robbins 2007), space and time (Corsín Jiménez 2003; Gell 1992; Ingold 2000; Munn 1986), the relation between crisis and temporal uprootedness (Game 1997; Vigh 2007), personhood as temporal compositions (Maurer and Schwab 2006), and the close linkages between materiality or technology and perceptions of time (Gell 1998; Küchler 2002). Furthermore, recent ethnographic studies have explored the particular ways that the future is envisioned and enacted upon, for example, in relation to economics (Guyer 2007; Maurer 2002), as imagined 'hinterlands' (Crapanzano 2004), or as perspectives from which to imagine the present (Miyazaki 2004; Nielsen 2008, 2011, 2014; Pedersen 2012). Finally, since the heyday of the Manchester School, the study of social situations and events has maintained a prominent status within anthropology (Burawoy 1998; Evens and Handelman 2006; see also Sahlins 1991; Strathern 1990). The particular study of events can even be seen in recent works that seek to question a one-sided emphasis on time as linearity (Das 2007; Hodges 2008). In these instances, it is by delimiting the fieldwork setting that a time of the study is established. Analytically, the detailed analysis of situations and events invariably delimits epochs, periods, durations, and their temporal extensions toward pasts and futures (cf. Gupta and Ferguson 1997a: 2).

In sum, whereas a shift toward increasing analytical attention toward time can be discerned, its relation to the field has generally been absent in anthropological debates until recently. What is at stake, then, is a need to acknowledge the temporal properties of the field, both in relation to concrete ethnographic work and as anthropological representation.

Beyond the Spatial Trope

As Bruce Kapferer (2006: 125) tells us, ethnographic research is based on actual social interactions, encounters, situations, and events that "are effectively moments of social life in the very process of formation." Stretched out between what was and that which will be, these moments (or 'temporal sites', in our terms) include surprise discoveries and hunches as mentioned above, which enable the ethnographer to engage with wider realities and thereby chart viable analytical terrains.[2] In a similar vein, many of the contributions in this collection (S. Dalsgaard, Lutz, Pedersen and Nielsen, Sjørslev) make clear that irrespective of the parameters with which we choose to delimit a given field, it has fundamental temporal properties that need to be examined *ipso facto* and not only by reference to a spatial trope. Identifying a set of temporal properties is, firstly, a matter of simply 'being present' for whatever period is necessary in order to establish a dynamic and mutually conditioned relationship between the questions we ask of our material and the concrete ethnographic circumstances of their problematization. Secondly, and this follows from the first point, it is equally a matter of identifying the precise juncture at which new insights are constructed from the relationship between research questions and ethnographic data. According to Strathern (1999: 6), such a juncture may fruitfully be understood as an "ethnographic moment" where the already known is transcended by establishing new associations between "the understood (what is analysed at the moment of observation)" and "the need to understand (what is observed at the moment of analysis)." What is emphasized, however, is the volatility of the relationship established between question and answer. As Strathern (1991: xxii) argues: "[I]nsofar as an answer generates new material or insights, then it necessarily draws on knowledge not available to the questioner ... This excess may well generate new questions that make the old ones uninteresting ... Each question in conjuncture with its answer, or each position from which a new position is created, in turn becomes a position that one leaves behind."

As more and more information is gathered, research questions invariably undergo a process of analytical displacement. It is therefore the researcher's immersion in an ethnographic field that comes to destabilize the premises that initially anchored the study. What is particularly interesting in relation to the present discussion, then, is the fact that the parameters that define the field undergo gradual transformations. Different aspects (both temporal and spatial) become relevant as more is learned about social life in a local environment.

Particular social configurations might assert themselves in radically new ways, for example, by shifting the analytic scale from economics to aesthetics and thereby also changing its analytically defined properties. In other words, if differentiation and change are integral to the field, the concept invariably loses its spatial anchorage. Here we might recall how multi-sited fields in Marcus's (1995) outline emerge by tracing a social phenomenon that traverses a number of connected sites or locations. Taking into account the internal differentiations of individual sites, it becomes untenable to maintain the notion of the field as resting on a spatial trope, that is, on the idea that lines can be drawn between locatable sites. Simply put, not only the object of study but also that which we take to constitute a site might already be in the process of transformation, and thus it is problematic (if not impossible) to trace associations between sites that supposedly display similar properties.

In order to appreciate analytically the internal differentiations of discrete sites, we consequently need to bracket the proclivity to consider the field as a spatial configuration and instead explore the analytical potentials of conjoining time and field in a conceptual assemblage. What emerges is a glimpse of the ways in which different moments co-exist, stretch out, and allow for indeterminate series of becomings (Grosz 1999: 25). Indeed, if that which is shared by different sites has not yet come into existence (Strathern 1999: 163), unrealized (but potential) futures co-exist with other times within the present (Nielsen 2011). What constitutes a temporal field, then, might be a particular rhythmic modulation within and across different sites and times, that is, a particular way in which the various sites change through their interconnections. In this collection, some of the contributions show how orientations in time (Otto), experiences such as waiting (Sjørslev, S. Dalsgaard, Lutz), or anticipatory hunches that connect emic and etic domains (Pedersen and Nielsen) open to the researcher fields that exist purely as oscillations between pasts, presences, and unknown futures.

Surely, if a temporal field comes together as an effect of how various sites differentiate, we need to reconsider the presence of the ethnographer in the field. According to Marcus (1995: 99), multi-sited ethnography acquires its analytical strength from the researcher's extended immersion in particular sites. We wish to suggest, however, that if individual sites can be considered also as temporal nodal points, it becomes problematic to privilege the spatial dwelling in a limited set of (physical) places, whose visibility derives from traversing phenomena, for example, when the ethnographer is following ideas, persons, or things. Borrowing a well-known Heideggerian concept, we might define this kind of ethnographic presence as 'temporal dwelling'. In "Building, Dwelling, Thinking," Heidegger (1971) describes 'dwelling' as a process of creating a meaningful environment through concrete, practical 'doings'. As a temporal concept, we take dwelling to constitute the ways in which past, present, and future are stitched together by the researcher to constitute a volatile durational assemblage composed by converging times. As such, the ethnographic present constituted by the interaction or encounter between fieldworker and field/informant becomes an "interstitial zone of time/space" (Handelman 2006: 106) from which the temporal field gradually emerges as a result of the fieldworker's attachment to other times and places. In a sense, temporal dwelling suggests a more flexible association with the field whereby the ethnographer is equally positioned in those futures and pasts, which have never been and might never be actualized, while still asserting some kind of effect in the present. Furthermore, it acknowledges that getting things wrong is part of the analytical endeavor. As most anthropologists know, a hunch is not always a prelude to a surprise discovery. Sometimes it is simply an irrelevant sensation caused by the ethnographer's inability to connect the temporal dots.

Temporalizing the Field

In his article "Reflections on Hope as a Category of Social and Psychological Analysis," Vincent Crapanzano (2003) discusses the pitfalls of assuming that different temporalities can be described through an inherently transparent vocabulary. "Can we assume that the structures of time … are universal?" he asks (ibid.: 11). Crapanzano continues to argue that rather than conceiving of time as a "smooth flowing continuum" (ibid.), that is, as the objective and unchanging ground, we need to grasp how different temporalities are produced and expressed both ethnographically and analytically in multiple and often contradictory ways.

Crapanzano's description of the inherent complexities of studying diverse temporalities may be taken as an apt starting point for the final synthesis of our discussion. If we follow his distinction between a social-cum-ontological production of time and an analytical-cum-methodological vocabulary through which the former emerges as a distinct object of study, the contributions to this volume are occupied precisely with exploring the interrelations between the two.[3] In particular, they emphasize a need to treat discrete temporalities recursively, that is, to allow temporal imaginaries to condition the analytical framework rather than vice versa. Instead of representing time as an implicit ground upon which other components figure, primary attention is given to the operations of time in the constitution of social life.[4] As such, several of the contributors (S. Dalsgaard, Sjørslev, Pedersen and Nielsen) show that different fields contain social perspectives as moments in time that can merge temporalities and thus equally erupt from time.

As stated above, based on the contributions, our hypothesis has been that the field may effectively be taken to constitute an emergent agglomeration of temporal sites, and it is in this (recursive) albeit perhaps counter-intuitive understanding that the notion is considered to be particularly pertinent. What might the implications be, then, for an anthropological approach to time and the field that (recursively) takes seriously the insights from the ethnographic accounts in this collection? First, time needs to be understood in relation to particular activities (cf. Gell 1992: 212). As William James (1909: 232) told us more than a century ago, time "comes in drops," and it is this emergent quality that more than anything characterizes its dynamics. Thus, functioning not merely as a 'smooth flowing continuum', time may be "braided" (Grosz 1999: 17) or "folded" (Latour 2005: 201) in numerous different ways. In a nutshell, we may argue that time is the principle of movement and change whose modus operandi is succession. Second, by opening space to time (*pace* Corsín Jiménez 2003), it becomes impossible to privilege either one as a priori stable ground upon which to explore social processes, since space and time are each other's ontological condition (cf. Massey 1992). The paradoxical joining of time and field in a conceptual assemblage thus guides our attention toward the diverse ways that sites and times may come together without attaining the fixity and/ or directionality that is often ascribed to each individually. A temporal field emerges, we argue, precisely by identifying certain sites, which derive their spatial (i.e., locatable) properties by actualizing particular temporalities across different settings—and not only through sequencing built on simultaneous spatial convergences (ibid.).

In order to unpack this argument, we refer to the analyses and ethnographic examples in this volume. Taken together, they embrace multi-temporality by demonstrating a wide range of conceptual linkages of time and field. Their inputs range from 'fieldwork techniques', as in the advantages of the longitudinal (and often episodic) study where field and fieldworker are transformed through forward-moving linear progressions that continuously shift in pace (Whyte), to the experience of rhythms and durations of (ritual) waiting time (Sjørslev). The common-sense sequence of knowing and the need to know is challenged by the anticipation associated with 'unfocused presence' (Sjørslev) and the temporal reversibility established through certain 'trans-temporal hinges' (Pedersen and Nielsen). But there are also temporal challenges related to ethnographic writing about continuously expanding narratives of living people's lived lives, which perpetually leaves the anthropologists in a position of being 'belated' (Marcus) or even 'out of conclusion' (A. Dalsgaard and Frederiksen).

Through the contributions, the reader also gets a sense of how attention to time and temporality is central to specific topics if one wants to understand what people do and why, or that temporalities can be crucial ingredients in the definition of the field in question (Walford, S. Dalsgaard, Otto, Lutz). Even if not spelled out, presence is a key organizing trope in several of the pieces because it is through presence and the present that time 'surfaces', to use the term adopted by Peter Lutz in his chapter. Whether the (repeated) unfocused presence of the anthropologist (Sjørslev) or the intermittent and cyclical presence of government big men in Papua New Guinea (S. Dalsgaard), presence is a precondition for knowing—but knowing often seems to depend on something apart from what is in the present moment, such as memory or anticipation. Indeed, as Ton Otto argues in his chapter, sharing the present (time) with informants is the basis for ethnographic fieldwork. But one also shares past and future, and thus understanding, expectations, and aims in life cannot be assumed. Herein lies perhaps the challenge of the temporal reversibility implied by trans-temporal hinges (Pedersen and Nielsen), boredom (Sjørslev), and the calibrations necessary for climatologists' predictions (Walford). Together, the contributions may take a step not toward answers but toward better questions about the multitude of interrelations of time and field that buttress the anthropology of the contemporary.

To present how the contributions develop the relationship between time and field, we have organized them according to three different angles. The first chapters explore how our anthropological subjects reflect on, act upon, and, perhaps ultimately, are constituted by different temporal orientations or 'situated temporalities'. If people's temporal orientations might be seen as particular ontological perspectives, we might fruitfully ask to what extent particular ontologies are constituted not only *in* time but, indeed, *of* time.

Antonia Walford explores the apparent binary of 'social' and 'natural' time based on how micrometeorologists and climate modelers 'make new knowledge' in their work in the Amazon. In calibrating their equipment, the micrometeorologists make use of past data to anticipate the range within which new data should fall. Past data are a scale and a model signifying how future data *should* be. They are a future-oriented 'model for' as much as a 'model of' past reality. However, time also enables the generation of prediction through the careful elimination of an infinite number of potential futures. For climate modelers and micrometeorologists in different ways, time is a priori and thus ontological as 't'—the base scale for all variations as variation happening over time and connecting past, present, and future in a meaningful relationship. Where 't' situates the concrete observations of micrometeorologists *in* time, it also works as the fundamental principle and scale situating their studies as research constituted *of* time.

Steffen Dalsgaard's chapter, which illustrates the temporal practices associated with the state in Papua New Guinea, is a call for the study of the state as a temporal entity as much as a territorialized one. The exchange events, which in Papua New Guinea bring the state into being, contain the temporal as well as spatial limits of the extension of the state. The state, personified by 'government men', exists in time as only intermittently present in people's lives through such events. In addition, interaction between public servants and citizens is often negotiated through social relationships and obligations that challenge the control of space and time often ascribed to state actors. In this way, the sociality of leadership and the state itself are as much made of time or temporal practices as they are situated in time.

The following chapters address the issue of 'different times'. They suggest a distinction between 'time as difference' and 'differences over time' (e.g., speed, change, and speed of change). Considering that people act on localized and possibly even clashing temporal orientations, time might be taken to constitute a decisive differential parameter distinguishing particular cultural fields. How do we analytically delimit and explore these temporal domains and, just as important, what are the implications for our understanding of what constitutes an ethnographic field?

Through their studies of young people, Anne Line Dalsgaard and Martin Demant Frederiksen argue for an anthropology more oriented toward possibilities and open endings. No one knows how the future will turn out, but many classic analyses of young people's situations (e.g., Willis 1977) have often emphasized the structural patterns of continuity—and thus hopelessness—rather than seeing the future as open to change and hope. Hope in particular is important in Dalsgaard and Frederiksen's account, especially when working with young people, because it seems crucial that anthropologists take informants' dreams and aspirations seriously. This entails acknowledging the way that hope is associated with agency and striving toward other potential futures—a striving that perhaps makes a difference over time by dreaming of a different time. In addition, the authors' attempt to analyze potential futures for their interlocutors tries to maintain an openness, but this poses the dilemma of how to close the chapter, since the future remains open and the lives of their interlocutors are still evolving. In this way, Dalsgaard and Frederiksen also address what has become a perpetual dilemma, that is, the slowness and belatedness of ethnography (Marcus, this volume).

Otto's chapter demonstrates different times by discussing the way that different temporalities or 'timescapes' exist simultaneously in a Papua New Guinean society and how these may be studied over time. The term 'timescape' refers to people discursively and practically stressing an orientation toward future or past in the way that they position themselves in the face of ongoing changes in the world around them. Like some of the other contributors (Sjørslev, Whyte), Otto argues for a long-term approach bringing the anthropologist into engagement with social relationships that will evoke sensitivity to contrasts in people's perspectives and draw out their different temporal domains. In his field, this is exemplified by conflicts between 'traditionalists' and 'modernists' arguing over the relative importance of past and future in shaping lives in the present. For an ethnographer, shared experiences may draw forth shared understandings—or the realization that the ethnographer and her or his collocutors do not share the presumed understanding.

The contribution by Lutz investigates how time matters in the field of Swedish old-age home care. To explore this question, he analyzes multiple 'space-timings' that affect the scheduled minutes of managed care, the care worker's own practices, and the elderly who receive home care. Inspired by Bruno Latour's comments on the ontological underpinnings of 'objective' time and 'subjective' experience of time, Lutz proposes the concept 'surfacing' as a way to think through the materializations of the space-timings. Rather than asserting an a priori 'objective' or clock time, he demonstrates how the time schedule is formed into a unique temporality by multiple actors. Lutz concludes that surfacing is relevant for conceptualizing temporal relationships, not only between the field and desk of home care (care work versus care management), but also between the fieldwork and analysis that anthropologists must mediate.

The final chapters discuss the timing and temporalities of fieldwork—what we have chosen to call 'methodologies of time and timing'. How are temporally protracted ethnographic studies expanded and/or contracted? What are the challenges of working in or with recurrent (cyclical) episodic times? And, finally, how do we tackle the analytical and methodological challenge of absences from and returns to ongoing and shifting 'ethnographic times'?

Inger Sjørslev writes about her gradual introduction to the syncretistic religion Candomblé in Brazil. In her account, her unfocused presence (i.e., boredom) had been the grounds from which meaningful figures (events, happenings) stood out during fieldwork. This constituted a rhythmic modality that momentarily connected ethnographer and informant in a unique temporal field. To identify these figures, though, requires recurrent visits and 'deep hanging out' through a prolonged interaction of shared time, involving varying tempos, between fieldworker and informants. In this way, Sjørslev compares ethnographic fieldwork to ritual, which creates generalized knowledge about the Other when the temporal (fieldwork) is the basis for the atemporal (analysis). Her success in learning about and with her informants stems in part from her time and timing, but also from being present at different times where 'nothing' happens.

Likewise, Michael Whyte argues that returning to the field and being 'updated' is an underestimated aspect of the long-term process of doing anthropology, which he demonstrates with reference to the 40-odd years he has been working in and out of Uganda. To re-enter the field is an act of continuously trying to re-establish coevalness between anthropologist and informants and become 'synchronized' with respect to social relations of one's field (cf. Fabian 1983). In this way, overcoming the social lapse between field visits can be turned into an advantage in the understanding of long-term shifting positions, discourses, and narratives. The social relationships of such 'episodic fieldwork' thus build on the significance of the absence and return of the fieldworker as an event in itself, which elicits information.

In the chapter by Pedersen and Nielsen, the focus of attention is on the multiple and overlapping temporalities of ethnographic fieldwork. Based on two discrete cases from Mongolia and Mozambique that explore the socio-economic effects of Chinese infrastructure projects, the authors introduce the notion of a trans-temporal hinge, which operates by bringing together phenomena and events otherwise distributed across time. Hence, a trans-temporal hinge might be any social configuration that the ethnographer encounters in the field that allows for a broader temporal assemblage to be composed.

The contributions are rounded off by Marcus's afterword, in which he reflects on time and the field. In line with his recent work on an anthropology of the contemporary (Rabinow et al. 2008), Marcus considers the issue of the belatedness of anthropology. The slowness of ethnographic work, dominated by a "norm of patience," is now challenged by the anxious demands of relevance—demands that are fundamentally temporal. Called upon to respond to concerns emerging in the present, ethnographic analysis cannot maintain a detached status as a "historical document in the making" or as a scientific endeavor to uncover eternal truths while claiming "all the time in the world" to do so. The urge for relevance arises because research subjects (informants, specialists, etc.) are increasingly found among the readership of anthropological accounts. The way to overcome demands for relevance seems to be to locate ethnography historically. By changing the temporal point of reference toward past events, the contemporary itself becomes a medium-term frame that negotiates the slowness of ethnography with the "permanent belatedness in relation to its object." Marcus relates the temporal matter of producing ethnography to the changing (political) relationships wherein representational practices are embedded. He thus concludes that "'being there' is perhaps no longer as important as 'taking one's time.'"

Acknowledgments

This volume has grown out of the workshop "Time and the Field," which was held in Sandbjerg at the August 2009 Megaseminar of the Danish Research School of Anthropology and Ethnography. In putting it together, we are indebted to the Danish Council for Independent Research for funding and to the contributors for their enthusiasm and comments. We also would like to thank those who participated without papers and especially Marilyn Strathern and Martijn van Beek for being discussants. Finally, we express thanks to Nigel Rapport, Signe Howell, and Aud Talle for having shared their work with us and to Nils Bubandt and the two anonymous reviewers, whose insightful comments helped us to polish the argument.

Steffen Dalsgaard holds a PhD in Anthropology and Ethnography from Aarhus University and is an Associate Professor at the IT University of Copenhagen. He is currently Deputy Chair of the Young Academy of Denmark. Since 2002 he has conducted research in Manus, Papua New Guinea, specializing in state and political leadership with a focus on tradition, exchange, and elections. He is currently working on two projects: democratic technologies (in Denmark and Papua New Guinea) and the introduction of carbon as a form of global value. Recent publications include articles in *HAU: Journal of Ethnographic Theory*, *Social Anthropology*, *Environment and Society: Advances in Research*, and *Social Analysis*.

Morten Nielsen is an Associate Professor in the Department of Anthropology at Aarhus University and coordinator of the interdisciplinary research network Urban Orders (URO). Based on his fieldwork in Brazil, Mozambique, and, most recently, Scotland, he has published on issues such as urban aesthetics, time and temporality, materiality, relational ontologies, infrastructure, and political cosmologies. Recent publications include articles in the *Journal of the Royal Anthropological Institute*, *HAU: Journal of Ethnographic Theory*, *Social Analysis*, and *Social Anthropology*.

Notes

1. As an example, we might take Veena Das's (2007) description of the spatio-temporal traces of the partition of India. She writes that "although the Partition was of the past if seen through homogeneous units of measurable time, its continued presence in people's lives was apparent in story, gesture, and conversation ... The sense of the present then was marked by a fearful anticipation. The survivors in the locality were living not only with memories embodied in the walls of houses, on the charred doors, in the little heaps of ashes in the street, but also with threats embodied in words and gestures" (ibid.: 97–98).

2. A parallel concern with multiple temporalities of a site can be discerned from Ssorin-Chaikov's (2006) analysis of gifts to Stalin as involving heterochrony.
3. For comparison, consider James and Mills's (2005: 14) argument that "[t]ime 'exists' for academic discussion, speculation, and comparison, only in the interplay of idioms we provide or invent for it through our languages, ceremonies, 'cultural' codes and technical inventions."
4. As argued by Munn (1992: 93): "[T]he problem of time has often been handmaiden to other anthropological frames and issues ... with which it is inextricably bound up. In short, the topic of time frequently fragments into all the other dimensions and topics anthropologists deal with in the social world."

References

Appadurai, Arjun. 1990. "Disjuncture and Difference in the Global Cultural Economy." Pp. 295–310 in *Global Culture: Nationalism, Globalization and Modernity*, ed. Mike Featherstone. London: Sage.

Boellstorff, Tom. 2008. *Coming of Age in Second Life*. Princeton, NJ: Princeton University Press.

Bourdieu, Pierre. 1977. *Outline of a Theory of Practice*. Trans. Richard Nice. Cambridge: Cambridge University Press.

Bourdieu, Pierre. 2000. *Pascalian Meditations*. Trans. Richard Nice. Oxford: Polity Press.

Burawoy, Michael. 1998. "The Extended Case Method." *Sociological Theory* 16, no. 1: 4–33.

Candea, Matei. 2007. "Arbitrary Locations." *Journal of the Royal Anthropological Institute* 13, no. 1: 167–184.

Clifford, James. 1997. *Routes: Travel and Translation in the Late Twentieth Century*. Cambridge, MA: Harvard University Press.

Coleman, Simon, and Peter Collins, eds. 2006. *Locating the Field: Space, Place and Context in Anthropology*. Oxford: Berg.

Corsín Jiménez, Alberto. 2003. "On Space as a Capacity." *Journal of the Royal Anthropological Institute* 9, no. 1: 137–153.

Crapanzano, Vincent. 2003. "Reflections on Hope as a Category of Social and Psychological Analysis." *Cultural Anthropology* 18, no. 1: 3–32.

Crapanzano, Vincent. 2004. *Imaginative Horizons: An Essay in Literary-Philosophical Anthropology*. Chicago: University of Chicago Press.

Das, Veena. 2007. *Life and Words: Violence and the Descent into the Ordinary*. Berkeley: University of California Press.

de Certeau, Michel. 1984. *The Practice of Everyday Life*. Trans. Steven Rendall. Berkeley: University of California Press.

Evans-Pritchard, E. E. 1940. *The Nuer*. Oxford: Oxford University Press.

Evens, T. M. S., and Don Handelman, eds. 2006. *The Manchester School: Practice and Ethnographic Praxis in Anthropology*. New York: Berghahn Books.

Fabian, Johannes. 1983. *Time and the Other*. New York: Columbia University Press.

Faubion, James D. 2009. "The Ethics of Fieldwork as an Ethics of Connectivity, or the Good Anthropologist (Isn't What She Used to Be)." Pp. 145–164 in *Fieldwork Is Not What It Used to Be: Learning Anthropology's Method in a Time of Transition*, ed. James D. Faubion and George E. Marcus. Ithaca, NY: Cornell University Press.

Fortun, Kim. 2001. *Advocacy after Bhopal: Environmentalism, Disaster, New Global Orders.* Chicago: University of Chicago Press.

Foster, George M., Thayer Scudder, Elizabeth Colson, and Robert V. Kemper, eds. 1979. *Long-Term Field Research in Social Anthropology.* New York: Academic Press.

Game, Ann. 1997. "Time Unhinged." *Time & Society* 6, no. 2: 115–129.

Geertz, Clifford. 1973. *The Interpretation of Cultures.* New York: Basic Books.

Gell, Alfred. 1992. *The Anthropology of Time: Cultural Constructions of Temporal Maps and Images.* Oxford: Berg.

Gell, Alfred. 1998. *Art and Agency: An Anthropological Theory.* Oxford: Clarendon Press.

Giddens, Anthony. 1990. *The Consequences of Modernity.* Cambridge: Polity Press.

Gluckman, Max. [1940] 1958. *Analysis of a Social Situation in Modern Zululand.* Manchester: Manchester University Press.

Grosz, Elizabeth. 1999. "Thinking the New: Of Futures Yet Unthought." Pp. 15–28 in *Becomings: Explorations in Time, Memory, and Futures,* ed. Elizabeth Grosz. Ithaca, NY: Cornell University.

Gupta, Akhil, and James Ferguson. 1997a. "Discipline and Practice: 'The Field' as Site, Method, and Location in Anthropology." Pp. 1–46 in Gupta and Ferguson 1997b.

Gupta, Akhil, and James Ferguson, eds. 1997b. *Anthropological Locations: Boundaries and Grounds of a Field Science.* Berkeley: University of California Press.

Guyer, Jane. 2007. "Prophecy and the Near Future: Thoughts on Macroeconomic, Evangelical, and Punctuated Time." *American Ethnologist* 34, no. 3: 409–421.

Hage, Ghassan. 2005. "A Not So Multi-sited Ethnography of a Not So Imagined Community." *Anthropological Theory* 5, no. 4: 463–475.

Handelman, Don. 2006. "The Extended Case: Interactional Foundations and Prospective Dimensions." Pp. 94–117 in Evens and Handelman 2006.

Harvey, David. 1989. *The Condition of Postmodernity: An Enquiry into the Origins of Cultural Change.* London: Blackwell.

Heidegger, Martin. 1971. "Building, Dwelling, Thinking." Pp. 145–161 in *Poetry, Language, Thought,* trans. Albert Hofstadter. New York: Harper & Row.

Hirsch, Eric, and Charles Stewart, eds. 2005. *Ethnographies of Historicity.* London: Routledge. Special issue of *History and Anthropology* 16, no. 3.

Hobsbawm, Eric, and Terence Ranger, eds. 1983. *The Invention of Tradition.* Cambridge: Cambridge University Press.

Hodges, Matthew. 2008. "Rethinking Time's Arrow." *Anthropological Theory* 8, no. 4: 399–429.

Holbraad, Martin. 2008. "Definitive Evidence, from Cuban Gods." *Journal of the Royal Anthropological Institute* 14, no. 1: 93–109.

Howell, Signe, and Aud Talle, eds. 2011. *Returns to the Field: Multitemporal Research and Contemporary Anthropology.* Bloomington: Indiana University Press.

Ingold, Tim. 2000. *The Perception of the Environment: Essays on Livelihood, Dwelling and Skill.* London: Routledge.

Jackson, Michael. 2002. *The Politics of Storytelling: Violence, Transgression and Intersubjectivity.* Copenhagen: Museum Tusculanum.

James, William. 1909. *A Pluralistic Universe.* New York: Longmans, Green.

James, Wendy, and David Mills. 2005. "Introduction: From Representation to Action in the Flow of Time." Pp. 1–15 in *The Qualities of Time: Anthropological Approaches,* ed. Wendy James and David Mills. Oxford: Berg.

Kapferer, Bruce. 2006. "Situations, Crisis, and the Anthropology of the Concrete: The Contribution of Max Gluckman." Pp. 118–155 in Evens and Handelman 2006.

Keesing, Roger, and Robert Tonkinson, eds. 1982. *Reinventing Traditional Culture: The Politics of Kastom in Island Melanesia.* Special issue of *Mankind* 13, no. 4.

Kemper, Robert. V., and Anya P. Royce, eds. 2002. *Chronicling Cultures: Long-Term Field Research in Anthropology*. Walnut Creek, CA: AltaMira Press.

Küchler, Susanne. 2002. *Malanggan: Art, Memory and Sacrifice*. Oxford: Berg.

Latour, Bruno. 2005. *Reassembling the Social: An Introduction to Actor-Network-Theory*. Oxford: Oxford University Press.

Marcus, George E. 1995. "Ethnography in/of the World System: The Emergence of Multi-sited Ethnography." *Annual Review of Anthropology* 24: 95–117.

Marcus, George E. 2006. "Where Have All the Tales of Fieldwork Gone?" *Ethnos* 71, no. 1: 113–122.

Marcus, George E., and Judith Okely. 2007. "Debate Section: 'How Short Can Fieldwork Be?'" *Social Anthropology* 15, no. 3: 353–367.

Massey, Doreen. 1992. "Politics and Space/Time." *New Left Review* 196: 65–84.

Maurer, William. 2002. "Repressed Futures: Financial Derivatives' Theological Unconscious." *Economy and Society* 31, no. 1: 15–36.

Maurer, William, and Gabriele Schwab, eds. 2006. *Accelerating Possession: Global Futures of Property and Personhood*. New York: Columbia University Press.

Mitchell, Clyde. 1956. *The Kalela Dance: Aspects of Social Relationships among Urban Africans in Northern Rhodesia*. Manchester: Manchester University Press.

Miyazaki, Hiro. 2004. *The Method of Hope: Anthropology, Philosophy, and Fijian Knowledge*. Stanford, CA: Stanford University Press.

Munn, Nancy. 1986. *The Fame of Gawa*. Cambridge: Cambridge University Press.

Munn, Nancy. 1992. "The Cultural Anthropology of Time: A Critical Essay." *Annual Review of Anthropology* 21: 93–123.

Nielsen, Morten. 2008. "In the Vicinity of the State: House Construction, Personhood, and the State in Maputo, Mozambique." PhD diss., University of Copenhagen.

Nielsen, Morten. 2011. "Futures Within: Reversible Time and House-Building in Maputo, Mozambique." *Anthropological Theory* 11, no. 4: 397–423.

Nielsen, Morten. 2014. "A Wedge of Time: Futures in the Present and Presents without Futures in Maputo, Mozambique." *Journal of the Royal Anthropological Institute* 20, no. S1: 166–182.

Olwig, Karen F., and Kirsten Hastrup, eds. 1997. *Siting Culture: The Shifting Anthropological Object*. London: Routledge.

Ong, Aihwah, and Stephen Collier, eds. 2005. *Global Assemblages: Technology, Politics, and Ethics as Anthropological Problems*. Malden, MA: Blackwell.

Otto, Ton, and Poul Pedersen, eds. 2005. *Tradition and Agency: Tracing Cultural Continuity and Invention*. Aarhus: Aarhus University Press.

Pedersen, Morten A. 2012. "A Day in the Cadillac: The Work of Hope in Urban Mongolia." *Social Analysis* 56, no. 2: 136–151.

Rabinow, Paul, and George E. Marcus, with James D. Faubion and Tobias Rees. 2008. *Designs for an Anthropology of the Contemporary*. Durham, NC: Duke University Press.

Radin, Paul. [1933] 1966. *The Method and Theory of Ethnology: An Essay in Criticism*. New York: Basic Books.

Robbins, Joel. 2007. "Continuity Thinking and the Problem of Christian Culture: Belief, Time, and the Anthropology of Christianity." *Current Anthropology* 48, no. 1: 5–38.

Sahlins, Marshall. 1991. "The Return of the Event, Again: With Reflections on the Beginnings of the Great Fijian War of 1843 to 1855 between the Kingdoms of Bau and Rewa." Pp. 37–99 in *Clio in Oceania: Toward a Historical Anthropology*, ed. Aletta Biersack. Washington, DC: Smithsonian Institute Press.

Ssorin-Chaikov, Nikolai. 2006. "On Heterochrony: Birthday Gifts to Stalin, 1949." *Journal of the Royal Anthropological Institute* 12, no. 2: 355–375.

Strathern, Marilyn. 1990. "Artefacts of History: Events and the Interpretation of Images." Pp. 25–44 in *Culture and History in the Pacific*, ed. Jukka Siikala. Helsinki: Suomen Antropologinen Seura.

Strathern, Marilyn. 1991. *Partial Connections*. Totowa, NJ: Rowman & Littlefield.

Strathern, Marilyn. 1999. *Property, Substance and Effect: Anthropological Essays on Persons and Things*. London: Athlone Press.

Turner, Victor. 1957. *Schism and Continuity in an African Society: A Study of Ndembu Village Life*. Manchester: Manchester University Press.

Vigh, Henrik. 2007. "Crisis and Chronicity: Anthropological Perspectives on Continuous Conflict and Decline." *Ethnos* 73, no. 1: 5–24.

Willis, Paul. 1977. *Learning to Labour: How Working Class Kids Get Working Class Jobs*. Aldershot: Gower.

Wulff, Helena. 2002. "Yo-Yo Fieldwork: Mobility and Time in a Multi-local Study of Dance in Ireland." *Anthropological Journal on European Culture* 11: 117–136.

Chapter 1

LIMITS AND LIMITLESSNESS
Exploring Time in Scientific Practice

Antonia Walford

This chapter will explore the implicit affinity between the past, finiteness, and certainty, on the one hand, and the future, infinite possibilities, and uncertainty, on the other. Drawing on fieldwork involving a scientific project in the Brazilian Amazon, it aims to demonstrate that these conceptual conjunctions can be teased apart ethnographically in order to render visible different ways of analyzing their relation to each other and what that might mean for the production of new knowledge. My interest in new knowledge is a direct result of considering the relation between the temporal configurations I encountered in two groups of researchers during my fieldwork (micrometeorologists and climate modelers) and the temporal configurations I found in the literature. The underlying proposition of this chapter is that new knowledge for anthropology inheres in the extent to which it can learn from its fields—about the notion of 'social time' and 'natural time', for example. However, the form that this new knowledge takes, I contend, is based on a particular way of figuring the relation

Notes for this chapter are located on page 32.

between certainty, the past, and finiteness or, conversely, between uncertainty, the future, and infinite possibilities. It is these conceptual associations that the chapter specifically addresses, or at least lays open to re-evaluation, through the ethnography presented—in this case, with micrometeorologists and climate modelers. As such, this exposition has ramifications for both the description of scientific knowledge practices and the extension of anthropological ones, pointing to the mutual constitution of both. I start with the literature and a discussion of the limitations of the trope of limitlessness as it pertains to the discovery of ever more possible temporalities.

Social Time and Natural Time

Time has been the subject of numerous social studies,[1] and it continues to fascinate social theorists. This body of work, sociologist Barbara Adam (1990: 16) tells us, for the most part demonstrates "a general conviction that all time is social time and an agreement that contemporary Western time needs to be understood in its historically developed uniqueness." This seems to be something of a definitive statement for the social sciences, the first part of which many scholars trace back to Émile Durkheim (1912). For example, Helga Nowotny (1992: 424) maintains that "Durkheim held as the most general conclusion that it is the rhythm of social life which is the basis of the category of time itself," and Carol Greenhouse (1996: ix) reminds us that "'[s]ocial time', as Emile Durkheim called it, names this long-standing inquiry into the varied means and ends people make of the logical and existential challenges of living in the company of others." Alfred Gell (1992: 4) suggests that, for anthropologists, it was only because Durkheim posited the possibility of social time "that the 'time' problem becomes interesting at all, i.e. when the possibility is raised that collective representations of time do not passively reflect time, but actually *create* time as a phenomenon apprehended by sentient beings." However, a common origin does not imply subsequent singularity. Durkheim's original insight now sits alongside a myriad of theories and descriptions of social time—collective, subjective, material, or otherwise. It is therefore of the utmost interest for anthropology to tease out ethnographically how time is figured in the practices of those studied, and this has been seen as one of the most revealing and reflexive possibilities afforded by fieldwork (cf. Fabian 1983).

However, there emerges from this body of work two general observations that I would like to concentrate on. The first is that social time, in any of its guises, is often defined as against natural time.[2] And whereas there is an increasingly complex and heterogeneous array of descriptions and theories as to the social, cultural, organizational, and ritual permutations of social time around the world, natural time remains a static concept belonging to an outdated vision of the natural sciences' own take on the matter (Adam 1990: 150). Natural time is "abstract, absolute, unitary, invariant, linear, mechanical and quantitative" (Orlikowski and Yates 2002: 685). It is against this formulation of natural time as itself 'timeless' that social time seems to gain its revelatory purchase. As Nowotny (1992: 426) puts it, a "conception of time as something 'external', which 'flows', as Newton thought, 'of itself and from its own nature' and which is somehow embodied in clock times, seems to have suited most social theorists as an external reference frame, against which 'social time' could be posited." Thus, although there are many different origins suggested for social time, including "rhythms of nature or society, information processing, the capacity for memory and expectation, sociality, language, and social synchronization" (Adam 1990: 15), it seems to be only against an invariant natural time that such descriptions gain analytical clout. Even framing Western time itself as a social time like any other necessitates that it be framed in terms of what it was imagined (even if 'incorrectly') to be.

The second general observation concerns the resulting limitlessness that the notion of social time affords analytically. If, as Adam suggests, it is no longer viable to reduce the time of others to representations of an invariant natural time, it follows as a corollary that there is no single origin beyond these interpretations and that Western time is as locally specific as any other. The term 'pluritemporalism', coined by Nowotny (1992) to refer to the conclusion that there are many different times that exist side by side, captures this idea of multiple (and multiplying) analytical possibilities. However, this necessary and indubitably fruitful realization carries with it its own load of uncertainty. The lack of the ability to scale makes analysis seem impossible, and the sense that interpretations are limitless or infinite makes any explanation seem incomplete. This problem is inherent in the Western act of making meaning, which has at its foundation the act of comparing or of determining what to take as context. As Marilyn Strathern (2002: 94–95) puts it, either "one can see through interpretation" to the reality behind, with the result that there is always too much interpretation, which obscures what is really going on, or there is never enough interpretation because "everything is interpretation" (ibid.: 94)—so there is nothing behind to see through *to*. What Strathern calls the 'oscillation' between these two views can be understood as reactions to the problems inherent in taking either one as context or background for the other. Although this creates the sensation of "very different views of the world" (ibid.: 88), these views are in fact related, as the one necessarily must be a background for the other to emerge as a figure.[3]

It is thus hard to make natural time disappear from social analyses. If anything, its denial is a frequent step in the establishment of its various opposites (i.e., the result of not enough interpretation). But if natural time is also an interpretation, this causes a dizzying consciousness of a multiplication of perspectives without any way to relate them (i.e., the result of too much interpretation) (cf. Strathern 1991). One gets the sense of endless repetition, which Nowotny (1992: 423) characterizes as a "sheer fragmentation of approaches which ramble through many subfields and facets, each one discovering anew time as a 'social construction.'" Adam (1990: 15) writes of the "incompatible array of definitions" and "incommensurable ideas about the source of our experience and concept of time," where "there are no signposts for orientation in this maze of conceptual chaos." In the end, accruing more and more perspectives does not seem to add up to anything, especially when the profusion of new perspectives seems to inhibit one's ability to countenance others. The overarching problem seems to be how to make new knowledge at all. Limitlessness in this sense has its limits.

What I would like to suggest is that an ethnographic investigation of the first observation may shed some light on the second. Thus, I will discuss the relationship among time, new knowledge, and certainty using some ethnographic work that I undertook in 2007 in Brazil with an international scientific project—the Large-Scale Biosphere-Atmosphere Experiment in Amazonia (LBA). I will start by exploring the relation between natural time and social time in the work of the researchers and technicians whom I accompanied. I will then address the same question in the work of LBA climate modelers. Investigating these questions ethnographically demonstrates the insufficiency of the premise that underpins both of the above observations, namely, that limits only act to reduce (potential, knowledge, possibilities). In fact, fixity and invariance of time are shown to be crucial for those with whom I worked. I therefore suggest that it is not necessary to deny what is invariant and privilege the infinitely variable in order to create new knowledge, ethnographically or scientifically.

The LBA

The LBA was established in 1998 through the combined efforts of NASA (the US National Aeronautics and Space Administration), the European Commission, INPA (the Brazilian National Institute of Amazonian Research), and INPE (the Brazilian National Institute for Space Research). The LBA describes itself on its website as "an international research initiative led by Brazil. LBA is designed to create the new knowledge needed to understand the climatological, ecological, biogeochemical, and hydrological functioning of Amazonia, the impact of land use change on these functions, and the interactions between Amazonia and the Earth system."[4] The LBA has set up research sites all over the Amazon and conducts a wide range of studies in diverse areas of scientific and ecological knowledge. It also maintains collaborative partnerships with many different institutions, inside and outside of Latin America, including, for example, various universities in the United States, the Max Planck Institute in Germany, and Leeds University in England. At the LBA's inception, it was stated that each project should have a foreign (usually North American, as it turns out) and a Brazilian principal investigator (PI), although the particular form that this policy takes in practice varies hugely, depending on the project.

At many of the research sites, meteorological towers have been erected that extend 20 meters above the top canopy of the forest (with some as high as 60 meters) in order to measure, by means of various instrumentation, the flux of carbon molecules between the biosphere and the atmosphere. As one Brazilian PI explained to me: "Is the Amazon giving out more carbon than it is taking in, or vice versa? That's the big question." I was informed by another researcher that the LBA was set up as a response, firstly, to the lack of data available to the scientific community on tropical biospheres and, secondly, to the realization that carbon uptake experiments conducted thus far were possibly being skewed by the fact that they were not long term. Researchers might be measuring not the total forest dynamic but only one tiny part of a cycle that constitutes the total. There is a strict policy that governs the management of the data that are collected at these research sites and during any research conducted under the aegis of the LBA. Data must be made available as quickly as possible to the Beija-flor data system, which has its base in São Paulo. From there, it is made available to any LBA researcher anywhere in the world.

The Micrometeorologists

Of the 10 weeks or so that I spent with the researchers of the LBA in 2007, one was in North Amazonia, 87 kilometers north of the town of São Gabriel de Cachoeira, at an LBA research site in the forest. I was accompanying a group of LBA researchers from three different disciplines: micrometeorology, biogeo-chemical cycles, and plant physiology.[5] We were camping in the forest, about 300 meters from the tower, sleeping in hammocks and starting the day at dawn. The micrometeorologists were there to "fix" the meteorological tower and its equipment. The tower has a "profile" of instrumentation that measures differ-ent variables pertaining to meteorology and carbon flux: air pressure, radiation, air and soil temperature, air and soil humidity, wind turbulence, and carbon concentration of the air. Different sensors are arranged along the tower, and the measurements are fed into either one of two small computers called datalog-gers, which are kept in sealed boxes on the tower. This information is normally then downloaded by a tower technician, put onto a CD, and sent to the LBA's headquarters in Manaus. The equipment on this tower, however, had been giv-ing incorrect measurements for some time: the datalogger that stores the soil data had not been giving readings for almost four months; the battery that runs the equipment on the tower did not stay charged as long as it should have; and one of the infrared gas analyzers (IRGA), which measure the concentration of carbon and water vapor in the air, decalibrated every time the battery unex-pectedly ran out of charge. There were also problems with the barometer, the soil humidity and temperature sensors, and a radiation sensor. The errors had been noticed by comparing the information being sent to Manaus with "what we already know." One of the micrometeorologists told me: "We spend 99 per-cent of the time fixing things. Nothing happens as expected. Three months of planning, just in order to fix a computer program!" No matter how much time they spent planning their trips, there were always surprises.

The data and the equipment producing it were often described by the micro-meteorologists as "surprising," "unexpected," "anomalous," "exceptional," or "mysterious." The soil humidity sensor had to be changed because the data it was supplying "do not correspond to what we expect." The data sent to Manaus over the past few months had been surprisingly low. As I was told, "It's horrible, because you end up not trusting the data." We had brought a new sensor with us from INPE and would take the old one back with us to be calibrated in the

LBA offices or possibly even sent to São Paulo. But it might not be the sensor at all. Before returning to the LBA offices in Manaus, the micrometeorologists had a few more ideas as to how to identify the source of the error. The sensor was swapped, but not before downloading the last readings it had sent to the datalogger "to compare before and after." We waited. The readings were still too low. The team was puzzled. They started the wearying process of checking the wiring that connects the sensor to the soil datalogger. One researcher sat in front of the soil datalogger, waiting to see if the readings made any more sense. They found that the wire casing had been worn through and water had got inside the wire. They were going to have to cut out the rusted part, solder it back together, and then reattach the wire with duct tape.

The head of the team explained: "You have to test each hypothesis. It doesn't make any sense that it isn't working." The soil humidity sensor was still not working, even though some connections had been newly soldered. We knew this to be the case because we had a sheet with a table "from the literature," and the readings were consistently below what the table told us they should be. It might not have been the sensor at all, so the team checked the program on the datalogger. All seemed to be in order. They then started the persnickety business of checking the wires in the soil datalogger, all of which have colors depending on which sensor they connect to. There was some discussion as to which color was which: "Is this green or turquoise?" They shouted colors to each other between the trees, verifying connections and channels. It seemed absurd for a moment. The wires were correctly connected. The head researcher looked at me. "Everything is possible," he said.

One of the remarkable aspects of the time I spent with the micrometeorologists was the rapidity with which they tested and moved on to new possible causes of error. This process involved assigning new identities to things and overcoming unexpected occurrences. There was a sense of a collective tinkering, a coaxing and cajoling of the instruments, whereby first one culprit was accused and then acquitted of being the source of the error. Their attention shifted back and forth between each possible cause, weighing up uncertainty in each case. Sometimes, I was told, "you don't know why, but it just starts working again."

To fix the equipment requires one to battle not only with wiring and computer programs but also with maintenance problems caused by wayward animals or plants—frogs fall in the pluviometers used to measure rainfall, and bees colonize the boxes meant to protect the dataloggers—or by the fact that the equipment comes from Europe and so is made for a temperate climate and not a tropical one. The 'working order' of the equipment had been determined in a certain way back in Manaus at a series of meetings prior to the expedition. It was based on information that is reified within the equipment that has been built to its specifications and is also very distant from that equipment, sitting in an instruction manual in a room somewhere thousands of kilometers away from the area of remote forest where the equipment is doing its work. How the micrometeorologists fix their equipment depends heavily on what information they can keep fixed along that route from office to forest.

Calibration and the Limits of Limitlessness

One of the most notable observations about the micrometeorologists' work is the way that they constantly refer to past data. The charts and tables, full of data collected and verified at a past time, are being used to 'scale' the instruments—to provide data in the present that make sense and can be trusted. Their instruments have to be calibrated in order to afford this scaling capacity. Calibration proceeds in broad terms by using one set of stable, verified, and known measurements to adjust other measurements in order to ensure their subsequent accuracy and therefore their trustworthiness. For example, both IRGAs have been calibrated under controlled conditions back in the laboratory in São Gabriel. Calibration[6] in the case of the LBA micrometeorologists involves running nitrogen through the IRGA and 'telling' it that this is 'zero CO_2' (carbon dioxide) and 'zero H_2O' (water vapor). With this zero as a fixed point, the IRGA is capable of recording variations in CO_2 and H_2O. This process might be seen as a limiting device, a way of eliciting only certain information from the limitless possibilities of information that exist. As to the other instruments the micrometeorologists work with, there are several different ways that a calibration is performed. Many are sent to a calibration laboratory in São Paulo, in the south of Brazil, where there are new instruments that are never taken to the field. These 'standard' (*padrão*) instruments are used to calibrate certain instruments that are brought back from the towers. When I asked about the procedure for calibrating these standard instruments, I was met with confusion. "No one calibrates the standard," I was told.

During a more recent trip to the LBA in 2010, I had the opportunity to sit in on some discussions about calibration. In this case, it was a pluviometer and a barometer that had been sent to the calibration laboratory at the INPE's Laboratory of Meteorological Instrumentation in the state of São Paulo. What the micrometeorologists at the LBA received, along with the instruments, were certificates of calibration. Each instrument requires a mathematical constant that corrects for the systematic errors that it makes when measuring. This constant is included in the computer program that converts the voltage generated by the instrument—for example, when a certain amount of rain enters it—into units of measurement that can be used as data, and in this situation no two instruments are exactly the same. Furthermore, over time and with use, these constants have to be changed slightly to make up for the wear and tear that the instrument suffers due to being out in the world. The micrometeorologists had to use the information on the certificate of calibration to work out the new constant. Thus, there is a constant updating to ensure that the instrument says what the micrometeorologists expect it to say.

In order to use time to afford certainty, it could be argued that the meteorologists are orienting themselves by using a conception of time that is necessarily linear and invariant, in which the relation between the past and present is already known. It might be said that by checking with past measurements, tables, and charts about which they are certain, they assume a linear relation between past and present. The present follows from the past in predictable ways, and this is why past measurements can be taken as a standard for present ones. In this approach, old certainties are the scales by which new uncertainties can be brought into line. Time would thus be an objective external notion that ensures the rationality of scientific work.

Yet a close examination of the calibration process seems to reveal concerted and active construction work. Calibration allows the micrometeorologists to bridge the distance between past and present, certainty and uncertainty. Calibration also provides a way to ensure that predictability is maintained, rather than taken for granted. Although no one calibrates the standard, depending on the instrument, the standard itself is also constantly being checked and verified by other standard instruments of different types. The ability of any instrument to measure correctly depends on the intervention of correction factors that have to be constantly updated. This immediately suggests that calibration has the power to construct what it measures. Sociologist of science Harry Collins (1985) has described how the physics community insisted that the physicist Joseph Weber calibrate the apparatus that he had designed to measure gravitational radiation, an elusive physical force thought to emanate from cosmic events. Physicists were skeptical about the rate at which Weber was asserting that the waves were arriving on Earth. By requiring Weber to calibrate his instruments according to previous knowledge of the subject, Collins suggests, they were able to ensure that his results were discredited. Collins writes that "[m]aking Weber calibrate his apparatus with electrostatic pulses was one way in which his critics ensured that gravitational radiation remained a force that could be understood within the ambit of physics as we know it. They ensured physics' continuity—the maintenance of the links between past and future" (ibid.: 105–106).

In a similar sense, temporal linearity, or cohesion, was being actively executed by the LBA micrometeorologists. They were painstakingly suturing past and present together into a seamless line, doing their utmost to correct the lack of linearity that was apparent in what their troublesome instruments were telling them. The constantly shifting attention, the varying tests and trials, and the continuous negotiation with the instrumentation seemed to reflect the lack of linearity that the micrometeorologists were trying to fix. This observation resonates with Andrew Pickering's (1993) notion of the 'mangle of practice', a concept he suggests as a way to think of the dialectic of resistance (by the instrumentation) and subsequent accommodation (by the scientist) that characterizes the stabilization of any scientific instrument or fact. For Pickering, the relation between scientist and instrument involved in this process is temporally emergent: they are mutually constitutive products of each other. Each reconfigures the other, and both emerge in "the real time of practice" (ibid.: 566), often in unpredictable ways. Practice in this way 'mangles' intentions and agencies, both human and non-human. It is concentrating on practice that allows an insight into the simultaneous co-production of human and non-human agencies and permits one to trace the apparently haphazard way in which scientific discoveries or inventions tend to come about. 'Temporal emergence' is one way in which an analysis of the practice of the micrometeorologists might make sense. A constantly shifting redefinition of goals and future possibilities, informed by the fluid properties of the present, is a particularly seductive way to describe what the micrometeorologists were doing because it allows a certain space for the multiple possibilities potentially inherent in any situation.

A focus on 'practice' has become a trademark of those approaches that seek to multiply the perspectives that can be brought to bear on a situation. In the context of ethnographic studies of science, such approaches, sometimes called 'constructivist', tend to emphasize the constructed ways in which stabilized outcomes come to exist as such. Temporal emergence therefore aims at unpacking the reifying practices of science. In the case of the micrometeorologists, the outcome—the source of the error and how it came about—is co-produced by the human and non-human actors involved. As such, it is in constant flux and thus can be either what is expected or what is not. Yet, I would argue, temporal emergence is not what the micrometeorologist meant when he told me that everything is possible. Although certainty is perhaps an unattainable state, and even though the present seems to flicker in and out of focus very rapidly, the past stays obstinately solid in the form of the tables and references that the micrometeorologists use. The idea of infinite possible causes of error is combined with a very finite and fixed sense of the desired outcome.

To say something new about time in scientific practice is interesting partly because we are already to a certain extent connected to the world we are trying to describe.[7] It is therefore difficult sometimes not to assume that one's taken-for-granted understanding can sufficiently explain what one is trying to understand. But attempting to describe the way that time is either invariant or constructed in the micrometeorologists' practice seems unsatisfactory because we have already defined these alternatives beforehand. To take a recent example, close attention to actors' practice in an organizational context has revealed that stable temporal structures that are only "apparently objective" are constantly being amended and restructured through practice, becoming cemented again by their consistent re-enactment and being "taken-for-granted" once more (Orlikowski and Yates 2002: 686). This then "bridges" what is called the "subjective-objective dichotomy" (ibid.). This bridge, however, relies heavily on the idea that the objective is only apparent. Likewise, a different sort of bridging practice, such as Pickering's temporal emergence, which attempts to annul the subjective and the objective binary through a notion of constantly shifting emergence, seems insufficient. Both of these fail, in different ways, to take into account the fact that the micrometeorologists do necessarily hold something very steady—that is, the linear and predictable relation between past and present—and how they do so.

What seems to me to be a more interesting and ethnographically fitting way to describe how the micrometeorologists figure time necessitates a shift in the way that we define the alternatives altogether. Perhaps like Annelise Riles's (2001: 92) description of "division within the boundaries," the fact that time is a priori does not in fact limit possibilities for the micrometeorologists. In this view, time is not a reduction at all, and therefore there is no need to describe it as 'apparently' objective. That is to say, even if one's interest is in capturing the complexity inherent in how these researchers work, it is unnecessary to deny outright the possibility of an a priori stability or fixity. Riles offers another way to think about limitlessness that does not depend on such a negation. I am moved to suggest a parallel here because the micrometeorologists do not describe their own activities by denying the invariant and fixed form of the relationships that they are trying to capture with their instruments, that are enshrined in the tables of past data, and that they expect to see in the data that the instruments are collecting. At the same time, the micrometeorologists are still making new knowledge in the form of the repeated instantiation of these very relationships. The limitlessness of the micrometeorologists' knowledge practice lies in the way that what there is to know is already given while also being what they are working on (ibid.: 109). In other words, it is not necessary to imagine information as being gained only by endlessly adding new perspectives.

Rather than linking the past to the present, the micrometeorologists reconfirm what is given from the start in order to make new knowledge. From this vantage point, the natural (given) and the social (constructed) are not irreconcilable; nor does the natural lose its status as a fixed given. Instead, the dualism is reshaped by paying attention to what the micrometeorologists themselves hold steady and what they work on, even if it is the same thing. The past, as a certainty, affords the creation of new knowledge exactly because it is fixed—and in this way, fixity can be seen as generative. The micrometeorologists' practice thus suggests that there is a limit to the social scientific imaginary of endless possibilities. But the idea of a limit can itself be transformed. I will indicate how through a brief look at the LBA climate and weather modelers, whose work environment is very different from that of the micrometeorologists. The modelers' work brings into relief the relation between certainty and uncertainty in the temporal context of prediction, in which limits themselves might seem limitless.

Prediction and Limitless Limits

The LBA has a small but growing number of climate and weather modelers, who spend their time in the LBA head office poring over models that run on the LBA's supercomputer. Although their work is very different from that of the micrometeorologists, they also contribute to the new knowledge that the LBA produces, in the form of predictions. Climate modelers work with mathematical models of the atmosphere that have been written using the equations of fluid dynamics. Time, which appears in modeling formulae as 't', is known as an 'independent variable'. Other climatic variables such as temperature vary with time, but time does not vary with temperature. It is a constant by which other variables can be measured. By keeping time steady and universal, the modelers can, in their own words, "time travel" to the extent that they can go forward in time with their predictions. But they can also do a "hindcast," that is, they can use previously observed data to test their model. If the model would have predicted what has happened, then it can be extrapolated to predict (into) the future. Time is unquestionably an invariant and given element in these models. It is not up for dispute.

In order to predict the weather, mathematical interpolations and extrapolations have to be made. Interpolation is the mathematical method by which one can find an unknown value that lies *between* two known data points. Extrapolation is the mathematical method by which one can find an unknown value that extends *beyond* a given data set. As one modeler explained to me:

> [Weather] prediction is not a linear direct extrapolation from today to tomorrow. It's not. This is wrong. Prediction has to be done in small intervals of time … normally, 150 seconds, two and a half minutes … Now imagine I want to make a prediction from here … I have an observation here, I have an observation here, so the inclination, this margin of variation of temperature, follows this straight line, right? Now, [for] an extrapolation for a short time period, you resolve it, and it gives this line here. You specify that there the temperature is 15. There you're getting it right, you're in the curve still. But if you use a long time period, your temperature is going to be here, so your temperature is going to fall here. The difference of error is very large, so you have to do your extrapolations in little intervals, based on this value … then based on this one, then on this one, and so you proceed very gradually.

However, despite this careful mathematical extension of information into the unknown, the inescapable problem in modeling is that of 'chaos'—the unpredictable way in which predictions lose their accuracy over time. The goal of a modeler is therefore to close this gap between what is 'observed' and what is 'expected', for when these are the same thing, the model is actualizing the future. But they know that the predictions they present are not certainties, by any means. As another modeler told me, "We will never be certain—only perhaps a little less uncertain." As Brown and Michael (2003) point out, in the case of modeling, it is our very instruments of prediction that confront us in the present with glaring uncertainties.

In climate and weather modeling, time does not run out. What in fact runs out is the predictability of the model. When the model is no longer able to predict convincingly, the modelers are confronted with the limits of their own knowledge. It could therefore be said that what runs out is knowledge, when it is envisioned as coming up against the infinite and unpredictable potential of future events. However, it is exactly these future events—conceived of in the present—that constitute new knowledge for the climate modelers. To generate a prediction, they construct models that, little by little, exclude the infinite potential inherent in the future in order to propose possible scenarios that are, as Paul Edwards (1999, 2001) points out, the major source of information in the discussions on climate change. The only way to verify such predictions is to wait until the events that they describe are in the past—that is, to wait until they are no longer predictions because they inhabit the same time as those scenarios that they aimed to predict. The future, made present, is no longer a space of infinite, limitless possibilities, but it is also a space of uncertainty. In this sense, perhaps, there can be a limitlessness to limits. To understand the work of the modelers, it is necessary to countenance this constructed space of prediction, in which new knowledge is inevitably uncertain but has definite and hard-won limits.

Whereas the micrometeorologists in my account make new knowledge exactly by reaffirming old knowledge, the modelers make new knowledge by proposing certain uncertainty. These very different knowledge practices challenge an understanding of time that posits two mutually exclusive poles—one finite, given, and certain, the other infinite, constructed, and uncertain. The ways that limitlessness and finiteness are configured in both practices also challenge the assumption that limitlessness, and its possibility of constantly multiplying perspectives, is the only way to make new information, or that certainty is a prerequisite for new knowledge. Understanding what is happening in the field, in this case, necessitates countenancing how certainty contains novelty and how uncertainty can be a form of knowing (see also Strathern 2005). In order to understand how time works for both the micrometeorologists and the modelers, it is necessary to uncouple natural time and social time from an oscillation in which one is never enough and the other is excessive.

Being able to reconceptualize the relation of the social to the natural in this way is integral to an anthropology that would seek to embrace the idea of there being as many temporalities as there are ontologies (see Henare et al. 2007; Viveiros de Castro 2002). This goal is implicit in the introduction to this collection, which calls for countenancing others' ontologies "not only *in* time, but, indeed, *of* time." Such a proposal necessitates the capacity to rethink constantly the relational dynamics that structure our descriptions. In an intellectual world that increasingly seeks to uncover the myriad differential relations inherent in it, ethnographic practice is a valuable means to negotiate these relations, not only because, as Fabian (1983) points out, it is the way (rightly or wrongly) for us to gain 'temporal distance' from those we study, but also (more broadly) because it is an instantiation of those very relations. The relation between analysis and data is another way to think of the relation between the constructed and the given or the social and the natural. As such, the ways that anthropology's interlocutors figure this relation should affect the way that anthropology itself comprehends and accounts for it. The field, in this sense, might itself be seen as a particular relation between relations that should be explored anew and reconfirmed each time. For example, there is scope to see analytical significance in how uncertainty for the climate modelers is not so much a lack of knowledge but rather a specific way of knowing. Taking account ethnographically of the generative limits of knowledge in the field therefore points to some of the ways that new knowledge in anthropology may come about.

Acknowledgments

I would like to thank the organizers and participants of the "Time and the Field" workshop, which was held in Sandbjerg at the 2009 Megaseminar of the Danish Research School of Anthropology and Ethnography. I would also like to thank Casper Bruun Jensen for his comments. The research on which this chapter is based was funded by the Núcleo de Transformações Indígenas (NuTI) at the Museu Nacional, UFRJ, and the Conselho Nacional de Desenvolvimento Científico e Tecnológico (CNPq), Brazil.

Antonia Walford is currently an Honorary Research Associate in the Anthropology Department at University College London. She completed her undergraduate degree in Human Sciences at Oxford University, her master's degree in Social Anthropology at the Federal University of Rio de Janeiro, and her PhD in Science and Technology Studies/Anthropology of Science from the IT University of Copenhagen.

Notes

1. In this chapter I draw on Adam (1990), Gell (1992), Greenhouse (1996), and Nowotny (1992), but there are of course many others.
2. Alternatively, Greenhouse (1996: 3) has given the inversely symmetrical suggestion that social time is posited not against natural time, but as linked to the social whole, in an equally "objective and natural world in which societies exist."
3. Greenhouse (1996: 1) describes this oscillation in social time as a paradox for anthropology, as it seems to be "both culturally relative and universal." She emphatically denies, however, that there is "some cultural universal at time's core" (ibid.) and suggests that this paradox is instead the result of "the double assumption that linear time ... really *is* our time and really is *real*" (ibid.: 2).
4. See http://lba.cptec.inpe.br/lba/?lg = eng (accessed 10 June 2010).
5. In this chapter I will be concentrating on the work of the micrometeorologists.
6. On subsequent fieldwork, I was informed that what the micrometeorologists referred to as 'calibration' was in fact formally known in metrology as 'verification', as it was not as stringent a process as the calibrations that are performed in the Laboratory of Meteorological Instruments in São Paulo. However, for the purposes of this chapter, this difference is not relevant.
7. Strathern (1999: 10–11) observes that "special knowledge which inheres, say, in theological or scientific expertise has never held quite the place in anthropological accounts as materials which appear esoteric *because* they require revealing (beg immediate interpretation)."

References

Adam, Barbara. 1990. *Time and Social Theory*. Cambridge: Polity Press.
Brown, Nik, and Mike Michael. 2003. "A Sociology of Expectations: Retrospecting Prospects and Prospecting Retrospects." *Technology Analysis and Strategic Management* 15, no. 1: 3–18.
Collins, H. M. 1985. *Changing Order: Replication and Induction in Scientific Practice*. Chicago: University of Chicago Press.
Durkheim, Émile. 1912. *Les formes élémentaires de la vie religieuse*. Paris: Alcan.
Edwards, Paul N. 1999. "Global Climate Science, Uncertainty and Politics: Data-Laden Models, Model-Filtered Data." *Science as Culture* 8, no. 4: 437–472.
Edwards, Paul N. 2001. "Representing the Global Atmosphere: Computer Models, Data, and Knowledge about Climate Change." Pp. 31–66 in *Changing the Atmosphere: Expert Knowledge and Environmental Governance*, ed. Clark A. Miller and Paul N. Edwards. Cambridge, MA: MIT Press.
Fabian, Johannes. 1983. *Time and the Other: How Anthropology Makes Its Object*. New York: Colombia University Press.
Gell, Alfred. 1992. *The Anthropology of Time: Cultural Constructions of Temporal Maps and Images*. Oxford: Berg.
Greenhouse, Carol. 1996. *A Moment's Notice: Time Politics across Cultures*. Ithaca, NY: Cornell University Press.
Henare, Amiria, Martin Holbraad, and Sara Wastell. 2007. "Introduction: Thinking Through Things." Pp. 1–31 in *Thinking Through Things: Theorising Artefacts Ethnographically*, ed. Amiria Henare, Martin Holbraad, and Sara Wastell. Oxon: Routledge.
Nowotny, Helga. 1992. "Time and Social Theory: Towards a Social Theory of Time." *Time & Society* 1, no. 3: 421–454.
Orlikowski, Wanda J., and JoAnne Yates. 2002. "It's about Time: Temporal Structuring in Organizations." *Organization Science* 13, no. 6: 684–700.
Pickering, Andrew. 1993. "The Mangle of Practice: Agency and Emergence in the Sociology of Science." *American Journal of Sociology* 99, no. 3: 559–589.
Riles, Annelise. 2001. *The Network Inside Out*. Michigan: University of Michigan Press.
Strathern, Marilyn. 1991. *Partial Connections*. Totowa, NJ: Rowman & Littlefield.
Strathern, Marilyn. 1999. *Property, Substance and Effect: Anthropological Essays on Persons and Things*. London: Athlone Press.
Strathern, Marilyn. 2002. "On Space and Depth," Pp. 88–115 in *Complexities: Social Studies of Knowledge Practices*, ed. John Law and Annemarie Mol. Durham, NC: Duke University Press.
Strathern, Marilyn. 2005. "Useful Knowledge." Isiah Berlin Lecture. *Proceedings of the British Academy* 139: 73–109.
Viveiros de Castro, Eduardo. 2002. "O Nativo Relativo." *Mana* 8, no. 1: 113–148.

Chapter 2

THE TIME OF THE STATE AND THE TEMPORALITY OF THE *GAVMAN* IN MANUS PROVINCE, PAPUA

Steffen Dalsgaard

As a social model for the organization of societies, the state has had a profound impact on the rhythms, schedules, temporalities, and timing of social interaction and events. Yet the most commonly accepted meaning of 'the state' in sociological literature is largely based on a spatial definition that describes it as an entity exercising sovereignty within a bounded physical territory. In this chapter, I stipulate that the study of the state in Papua New Guinea (PNG) demands as much attention to temporality as it does to spatiality and materiality (cf. Munn 1992). The state can be experienced by rural people in PNG as personified in the politicians who control its resources, which they give as personal prestations to kin, followers, or voters. This entails an experience of the state as both facilitated and

Notes for this chapter are located on page 47.

limited by the presence of the politicians and by the duration of their attention. It is usually argued that the state has its existence and is reproduced as a social and cultural model *over* time and thus exists *in* time through various forms of institutionalization (Bourdieu 1999). I will argue that the personification, on the other hand, implies a challenge to the institutionalization of the state by causing temporal limitations to the ways that the state is present in people's everyday lives. To understand the way that people culturally relate to the state is not only a matter of location—of *where* it is (cf. Gupta and Ferguson 1997). It is as much a matter of timing—of *when* it is. This relates to whether, how, and when people feel included in or excluded from the distinct spatial and temporal dimensions of the state. Understanding this cultural and symbolic nature of the state involves paying attention to the relationship between its temporal and spatial presence. These cannot be regarded as two separate forms of existence (Massey 1992). How does the state exist temporally to people when its presence relies on events and personification rather than permanence in material and spatial terms? In other words, how, in practice, is the state made *of* time?

In discussing this issue, the chapter analyzes the temporality of practices associated with the state in Manus Province, PNG, where I have done a total of 23 months of ethnographic research since 2002. Manus is the smallest province in the country in terms of land area, and, with approximately 50,000 people, it also has the smallest population. As an island province, it is geographically isolated from the rest of country. After World War II, Manus came to the forefront of the territory's modernization, in part brought about by demands from the Paliau Movement (e.g., Otto 1991), but Manusians have since then gradually come to see themselves overtaken by the larger provinces that are endowed with more natural resources. Today, Manus people at times refer to their home province as being PNG's 'last place'—that is, the most remote and the one most often left out (Dalsgaard 2011).

Representations of the state in Manus have been formed through two distinct and contrasting processes: personification and institutionalization (Dalsgaard 2010). Whereas the former refers to a local and emic notion of the politicians of the state appearing as the state itself (see Clark 1997), the latter is an etic view of the state as knowledge forms, laws, and practices that have become accepted locally and are continuously reproduced through internalization as social dispositions (Bourdieu 1977). In this sense, the state has fostered what Ton Otto (1991) has referred to as an 'institutional domain' (in Tok Pisin *gavman*, i.e., 'state' or 'government') spanning across local, provincial, and national dimensions. *Gavman* is regarded as competing with other domains, such as tradition (*kastam*) or the missions (*lotu*).

While the institutionalization of the state (matched with recurrent funding for state activities) gives consistency and even a sense of permanence to the state over time, personification results in a limitation in the duration of state presence. Personification refers to how PNG people, particularly in rural areas, mainly experience the presence of the state through powerful 'big men' politicians, whom I analytically call 'gavmen' (government men).[1] These gavmen stand for—and to some extent are—the state due to their personal control and distribution of its resources as gifts in the same way that the classical big man has been described as *being* 'society' based on his abilities in exchange (e.g., Sahlins 1963). As with the big man, the gavman does not embody an enduring social form, and the social coherence of his group dissipates upon his demise. While the state in the abstract and objectified sense remains as an institutional-ized entity, the subjective experience of the state, as undergone by rural people via the gavman, fades when the gavman is no longer in office. With no gavman to provide a direct link between a rural population and the center of govern-ment power, the state is reduced to a precarious existence that diminishes with the deterioration of the institutions it has left behind.

To elucidate how the state can be considered temporal, I rely on a notion of 'presence'. Derrida has criticized the historical discussion of time in philosophy for relying on presence as a dominant value, which fuses together "evidential, spatial, and … temporal motifs" (Wood 1989: 3). Without entering into this debate of time in relation to metaphysics (ibid.), I do take it as an invitation to clarify what I mean by the term. That is, I do not intend to imply a one-to-one relationship between presence and 'the present' (i.e., temporality), but to stress that presence may also involve exactly evidentiality or spatiality (i.e., material-ity) when talking about *gavman*. In the ethnographic record from Manus, it is possible to find observations of how materiality is valued as evidence over 'talk' (see Dalsgaard 2009; Otto 1992). The tangible thus validates the pres-ence of that which is conceptual and 'ephemeral'. To be sure, most Manusians have no doubt that there are powerful and resourceful government men around somewhere, even if they are physically absent at a given point in time, but it is the attention and goodwill of the gavmen that must be attracted in order for state presence to be legitimate and sincere. This state (and gavman) presence is uncertain, so it must be 'made present' through gift-giving, which is an indispensable part of nearly all events, including those in which government officials participate. In speeches there will be references to the past (previous exchanges, alliances, or genealogical links, but also sometimes *kastam* or 'tra-dition'), which call to the fore old 'debts', but the gifts are nonetheless planned attempts to attract future counter-gifts of (typically) government services or development. Thus, presence entails orientation, which extends beyond what is evident in the present (cf. Otto, this volume).

I thus think of presence in terms of how my empirical material debates the existence of *gavman* as being exactly something of the (temporal) pres-ent. This implies a conceptualization of presence that also depends on what it is *not*—that is, 'absence'—because the state is not taken for granted in PNG. It is not something that has been around in the past, nor is it expected to be automatically present in the future. Despite the historical processes of institutionalization (see Otto 1991), the temporalities of intermittent interac-tion between gavmen and public servants give the state an ephemeral guise. Below, I will consider the temporalization of the gavman and the event-based experiences of interacting with state agents before discussing these matters in light of recent concerns in anthropological studies relating the state to spatial-ity and temporality.

Events and Exchanges

As discussed by Inger Sjørslev (this volume), fieldwork entails a lot of waiting. This is also the case when working with public servants and politicians in PNG. My initial interest in studying the state was partly aroused by the way I was helped to navigate red tape in order to get a research permit. Once I had arrived in Manus for this project, waiting became an integral part of my research, although it did not necessarily involve boredom or even 'unfocused presence' (cf. Sjørslev, this volume). Waiting for meetings with public servants, as well as waiting for and during 'state events', soon turned out to be a frequent occurrence. But it was an opportunity for conversation with other people who were also waiting, and these events, during which state leaders appeared to the public, became a central aspect of fieldwork and of its rhythms. They revealed how people attempted to control a social situation by 'breaking' such rhythms or by manipulating them to their own advantage, which I began to find interesting.

In practice, the personified appearance of the state in the guise of the gavman is presented through temporally delimited events that usually last an afternoon. When a rural community is in need of funding for development, the people's path to procure the funding is to approach the relevant administration (typically the provincial one in Manus) and wait for their turn. This procedure takes a while, and success can be nearly impossible unless community members have personal relations with a senior administrator in the relevant department. A much more direct approach is to invite a gavman. This can be one of their members of Parliament (MPs) or, if this is not possible, the president of their local level of government. The gavman is typically invited to celebratory events, such as the launching of a community project, the opening of a building or a wharf, or possibly the graduation of the students of the local school. Such events display the local community as active agents in the eyes of the gavman, because he comes at a time when something has already been completed or achieved. At the event, the gavman is presented with gifts, but he is also given the opportunity to respond to more or less subtle requests for funding. In essence, the gavman is put in a situation where he can hardly respond negatively without contradicting the statement about his importance, which the villagers have made by showing him their hospitality.

A thorough analysis of the typical structure of a celebratory event taking place in Manus would exceed the limits of this chapter; however, as a guide for the reader I will mention the usual content and character. Events can initially be looked at from the vantage point of anticipating the preparations and the build-up of excitement (see Bourdieu 2000), and then from the point in time when the event is concluded and people are discussing the status and success of its outcome. Within the time span of the event itself, a number of actions are expected to take place. No event happens without speeches, which often outline how those who have been brought together have been linked through relations of exchange in the past. Food is always distributed, and sometimes there are gifts of other material objects. Often there are different forms of entertainment, such as choir songs, drama, or dancing to the beat of traditional log drums (*garamut*). These events thus take a form that incorporates elements of traditional gift exchange ceremonies. Many hours of organizing, planning, and discussion are involved in order to time the appearance of the visiting gavman and the groups to be assembled. The event itself follows as a climax to this longer time span of preparations, and afterward its success may be debated by those who were present or who heard about it. In other words, events contain their own space-time (cf. Munn 1992).

The appearance of a gavman and his attention to a specific village are fundamentally transitory. Yet the visiting gavman leaves behind gifts that may be of varying duration. Such gifts can be in the form of funding for the construction of buildings (classrooms, churches, clinics), for infrastructure (roads, wharves, shipping opportunities), and for sanitation (water tanks), or for other forms of material longevity in projects classified as 'development'. In some cases, the gavmen may hold feasts to celebrate certain achievements, such as the construction of the aforementioned developments (no matter who funded them) or the gavmen's own candidacy or election to Parliament, or to mark future ambitions and aims of development by launching projects or plans for projects.

The concern with the short-lived presence of politicians is mirrored in people's perceptions of the contrast between traditional and ideally hereditary leadership (called *lapan*), on the one side, and the growing electoral success of big men who govern through short durations of massive expenditure, on the other. One man commented to me that democracy was "democrazy," adding that "the culture of elections today ... you get into a car, get a cigarette, a beer you drink, and it will keep you going in the short run. If you vote for your blood, it will last a long time." The influence of the *lapan* (traditional leaders of villages and kin groups) has historically been and still is described as one based on achievement, but at the same time a strong ideology of ascribed rank deriving from bloodline seniority affects an individual's status (see Otto 2002; Schwartz 1963). This ideology is often invoked as a counter to what many Manus people describe as the negative influence of money and consumables, which fail to sustain people in the long run, but can be obtained in bulk every five years when a gavman seeks re-election. A village is fortunate if one of their kinsmen or allies is voted into office, because this assures their access to government resources that can help them 'develop'. Yet at the same time there is much anxiety about the continuity of representation in office due to the five-year electoral cycle and because historically the rate of members who serve more than one term has ranged from 20 percent to 60 percent (May 2008: 4).

The Temporal Limitation of Personal Relations of Exchange

Rural people's access to state resources depends on their personal relationship with either a senior public servant or a politician, preferably an MP. This personal relationship may be direct or indirect via what Manus people refer to with the spatial metaphor 'road'. Exchange takes place as a result of roads of kinship relations or past exchange relationships (cf. Dalsgaard 2011; Schwartz 1963:

59). No matter which relationship rural people may be able to evoke, a request for government funding depends on this activation of the social relationship with a gavman. Relationships that are not maintained over time will lapse and be forgotten, but they can be reactivated with appropriate gifts. As with many other forms of sociality in PNG, the general maintenance or activation is facilitated by exchange (Dalsgaard 2010). Giving gifts and thus eliciting responses or counter-gifts is a way for people to engage with the state, by exploring its limits, its potential resources, and its capacity to use them (cf. Strathern 1999) and obtaining access to those resources by attempting to articulate moral concerns with reciprocity.

The interests involved in the gift exchange, which people use to get state attention and to elicit development funding, is best demonstrated empirically. From here, I will first outline the material and spatialized presence of the state, because this forms the background to its temporal presence in the gift exchange. I will then return to the issue of temporality and the strategic control of time and space involved in practical interaction between the state and its citizens.

The spatiality and materiality of the PNG state is focused on the capital of Port Moresby where the buildings of Parliament and the offices of the various ministries and departments are located. Provincial administrations exist as mini-centers of power and resources in between the national center and rural areas. Despite the roll-out of some local level government services (e.g., clinics, postal service) in townships around the province, these are often defunct, and people frequently have to travel to the provincial capital or even farther to get what they need. Finally, the combined representations of the state stretch out into the villages through the institutions of education, health, and law (e.g., schools, community health orderlies, magistrates), but they also include values such as money and titles (cf. Bourdieu 1999). Some of these forms are unstable. Although they persist over time, their gradual deterioration is obvious in everyday discourse. Crime (*raskols*) and delinquency, for example, are regarded by locals as being on the rise in both urban and rural areas (Dinnen 2001; Goddard 2005). Some traditional leaders have responded with attempts to assert their own village sovereignty over the law by taking it into their own hands. Manus people also are concerned that the education system, which has been the road to success for many Manusians in the past (Carrier and Carrier 1989), is failing to provide the desired upward social mobility. Many high school graduates end up returning to the village because jobs are scarce and the combination of a funnel-shaped education system and social pressure from fellow students on those performing too well results in only the most adept and determined students advancing to the university level (Demerath 2000).

While the state has a materialized presence in the villages, in particular in the shape of school buildings and aid posts, there are two problems with these state representations that give them an air of temporal limitation and make state presence uncertain over a continuous period. Firstly, infrastructure and buildings are often in a state of disrepair and lack maintenance. The state thus appears to have a duration that expires as the constructions slowly fall into dilapidation. On two islands in Manus, where I conducted a lot of my fieldwork, the aid posts often had no supply of medicine, and the buildings were in a state of decay. While one of the communities (Mbuke) had put effort into maintaining some parts of these buildings, they lacked funds for materials. They tried to meet the costs with various fund-raising activities. While this gave the community ownership of the aid posts in the sense of commitment, it also lifted the responsibility for their upkeep and therefore the legal ownership of the aid posts as assets away from the state and onto the local community. Schools on these islands were better off and better maintained as long as there were teachers and students.[2] This was also a community effort. The Mbuke people had built a new double-story building with four classrooms and a couple of new teacher's houses. The provincial government provided a small contribution to cover some costs, but most of the project was paid for by local fund-raising schemes and by remittance contributions from Mbuke emigrants. One of the traditional leaders in Mbuke commented: "The government of the day has no money. We need to do this on our own." Similar stories could be told about the acquisition of water tanks. One of the Manus MPs had promised several large tanks, but the effort did not succeed, and again the gavman (and thus the state) was regarded as having failed. The general attitude was that "the government doesn't see [i.e., recognize] us."

Secondly, the constructions, viewed as gifts to a community, are often claimed by a 'sponsor' or 'donor', who 'made' them or gave them to the villagers. This donor is not tied to the abstract notion of the state but is recognized as a concrete politician, who made a choice and allocated the resources to construct the building in question (see also Clark 1997). One notable example of this is the naming of the donor even with what would be regarded, from an etic point of view, as public or state property. In 2006, one of the incumbent MPs for Manus, Charlie Benjamin, had used his development funds to purchase a car for the police in the provincial capital of Lorengau and a new ambulance for the Lorengau General Hospital. Both vehicles appeared on the roads of Lorengau with an inscription on the side: "Donated by Hon. Charlie Benjamin MP Member for Manus." With this naming on state property, the state becomes personified. Charlie Benjamin was not just occupying the office—he *was* the office. While there are no examples in Manus of such personal donations being taken back by the donor when he loses the office,[3] it does mean that the state is not recognized as the donor. It is the MP. When the donor is no longer in office, the gift can no longer be said to have been given by the state.

With these challenges to the identification of the state and to a permanent state presence in people's lives, it is common to hear complaints about the ephemerality of the state. People lament the lack of government attention and funding for the maintenance of state or community assets. Sometimes they express nostalgia in relation to what they had before. When I first arrived in the village of Lipan on Baluan Island in 2002, the closest thing the village had to a center was the school and the neighboring playing field. The village was spread out along the coast, so it was difficult to speak of the school grounds as a spatial center even if it was a social one, at least for schoolchildren. Several of the buildings on the school grounds, as well as some of those nearby, had housed a local administration, a co-op, and the local patrol officer (*kiap*) when Lipan had been the center for the Baluan Council in the early 1950s. The Baluan Council was allegedly the first native council outside the capital Port Moresby. During my fieldwork, one man in particular lamented how Lipan had had electricity from a generator when he was a child, and that they had had their own *kiap* stationed there when the village had been the home for the council. He expressed to me his hopes that Lipan and Baluan would once again become a center in Manus as he thought it ought to be because of its legacy of being the birthplace of the Manus prophet Paliau Maloat.[4] Paliau was regarded as the founder of the council, which was the first form of participation in government for Manus people. This lamenting of the past was also a lamenting of the absence of the state—or at least the absence of the power and centrality associated with the state. Now Baluan villagers experience living on the periphery of Manus and PNG. Much of the work that goes into local ceremonial or festive initiatives is thus aimed at drawing the state's attention or getting external resources including those available to migrant kin (Carrier and Carrier 1989; Dalsgaard and Otto 2011).

From this it can be concluded that there is an acute awareness of the transitory nature of the state—of the non-permanence of its attention and of its representations. The state is there when the gavman is there. As a result, enormous resources go into making the state present via the gavman. Whenever there is an appropriate event for celebration, an important VIP—usually a politician and preferably an MP—is invited as a guest. Paying for the transport of the invited VIP is often the most costly item on the agenda, but it is necessary to have a prominent guest to give the event a proper appearance, that is, to 'look good'. While political opponents may argue—particularly if nothing is elicited or the result is less than hoped for—that such events are merely for show (*bilas*), the appearance of the gavman confirms people's membership in the PNG state and thus, in a way, the citizenship of the villagers hosting the event. The gavman's presence may be enduring if it results in the financing of buildings or development projects, or it may not if his gifts are in the form of food and beer. These gifts (food in particular) can be given when a politician organizes feasts himself, for instance, during electoral campaigns (cf. Standish 1991). Yet this consumable form of a gift is metaphorically said not to leave anything tangible behind except *pispis na pekpek* (urine and feces). The memory of the feast may count as a manifestation of how many relations the organizer can assemble, thus adding to his or her reputation and status. However, such status wanes if the event cannot immediately attract resources that are of a more permanent nature or ensure a future response—something that cannot be known at the time an event is staged. It is evident that state events here are future-oriented by imposing obligations upon the recipients in their attempts to attain permanent, or at least long-lasting, durable assets. Herein lie both the power and the uncertainty of the present— and here I refer to the present as both temporality and a gift. The reciprocation is always uncertain in terms of quality, quantity, and timing (cf. Bourdieu 1977). This is especially so regarding exchange relationships with politicians, whose attention is being sought by different groups of their constituencies. It is thus only in retrospect that the gift can be deemed to have been successful.

Bureaucratic Space and Time

The previous section argued that the work of exchange through personal relationships enables rural people to elicit funding for development projects from
their MP. This is the best way for rural people to be 'seen' (i.e., recognized) by
the state and to count as 'citizens' (Clark 1997). Personal relationships are also
regarded as the most effective road to interaction with public servants, which
is what I discuss in this section.

Anthropological theories about bureaucratic practice situated in a Euro-
American perspective on the state tend to ascribe control of space and of time
to bureaucrats and bureaucracy. On one level, this addresses the institutionalization of the state as mentioned above, whereby the introduction of taxonomic regulations via clock time (with scheduling and calendars), production
demands, access to specific resources, and the timing of state events facilitate
control over people's time and even their private daily rhythms (Greenhouse
1996; Handelman 2004; Verdery 1996). In Manus, such temporal orderings add
to the perception of the institutionalized understanding of the state through the
category of *gavman*. My interest is at another level, asking how time in practice
is used and controlled in the actual interaction between bureaucrats and clients
who all draw upon various social obligations and categories as resources (cf.
Handelman 1976; Herzfeld 1992).

Control of this social interaction between state and citizen is difficult to sustain for provincial public servants in Manus. During fieldwork, I spent several
months working in and with the Manus Provincial Administration in Lorengau.
Being in the administration offices every day, I noted the work patterns of many
of the employees: several were often late or not present at all during the day.
While there were many reasons or excuses given for these absences (some better
than others), one in particular is of relevance to my argument. On this occasion,
it was almost midday before the executive officer of one of the local level gov-
ernments arrived.[5] He told me that he had been held up the whole morning by
clients who had come to his house, the first one appearing while he was having
breakfast. The private house of the public servant is not 'private' in the sense of
being secluded from work obligations. Since the public office is seen as personal,
it extends to wherever the public servant goes. A person who knows where a
public servant lives will often feel that it is legitimate to go there to ask for help
with a government errand. In addition, several public servants spend a significant amount of their office hours hanging out at Lorengau's market, chewing
betel nuts, flirting with passers-by, or taking care of business—either their own
or that of some of their clients. When a frustrated client had come in vain to the
administrative office, he summed it up as follows: "Their office is in the street."

In order to control time or the tempo of the interaction (cf. Herzfeld 1992:
162), the bureaucrat must also be able to control space. But Manus politicians
and public servants can be sought out in their homes and in the streets by clients (typically extended kin or exchange partners) because they do not control
social and/or moral obligations. Such obligations transcend the spatial and conceptual boundaries of the state. Bureaucrats cannot separate their obligations

to their employer from those to their personal associates. Thus, they do not control the timing of their work unless they can devise effective delaying tactics or strategies of avoidance (ibid.: 165). This inability of the public servant to control space and time was more severe for the junior public servants than for the senior ones. But even MPs, while having better opportunities to devise strategies of avoidance by referring to being 'busy' or 'in a meeting' or even by staying away in Port Moresby, could not remain aloof from clients altogether. Nor did they want to, if they intended to be re-elected. Several informants told me that they preferred leaders who would sit and eat with them or go fishing with them. They wanted leaders who could be found at the market and who were thus approachable by the common man or woman. To live up to such expectations, one candidate in the 2007 parliamentary election went so far as to state in a speech that his office was like an automated teller machine, in the sense that it was open to people 24 hours a day. He had to give what is often the most precious asset of someone trying to make a career in the modernized world: he had to 'give time' (cf. Bourdieu 2000).

In this way, while state agents from the colonial era up to the present have introduced measures that attempt to control villagers' utilization of time (such as the clock, the calendar, and the subsidization of certain forms of production that demand specific schedules), they have not managed to introduce a 'dominant time' (cf. Rutz 1992: 4–5; Verdery 1996). This is so partly because many rural households in PNG still have a degree of food self-sufficiency and thus cannot be coerced into specific rhythms of production and consumption, and partly due to the morality and hierarchies embedded in personal social relationships as mentioned above. The timing of exchange events outlined earlier is controlled by the most high-ranking participants: it starts when they arrive. This goes for traditional exchange ceremonies as much as for government meetings, and 'ritual waiting' can be imposed by traditional leaders as well as government leaders (cf. Verdery 1996: 49). The situation is reversed when clients seek out a politician or a public servant. While state agents may try to control where and when to meet, they are not in a position to turn away clients, who can draw upon social and moral ideals of how a 'good kinsperson' or a 'good leader' is supposed to behave. It is regarded as immoral if one does not listen to a person's plight or if one is not there for people who are in need. That is, one's house must always be open, and one must always take the time to deal with visitors. I heard tales of how public servants or politicians would try to hide from kin or clients. But even if they should flee to Port Moresby, they cannot avoid requests, which today are facilitated by the increasingly extensive mobile phone coverage of urban and even some rural areas.

Space, Time, and the State

In the final part of this chapter, I will relate the above analysis to recent theoretical and ethnographic interests in the spatiality and temporality of the state as a field of study. One notable reason for this recent anthropological interest in the state is the perception of changes in the conditions by which the Western state can exist and exercise its powers in a period that is seen as being characterized by an increase in space-time compression and globalization (Ferguson and Gupta 2002). Similarly, the applicability to post-colonial states of traditional characteristics of the nation-state, such as the claim to monopoly on the exercise of violence within a limited territory, has been questioned by some of the theories evolving from the concerns with global reconfigurations of the role of the state (Hansen and Stepputat 2006). As a 'field', the state is particularly problematic to delimit in spatial terms when its ultimate extension—its national boundaries—is challenged by processes involving the increased mobility of people, goods, media images, and so forth (Appadurai 1990). Where does one locate the practical and social boundaries of the state when its lack of sovereignty and ability to control global processes calls the legitimacy of the nation-state itself into question (Hansen and Stepputat 2006)? On the one hand, the state is where its offices and officers are. It is materialized and thus spatialized in the buildings, titles, resources, and everyday practices of a bureaucracy that controls numerous forms of cultural and symbolic production through social interaction (Ferguson and Gupta 2002). On the other hand, the state is in many countries 'everywhere' as a dispersed internalization of knowledge and practices through discipline (Foucault 1977) or through forms of capital (Bourdieu 1999). While the state can be perceived by its subjects to have a center (a capital city with government offices), its value systems also transcend boundaries in space when people in the margins accept the necessity of taxation, the symbolic capital of the state's insignia, and state money (ibid.).

Anthropological debates relating time and the state have predominantly been expressed as the passing of time that permits people to exercise agency over the state, or vice versa (e.g., Rutz 1992; Verdery 1996). The contention is even made that time has agency in and of itself. Time has been seen as that which provides the potential for change and thus for historical praxis, while its conceptual opposite, space, has been regarded as 'static' (Coronil 1997: 24–25). Because of the recent attention in academia to historical contexts and contingency, Fernando Coronil has argued that time has been overemphasized in the study of the state (ibid.). However, when it comes to delineating the state as a site for research, it is rather spatiality that has been overemphasized (Ferguson and Gupta 2002; Gupta and Ferguson 1997). Reasons for this include the attention given to globalism and the confusion over temporal and spatial scaling. Marilyn Strathern (1999: 204) contends that when "distance is measured in time ... the globe seems smaller, and speed becomes a short-hand for space-time compression." As I have argued above, delineating the practices under study purely in spatial terms (of location or site) misses the entwined concerns of practically negotiating the spatio-temporal distances between the state and its citizens.

I have looked at the temporality ascribed to the state from the perspective of its presences and absences (gavmen, materiality, and the approachability of MPs and public servants). This involves a perspective on several time-related practices (e.g., state longevity based on representation or the anticipation of state presence due to the strategic manipulation of social relationships) as much as on the spatial extension of the practices, events, and material representations associated with state agency. In this approach, I see everyday practices that involve the manipulation of time and people's temporal orientations as crucial elements (Bourdieu 1977; Herzfeld 1992; Munn 1992; Rutz 1992; Verdery 1996). As demonstrated by Pierre Bourdieu (1977, 2000), among others, gift exchange involves a manipulation of social relations through tempo. It is this temporality of the gavmen—that they have limited time because of their almost unlimited social obligations to other communities and social relations of different domains—that demands a constant work of exchange to attract a gavman's attention to villagers' needs for development. In Manus, where the procurement of power and of resources is facilitated through exchange, temporally delimited events often take center stage in the social interaction with resourceful others, including the state. Studying exchange and celebratory events as expressions of practice and process entails the recognition that the field itself is temporally situated. Such events are in many ways the main mode of socially organizing and displaying one's capacity for agency (cf. Strathern 1999). Without mass media and its broad public reach, most people in PNG experience government agency by being in the audience at events. This is where the actions of the state materialize and where villagers can witness developments the moment that they take place. It is by anticipating and participating in gavman events that one comes to play a role in the spatial reach of the state. At the same time, these events are at the center of the temporal outlook through which villagers perceive of the state and its realities. They are occasions when people come to enjoy and participate in social relations involving the state and where it is present in their lives.

Conclusion

In Manus, the contemporary dominant imaginary of the state is informed by the temporality of practices and events that include people as members of the state for a limited period of time. A spatio-temporal 'state effect' is created by gavmen as a nexus for exchange between the PNG state and rural populations. Through their activities, the gavmen maintain for a limited amount of time the illusion that the state can appear to be 'coherent' and can fulfill the will and the common good of the people. Their ability to assemble, in both space and time, the resources (human, monetary, material) needed for the conduct of a 'government event' gives the appearance of a coherent state.

Identified as a crucial part of the study of the state in Manus, exchange events present an assemblage of intentions and imaginaries that extend beyond both the time and the space in which they are conducted. *Gavman* exchange events display people's different temporal orientations. Along with the interaction between bureaucrats and their clients, they entail the spatio-temporal effect of the state by generating both its reach and its presence. The organizers invest enormous resources in such events, but doing so is necessary in order to achieve success and recognition. The participants identify the events as important, and therefore the prominence of these events is central to the emic understanding of the state's performance.

At the same time, personal relations of exchange, which are in the making during the events, also characterize many of the everyday bureaucratic interactions between public servants and clients. These are more difficult to identify and follow unless the researcher realizes that both the boundaries of time and the space of the state are dissolved when personal relationships can be entertained between public servant and client. Public servants are all potentially 'street-level officers' when they can be pressured to conduct business with clients not solely in office buildings but just as often at the market or in the home of the public servant. The people in need of bureaucratic help are not so much 'clients' as they are kin or acquaintances. They thus draw upon taxonomic resources and obligations located outside the state sphere and manage to defy the state's spatio-temporal segmentations of the world (cf. Bowker and Star 1999). This challenges the ethnographic fieldworker to examine not just the policies and official case documents that legally frame this interaction (cf. Handelman 1976), but also the expanded space of the public servant as a person and the temporalities embedded in historical structures of kinship, morality, and exchange.

Solely discussing the territoriality of the state or analyzing its spatial distances or locations misses half of the equation about how the state is practically constituted, both in the lives of its citizens and as a field and object of ethnographic inquiry. Analyzing the relationship between spatiality and temporality helps the researcher understand the specific cultural interpretations of the state that come into play and reveals how the state is constructed as a field both *in* time and *of* time.

Acknowledgments

This chapter could not have been written without the generosity of those people with whom I have worked in Papua New Guinea and in Manus in particular. My gratitude goes to them, but also to Morten Nielsen, Michael Whyte, two anonymous reviewers, and the participants in the workshop "Time and the Field" at the 2009 Megaseminar of the Danish Research School of Anthropology and Ethnography. The fieldwork for this chapter was funded by the Faculty of Humanities at Aarhus University, Carlsbergs Mindelegat for Brygger J. C. Jacobsen, Bikubenfonden, and the Danish Ministry of Science, Technology, and Innovation. It was written while affiliated with the Ethnographic Collections at Moesgård Museum, Aarhus.

Steffen Dalsgaard holds a PhD in Anthropology and Ethnography from Aarhus University and is an Associate Professor at the IT University of Copenhagen. He is currently Deputy Chair of the Young Academy of Denmark. Since 2002 he has conducted research in Manus, Papua New Guinea, specializing in state and political leadership with a focus on tradition, exchange, and elections. He is currently working on two projects: democratic technologies (in Denmark and Papua New Guinea) and the introduction of carbon as a form of global value. Recent publications include articles in *HAU: Journal of Ethnographic Theory*, *Social Anthropology*, *Environment and Society: Advances in Research*, and *Social Analysis*.

Notes

1. The term 'gavmen' is my pluralization of *gavman* as a personified entity. To distinguish between personified and institutionalized forms, I italicize the latter throughout the chapter.
2. However, every village has stories of school teachers staying away or skipping work and of the lack of school materials (books and so forth).
3. The journalist Sean Dorney (2000: 45) gives an account of a group of people in Southern Highlands Province who tore down a high school that the former MP, whom they had supported, had funded. They argued that the new MP could build his own school.
4. This villager has to date initiated several activities aimed at promoting Baluan. Among other things, he was the main organizer of a large cultural festival held in Lipan in 2006 (see Dalsgaard and Otto 2011).
5. The person was de facto head of the administration of a local level government and in practice a secretary to the elected president of the local level government.

References

Appadurai, Arjun. 1990. "Disjuncture and Difference in the Global Cultural Economy." *Theory, Culture & Society* 7, no. 2: 295–310.

Bourdieu, Pierre. 1977. *Outline of a Theory of Practice*. Trans. Richard Nice. Cambridge: Cambridge University Press.

Bourdieu, Pierre. 1999. "Rethinking the State: Genesis and Structure of the Bureaucratic Field." Trans. Loïc J. D. Wacquant and Samar Farage. Pp. 53–75 in *State/Culture: State-Formation after the Cultural Turn*, ed. George Steinmetz. Ithaca, NY: Cornell University Press.

Bourdieu, Pierre. 2000. *Pascalian Meditations*. Trans. Richard Nice. Oxford: Polity Press.

Bowker, Geoffrey C., and Susan L. Star. 1999. *Sorting Things Out: Classification and Its Consequences*. Cambridge, MA: MIT Press.

Carrier, James G., and Achsah H. Carrier. 1989. *Wage, Trade, and Exchange in Melanesia: A Manus Society in the Modern State*. Berkeley: University of California Press.

Clark, Jeffrey. 1997. "Imagining the State, or Tribalism and the Arts of Memory in the Highlands of Papua New Guinea." Pp. 65–90 in *Narratives of Nation in the South Pacific*, ed. Ton Otto and Nicholas Thomas. Amsterdam: Harwood Academic Publishers.

Coronil, Fernando. 1997. *The Magical State: Nature, Money, and Modernity in Venezuela*. Chicago: University of Chicago Press.

Dalsgaard, Steffen. 2009. "Claiming Culture: New Definitions and Ownership of Cultural Practices in Manus Province, Papua New Guinea." *Asia Pacific Journal of Anthropology* 10, no. 1: 20–32.

Dalsgaard, Steffen. 2010. "All the Government's Men." PhD diss., Aarhus University.

Dalsgaard, Steffen. 2011. "The Battle for the Highway: Road, Place and Non-place in Manus, Papua New Guinea." *Paideuma* 57: 231–249.

Dalsgaard, Steffen, and Ton Otto. 2011. "From *Kastam* to *Kalsa*? Leadership, Cultural Heritage and Modernization in Manus Province, Papua New Guinea." Pp. 141–160 in *Made in Oceania: Social Movements, Cultural Heritage and the State in the Pacific*, ed. Edvard Hviding and Knut M. Rio. Oxford: Sean Kingston.

Demerath, Peter. 2000. "The Social Cost of Acting 'Extra': Students' Moral Judgments of Self, Social Relations, and Academic Success in Papua New Guinea." *American Journal of Education* 108, no. 3: 196–235.

Dinnen, Sinclair. 2001. *Law and Order in a Weak State: Crime and Politics in Papua New Guinea*. Adelaide: Crawford House Publishing.

Dorney, Sean. 2000. *Papua New Guinea: People, Politics and History since 1975*. Sydney: ABC Books.

Ferguson, James, and Akhil Gupta. 2002. "Spatializing States: Toward an Ethnography of Neoliberal Governmentality." *American Ethnologist* 29, no. 4: 981–1002.

Foucault, Michel. 1977. *Discipline and Punish: The Birth of the Prison*. Trans. Alan Sheridan. Harmondsworth: Penguin.

Goddard, Michael. 2005. *The Unseen City: Anthropological Perspectives on Port Moresby, Papua New Guinea*. Canberra: Pandanus Books.

Greenhouse, Carol. 1996. *A Moment's Notice: Time Politics across Cultures*. Ithaca, NY: Cornell University Press.

Gupta, Akhil, and James Ferguson. 1997. "Discipline and Practice: 'The Field' as Site, Method, and Location in Anthropology." Pp. 1–46 in *Anthropological Locations: Boundaries and Grounds of a Field Science*, ed. Akhil Gupta and James Ferguson. Berkeley: University of California Press.

Handelman, Don. 1976. "Bureaucratic Transactions: The Development of Official-Client Relationships in Israel." Pp. 223–275 in *Transaction and Meaning: Directions in the Anthropology of Exchange and Symbolic Behavior*, ed. Bruce Kapferer. Philadelphia: Institute for the Study of Human Issues.

Handelman, Don. 2004. *Nationalism and the Israeli State: Bureaucratic Logic In Public Events*. Oxford: Berg.

Hansen, Thomas B., and Finn Stepputat. 2006. "Sovereignty Revisited." *Annual Review of Anthropology* 35: 295–316.

Herzfeld, Michael. 1992. *The Social Production of Indifference: Exploring the Symbolic Roots of Western Bureaucracy*. Chicago: University of Chicago Press.

Massey, Doreen. 1992. "Politics and Space/Time." *New Left Review* 196: 65–84.

May, Ron. 2008. "The 2007 Election in Papua New Guinea." SSGM Briefing Note 2008/7. Canberra: RSPAS, ANU.

Munn, Nancy. 1992. "The Cultural Anthropology of Time: A Critical Essay." *Annual Review of Anthropology* 21: 93–123.

Otto, Ton. 1991. "The Politics of Tradition in Baluan." PhD diss., Australian National University.

Otto, Ton. 1992. "The Paliau Movement in Manus and the Objectification of Tradition." *History and Anthropology* 5, no. 3–4: 427–454.

Otto, Ton. 2002. "Chefs, big men et bureaucrates: Weber et les politiques de la tradition à Baluan (Papouasie, Nouvelle-Guinée)." Pp. 103–129 in *La tradition et l'État: Églises, pouvoirs et politiques culturelles dans le Pacifique*, ed. Christine Hamelin and Eric Wittersheim. Paris: L'Harmattan.

Rutz, Henry J. 1992. "Introduction: The Idea of a Politics of Time." Pp. 1–17 in *The Politics of Time*, ed. Henry Rutz. Washington, DC: American Anthropological Association.

Sahlins, Marshall. 1963. "Poor Man, Rich Man, Big-Man, Chief: Political Types in Melanesia and Polynesia." *Comparative Studies in Society and History* 5, no. 3: 285–303.

Schwartz, Theodore. 1963. "Systems of Areal Integration: Some Considerations Based on the Admiralty Islands of Northern Melanesia." *Anthropological Forum* 1, no. 1: 56–97.

Standish, William. 1991. "Simbu Paths to Power. Political Change and Cultural Continuity in the Papua New Guinea Highlands." PhD diss., Australian National University.

Strathern, Marilyn. 1999. *Property, Substance and Effect: Anthropological Essays on Persons and Things*. London: Athlone Press.

Verdery, Katherine. 1996. *What Was Socialism, and What Comes Next?* Princeton, NJ: Princeton University Press.

Wood, David. 1989. *The Deconstruction of Time*. Atlantic Highlands, NJ: Humanities Press International.

Chapter 3

OUT OF CONCLUSION
On Recurrence and Open-Endedness in Life and Analysis

Anne Line Dalsgaard and Martin Demant Frederiksen

Endings

In the end, the business card actually turned into a business.
~~In the end, the business card actually turned into a business.~~
In the end, the business was substituted by a non-existing website.
~~In the end, the business was substituted by a non-existing website.~~
In the end, nothing really happened.
~~In the end, nothing really happened.~~

In the end, he became a decent worker at the factory.
~~In the end, he became a decent worker at the factory.~~
In the end, he was caught by the police and arrested for theft.
~~In the end, he was caught by the police and arrested for theft.~~
In the end, he took another shower.
~~In the end, he took another shower.~~

References for this chapter begin on page 61.

Recurrence

It began with a review of literature on marginalized youths. At the time, Martin Demant Frederiksen had finished his fieldwork in Tbilisi for his master's thesis and had to write an exam paper on a topic of his choice that related to his research. Martin contacted his future supervisor, Anne Line Dalsgaard, and together they discussed the possibility of turning the review into a comparative analysis based on his work on young people in Georgia and her work in Brazil. The writing began as an attempt to criticize the then current tendency within anthropology and related fields to consider marginalized youths as either victims of structural constraint or agents in their own lives. They took as their point of departure the stories of two individuals, Rezo and Fábio, whom they knew well and whom they saw as being neither victims nor efficient agents. The first draft eventually turned into a grant application with two colleagues to do research on questions of youth, marginality, and futurity. The project was funded, and Martin and Anne Line both returned to their field sites where new data emerged. Of course, the lives that they had focused on during previous fieldwork had moved on while they had been away. The initial conclusion of the first draft had to be changed, and so a new draft was written. Meanwhile, they had become interested in writing styles and questions concerning the anthropologist's possible responsibility in relation to the lives she or he describes.

A year or so went by. The stories of the two young men in Georgia and Brazil moved on yet again. Anne Line lost contact with the informant she was writing about and presumed he had gotten himself into serious trouble. Martin, on the other hand, had heard from his informant that he had, after several years of disappointment, finally succeeded in establishing an actual business. Yet another draft, with new endings, was written and later discussed at a workshop entitled "Time and the Field." Comments from other participants were included, and new ideas for restructuring the argument and ending were written into the text. The initial literature review was taken out, as it was no longer relevant. An invitation to submit the piece as part of a special issue of *Social Analysis* was accepted, and it was finalized and sent in. Almost a year passed without notice, during which new fieldwork, new data, updates on the worries and troubles of informants, as well as their missed chances and new prospects, all came about. When the anonymous reviews were received, certain things no longer seemed right. A new argument emerged out of corrections and adjustments, and a new theory had to be found. Once again, this meant beginning anew.

Holding On

A business card. He holds it in his hand as he approaches the anthropologist in the underground passageway. He is a tour guide, or at least he hopes that one day he will be. The card features an image from the animated film *Ice Age 2*: a small animal is clinging to a cliff, denying the fact that it is, inevitably, going to fall.

"Life is adventure or nothing at all," the card reads. The man approaches the anthropologist with the words "Could you help me? I have this business." The anthropologist looks at the business card and wonders why the web address has been crossed out and there is no office address. Does the business exist or not? It is hard to tell; maybe it does and does not at the same time. In the Republic of Georgia, in the capital city Tbilisi where the man lives, chances are few. He has an education but lacks the network and connections that are so vital in the country if one wants to advance or get a job. But what if he had his own business? Or it at least seemed as though he did? Would the foreigners living in the expensive city center hotels then maybe consider hiring him as their tour guide? Could he get business by pretending to have one already? Or is he, like the animal on the card, simply clinging to a cliff with his nails, destined to fall? Is he merely living in the future with no reference to his present situation, or is he making a future? Rezo is his name.

Somewhere else. A shower. A young man, brown skinned, with a hideous scar on his right thigh. He lives in one of the poorer parts of Brazil in circumstances that are not conducive to being well-groomed. The house in the *favela* (shanty town) where he lives is hot during the daytime, and the steps up the hillside to get there are many. He used to work in a factory, carrying heavy loads, and he dreamed of becoming a truck driver to escape from the meaningless toil and the commandments of others. To be allowed a driver's license at the factory, he needed to talk to the right people. But how? One day, during his lunch break, he sat down at the table next to Mauricio, a superior with influence. But Mauricio got up and moved to another table. "It was my smell of sweat. Brazil is divided into those who smell of sweat and those who do not. Like Mauricio." The young man refuses to be what they turn him into. But can he wash off a predestined future? The question is asked in every shower, in the changing of shirts, and in the honesty he projects, because he is the kind of person who could just as well be a reliable truck driver. Fábio is his name.

Introduction

Every moment has the potential to lead to something new; the question is how this potential is released. One may wait for the unexpected to emerge, assuming that "there is always the possibility, as in any mystery story, that factors will emerge and come into play of which one has no inkling, and that these unforeseen factors will free the future from the impress of the past" (Jackson 2005: 14). One may passively wait for 'luck' or 'miracles' in what Ghassan Hage (2003: 12) calls a "hope against life." And, in a way, this is what Rezo and Fábio do. They wait for the right moment to appear, the moment when someone calls Fábio forward and acknowledges his honesty and hard work, and the moment when Rezo meets the right kind of tourists, ready for a dubious adventure. But they do not do so passively. In their revisiting of the recurring experience of setbacks, of impossibilities, there is a manifestation of a vibrant life, of a kind of unjustified promise. They could just as well give up, but they do not. They begin again. The potential of every new beginning is not an empirical fact. It may rather be an empirical non-fact, since a potential cannot, by definition, have the factive quality of a fact. A potential is a capacity of being or becoming, and as such it challenges the established way of arguing in anthropology for the credibility of our analysis. How do we write about something that is present by way of absence or, rather, by way of not yet being a fact?

Anthropologists have written about the subjunctivity and managing of uncertainty in human life (Good and Good 1994; Steffen et al. 2005; Whyte 1997). These analyses have argued that agency unfolds in even the most difficult situations—that "[h]umans are never merely victims of fate" (Jenkins et al. 2005: 11) and that people generally struggle to achieve some sense of control in life (Jackson 1998). These studies have emphasized the negotiation of uncertainty and the often ingenious handling of it. However, ours is less an interest in negotiation and problem solving in relation to the question of agency and more a look to the manifestation of the subject over time. We simply ask how we can understand the loops in the trajectories of life that we observe, if not as repetition alone. Or, put differently, is there more to recurrence than mere repetition? Drawing primarily on the work of Hirokazu Miyazaki, we think of the process of repetition as a "method of hope ... predicated on the inheritance of a past hope and its performative replication in the present" (Miyazaki 2004: 139). However, where Miyazaki looks at hope in a ritual, that is, in a collective context, we try to understand a subjective process by way of his insight.

Our data stem from ongoing fieldwork in the Republic of Georgia and in Northeast Brazil. Life in the two chosen regional contexts is marked by poverty and disappointment, and young people in particular find it hard to uphold aspirations for the future. Even though Brazil today is experiencing enormous growth and reimagining of the future, this does not change Fábio's situation. He and many others of his age grew up in the depressing 1980s and early 1990s, and they had little to look forward to when they were younger. Similarly, although more stable today than in the 1990s, the social and political situation in the Republic of Georgia continues to leave few, if any, options for Rezo.

Stories

Rezo was 20 years old when Martin first met him in an underway passage. What distinguished Rezo from his peers was that, in describing his own situation, he acknowledged that his chances were near nil. As he noted on one occasion, "It is not really nice to talk bad about the country you live in but ... Georgia has some problems you know. For example, if you want a job, you have to know somebody, you know? Have relations." Rezo was referring to the fact that getting a job often depended on having a connection to someone who could either hire you or make sure that you were hired. It was clear to him that he did not have any such relations and did not see himself as having any obvious chances. He had begun to distrust the entire official system, and, due to changes in the educational sector, the courses he had taken in 'hospitality and hotel training' were considered 'too old' to be of any real use (although he had graduated only recently), making it impossible for him to find a job in the hotel industry. Furthermore, the hopes for the future expressed by the Georgian government and various institutions taking care of unemployed or homeless youths did not fit with his situation. But in some respects, it seemed that the recognition of not having any real chances and of the apparently hopeless situation motivated Rezo to continue to be on the lookout.

When Martin returned to Tbilisi after a year's absence in the spring of 2007, Rezo was thus still looking for a job, still looking for a girl to marry, and still walking around the city in search of possibilities—or looking for possibilities to find him. He was, in this sense, not different from many other young men in Tbilisi who were waiting for a chance to move on in life—except for one thing. He proudly carried a business card in his pocket. The business, he explained, did not actually exist yet. He did not have an office, and he had crossed out the web page link on the card because it linked to a non-existent page. And if he managed to get some customers, he was not sure what he would do or where he would take them. Still, he found that in order to *do* business he needed to *have* a business, and the business card served as an intermediate stage, an imagined future that was yet to become concrete. The image of the 'squirrel rat' from *Ice Age 2* was striking. In the movie, the rat is on a continuous chase to protect a small nut and to regain it when it is lost. For reasons that Rezo probably did not have in mind, the image of the squirrel rat seemed to correspond well to his situation. On the one hand, here was a young man desperately trying to hold on to something, but it was also an image of the fruitless end result of the eternal chase—with a possible business substituted for a nut. But this, of course, was Martin's interpretation, not Rezo's.

In Brazil, Fábio had almost given up waiting for the future that he wished for—a truck driver's license and a job as a driver. Even so, the possibility that he could as well have become a truck driver, if he had had a little help, seemed to change the situation he was in—or at least to keep it open. He was almost pre-destined to prison and an early death: when he was still young, he got involved in criminal activities like so many young boys in the neighborhood where he lived (Dalsgaard 2004; Dalsgaard et al. 2008). His brother was killed when they were out stealing. His friend was killed when they were high on drugs together, riding on the roof of a train. Fábio himself later went to prison when he was caught selling drugs. Although he got out with the help of a lawyer who could see his potential, he was soon wanted by the police again. Through the years that followed, he got himself into more and more criminal activities, and at the time of writing he is wanted by the police for having been part of a gang that has committed several serious crimes. And yet he somehow escapes the lot that befalls others like him. When Anne Line first met Fábio, he had already lived longer than many of his age mates. Through all that he has been involved in, he has, to some extent, been able to stop and withdraw when withdrawal was still possible. People help him despite the things he has done. They hide him, set him up with a job as a construction worker in the city he has fled to, and get him false papers when he needs them. According to his mother, this willingness to help springs from Fábio's sincere attitude, which people recognize and respect. The sincerity seems to be a result of his self-respect, which shows in small, everyday acts.

What is self-respect? In Georgia, it is your behavior when you toast a friendship, those who died, or those who will come. It is generosity toward friends, which is always an active choice (Frederiksen 2013). In Brazil, it is the simplicity with which you meet everyone, without anger or resentment, and the cleanliness that even the poorest can produce. It is the ability to resist 'heating up the head', as people say, like when Fábio said: "I will conform and continue my life forward, not look back. Because if a person looks back at the things he already did, what will you get? Nothing! You have to look forward ... you have to try!" Self-respect is thus closely related to the respect or recognition bestowed by others, but every moment involves a choice and is inherently dangerous, as recognition from others can be withdrawn. Recognizing the potential of a moment is thus also a hesitation to conclude. Somebody may see who I really am, despite the neglect and disregard of others.

Fábio seems to have let in some hope by allowing the agency of God a place in his life, while staying as clean and prepared as possible. His acts are not conspicuous. They mainly consist in withdrawing and not despairing, and thus staying alive against all odds. But something in him is active, as if the pain of knowing his situation keeps him awake. Rezo mimicked something that did not yet exist: the business card contained Rezo's hope of something coming into being, a not yet that, although non-existent, provided him with an incentive to keep striving. Moltmann's (2004) notion of hope as that which has no place 'yet' (but is immanent) seems pertinent here. Neither of the young men is in a safe haven, though. When Anne Line last heard from Fábio's mother Neide, she was angry with him because he kept asking for money through his girlfriend, who phoned Neide. Fábio could no longer work where he was, his girlfriend was tired of supporting him, and Neide had her own worries. Frustration was building up on all sides, and Neide was afraid that Fábio would do "something stupid" and get caught by the police. Rezo managed to get his first customers, and the tours went well, regardless of the fact that he had no previous experience of actually conducting tours outside Tbilisi. In e-mails and phone calls, he told Martin how he still had a long way to go; he wanted to learn foreign languages and to create a website. He was not sure how to accomplish this, but his endeavor no longer seemed destined to the wild goose chase that might never end, as Martin had originally assumed. Rezo had in fact succeeded in turning his imaginary vision of his own future into a present reality that offered him direct possibilities and gains. But when the conflict between Russia and Georgia broke out in August 2008, it dealt a serious blow to the tourism industry in Georgia (Frederiksen 2011). E-mails from Rezo stopped.

Both stories could end here with the conclusion that Fábio managed to stay clear of prison due to his hope of one day becoming a truck driver, while Rezo managed to get a business started against all odds. But it does not seem right to end here. Fábio and Rezo have to face new mornings with sincere doubts and risks. Both are likely (as our knowledge of them indeed has shown) to return to previous conditions and practices—showering, distributing business cards, or doing whatever is needed to hold on to their potential. It is this process of recurrence—the continual setbacks and the starting anew—that has caught our interest. Something occurs in the recurrence. A kind of continuity appears. It may be imagined, but it nevertheless has real consequences (cf. Jenkins et al. 2005: 10).

Hope

In his book *I Am Dynamite*, Nigel Rapport (2003: 14) writes that "construing and pursuing one's life as an individual project is a route to a dignified and accomplished life." This ongoing accomplishment is, to Rapport, the unfolding of an existential power, "the force, the will, the energy, in a word the agency, whereby individuals produce effects in their worlds—effect worlds, in fact" (ibid.: 75). While the individuals that Rapport takes as his "Everyperson" (ibid.: 15; cf. Rapport 2010) are people who, at least so it seems, are more capable and single-minded than Rezo and Fábio, we find that Rapport's insistence on the potential openness of every life has a bearing in relation to our cases as well. Neither Rezo nor Fábio moves through life as an "individual as projectile" (Rapport 2003: 149), but both possess an individual project, a 'distinctness' that manifests itself through their various acts (or non-acts) in a continual process of becoming, almost as an active waiting (cf. Jeffrey 2010).

From a common-sense perspective, human life is at all times open-ended, since no one, per definition, knows the end before it is reached. Hence, we may argue that as long as we in our analysis hold on to one view of what the future might bring, be it solely pessimistic or hopeful, we do not fully capture life as lived. A finished story is somehow 'over', lifeless. As John Berger (1982: 284) sees it, stories walk like men, and the suspense does not relate to the plot as much as to the passage from one step to another. Thus, knowing the end is not as interesting as following the process. What will happen next? This openness entails hope, because as long as the story has no conclusion, it can always be different. In both our fields, daily life is filled with seemingly mundane routines—or recurrences—that partake in upholding this openness to the world and the future. It is the propensity for change and the potential of each moment, we believe, that must be kept in mind while engaged in anthropological writing.

Indeed, hope is praxis, keeping things open, as Miyazaki (2006) writes, and not an emotional state of positive feeling about the future or a religious sense of expectation. It is a method of radical temporal reorientation of knowledge, a process of looking forward instead of backward, as Miyazaki (2004) describes it in relation to a gift-giving ritual in Fiji. The ritual was not designed to generate hope, as Miyazaki initially understood it; rather, it was in itself a hopeful praxis, where the maintenance of a prospective perspective was at the heart of its performance. Hope, he understood, was the submission, ritual after ritual, to keeping the future open by holding one's agency in abeyance, leaving the fulfillment of the story to higher powers. There are, we believe, striking parallels between Miyazaki's description of gift-giving rituals and the lives of Fábio and Rezo. The maintenance and repetition of everyday routines, such as Fábio taking his showers and Rezo polishing his shoes before venturing out onto the streets with his business card, are both forms of hopeful praxis that render their lives—and stories—open.

There are, writes Richard Wilk (2009: 144), "subtle and often subjective differences between the routines which make life possible, and those which make living miserable." In the repetitive gestures involved, for instance, in t'ai chi, repetition is aimed at perfecting and refining the act that is repeated (ibid.). But the return to and repetition of a previous condition or action (i.e., recurrence) may also be conducive to change. It is, we believe, in this sense that we can understand recurrence as a practice of hope. Indeed, hope and hopelessness are mutually related—two sides of the same coin (Crapanzano 2006: 17; see also Zigon 2009). At times, in a paradoxical manner, there is no way out of hopelessness but by accepting it as part of life. We often find hope in that which is *not*—not only because hope is the 'not yet', but also because hope has to do, in many cases, with not doing something that one would otherwise have done.

Repeated acts or withdrawal from action may have the quality of similarity, but they are not necessary identical—and this is the crucial point. Repetitions rarely (if ever) take place in a social vacuum. The social context in which they occur may change, and coincidence may allow for 'vital conjunctures' (Johnson-Hanks 2002, 2005) that, seen in retrospect, transform the trajectory of a life. The repeated acts may be interpreted in ways that result in alteration. For instance, Fábio's insistent showering may be recognized by others as a sign of decency, which changes their perception of him as a person, and Rezo's distribution of his business card may be read by a passer-by as a sign of persistence, qualifying him for a job. It is impossible to foresee such potentialities in any exact manner, but their possible presence is at the very heart of the hopeful aspects of recurrence.

In his article "A Day in the Cadillac," Morten Pedersen (2012) describes a hopeful day with a group of young men in Ulaanbaatar, Mongolia, and argues that otherwise heterogeneous and disparate impressions of self and situation are gathered into fragile assemblages during such moments of hope when one is seen by oneself and others as a whole person. Such moments of joyful realization and prospect are probably not absent in Rezo's and Fábio's lives, even though we have not been part of them. But we have found a different kind of wholeness: one that emerges out of a continuous process of revisiting (our informants' setbacks as well as our returns to the field). The process of revisiting leaves impressions that add up to more than their sum, as if in a montage, where the simultaneity of often different impressions creates the impression of something otherwise not perceptible (Dalsgaard 2013; Eisenstein 1972: 90). This impression of encompassing wholeness belongs to the viewer, and, therefore, what we try to grasp here does not necessarily contradict Pedersen's description of his friends' moments of coming together. Ours is an interest in the persistence that keeps Rezo and Fábio going. The 'viewer', as we see it, is not only us, the visitors, but also Rezo and Fábio, who are witnesses to their own lives. However, the existence of this inner continuity is inferred by us and not empirically justified, except for the fact that it manifests itself over time as persistence despite setbacks. As the filmmaker Sergei Eisenstein (1972) writes, only when time is introduced may a kind of wholeness emerge as a sensed overtone. Motion and rhythm are needed for this unifying overtone to appear: "In the three-dimensional space it is not spatially possible to represent it; only in the four-dimensional space (three plus time) does it emerge and exist" (ibid.: 106–109; our translation).

Writing

As stated at the beginning, the pattern of recurrence in the two stories only appeared to us as we kept returning to the field. In revisiting our fields, we have both returned to social realities we know well and interviewed young people we have known for a decade or more. Thus, we are addressing a question related to longitudinal studies: Is it the same continuous social reality we return to? If so, what is the character of the continuity? And if not, how do we allow for the unexpected to occur when experience tells us how things are most likely to develop?

In our analyses, we, the anthropologists (and markedly within youth studies), tend to become the judges of whether the hopes of our informants should be deemed prospective or deceptive. In other words, we tend to write analyses that are either too pessimistic or too optimistic because we wish to determine the future or come to terms with it in a very literal sense. This, we believe, is a problematic that can be traced back to the traditions of narration that dominate our ideas of good analysis. The full meaning of a story, Hannah Arendt ([1958] 1998: 192) tells us, reveals itself only when it has ended. It is therefore not until after the fact that we can fully grasp what was at stake in a given context. With a focus on the future, however, it is impossible to get beyond the fact, as the future continuously turns into something that is new and not yet tested. Every time we returned to the field, our conclusions or 'endings', so to speak, were put to shame by the course of events.

The method of fieldwork allows us to follow people in the present and to listen to their stories about the past. But the stories and lives of our informants do not come to a halt when we as fieldworkers return to our universities and are required to 'get something out of' the days we spent in the field. For our informants (and for us while it happened), the moments we spent together were open-ended and part of the process of life, but for the analytical mind, 'life as lived' is soon turned into a past from which we distance ourselves and that we objectify. Reflection upon past moments is inherent in meaning-making (cf. Muzzetto 2006), but for our informants reflection is still part of an ongoing process. In our analyses, however, we are seldom aware of the future-oriented aspect of reflection, of the consequences of our thinking. This temporal inequality is a crucial difference between lived moments and written, and hence objectified (maybe even reified), pasts that can be taken into account in analysis. As long as the future is open for our informants, the new and unexpected may still happen. One way of coming to terms with this, we believe, is to let the time of the field, including recurrence and potential, be reflected, not only in our analysis of the field, but also in the text itself.

Such a focus on the relation between field, time, and text in some ways relates to Johannes Fabian's (1983) much-quoted volume *Time and the Other*. Here Fabian argues for a style of writing that incorporates concepts of history and time as a means of portraying coevality between ethnographer and informants by, among other things, avoiding the ethnographic present that freezes societies in time. As Kevin Birth (2008: 4) sums up Fabian's argument: "Stating that 'The X are matrilineal' implies that the X have always been and always will be matrilineal even though all societies change ... Thus, the ethnographic present removes the Other from the flow of time and denies the human propensity to change." We agree with Fabian that freezing our informants in time denies them the propensity to change in the future, but we wish to take his argument one step further in stating that 'freezing in time' is not just a matter of grammar. Our narrative style that leads toward conclusion is a much stronger denial of openness and change, at least in the way that anthropologists usually employ it.

Conclusions about the present most often involve implicit predictions about the future, but it is difficult, perhaps even hazardous, to predict what will happen to persons or societies, as Jeremy Boissevain (1992) has found. Returning to the same field over a period of years made him aware of the relativity of the social life he was studying. When returning to the field after a period of several years, and looking back on his previous work, he could see how his attempts to predict what might happen did not correspond to reality. The relativity of the moment makes it impossible to foresee exactly what the moment will turn into. Boissevain concludes that it is essential to place one's analysis "in a time frame that provides a longer perspective than the few years you have personally experienced. This means more history, more examination of the past" (ibid.: 78). But as Birth (2008) has so precisely observed, the past is never just one, and to give it a place in analysis means first of all knowing which past is at play in the given lives under study. Which personal experiences, concepts of time, and culturally shared ideas are being combined? Placing ourselves and our informants in time—sometimes shared, sometimes not—is thus as much a phenomenological endeavor as a historical one.

Likewise, a focus on futurity is necessarily phenomenological since even the discourses about future outcomes are lived, insofar as they are meaningful to somebody (Frederiksen 2013). To write in a future-oriented way does not imply prediction. In fact, it means quite the opposite, namely, that anything can happen, be it felicitous or not, as the future is inherently unknowable. Indeed, as Miyazaki (2004: 8) notes: "The retrospective treatment of hope as a subject of description forecloses the possibility of describing the prospective momentum inherent in hope. As soon as hope is approached as the end point of a process, the newness or freshness of the prospective moment that defines that moment as hopeful is lost." A main objective of this chapter, therefore, has been to explore whether it is possible or maybe even necessary to deploy a sense of open-endedness in our analyses, thus highlighting the fact that life is a process that continuously extends into the future.

Endings?

For Rezo's and Fábio's stories to be finished, it would mean that they had died. Fábio is certainly on thin ice, as he is sought by the police, and although Rezo might have made progress with his tourist agency, he will be eager to achieve further success and will have to fight to keep his business going amid the challenges of the societal changes surrounding him, not least the recent war with Russia that turned many young Georgian men's lives into a question of life and death. We cannot know if Fábio and Rezo (or we) will be here 10 years hence. When Anne Line is back in Denmark, talking with Fábio's worried mother on the phone leaves hope open yet also demonstrates that things are not well. Had he been safe, his mother would not have called or been worried about where he is. Fábio is not safe—but, on the other hand, he is not dead. Receiving Rezo's e-mails is likewise keeping a hope alive. And yet, would Rezo write if he had better things to do? Are the recently missing e-mails in Martin's in-box a sign of trouble or of animated progress? These omens are full of promise but also of uncertainty, and they give rise to questions that keep the relation to the field vibrant. The unfinished relationship is productive, like a stone in the shoe that keeps disturbing us. Indeed, as Anthony Cohen (1992: 2) has observed, the writing of ethnography is a provisional endeavor in the sense that our understanding of what took place during fieldwork is likely to change over time. A good example of this is Renato Rosaldo's (2004) classic description of bereavement among the Ilongot and how his understanding of data changed over time as a result of the death of his wife. Rather than seeing this instability as a troublesome aspect of knowledge production, we (and Cohen) find it to be an inescapable condition to be met and explored creatively.

In constantly rewriting this text, new endings have been designed in order to test various possibilities, and these have in time opened up new questions and perspectives that have come to life. Numerous sections and paragraphs have been written only to be cut out later, used for something different or left in a drawer. The recurrence has in many ways created its own form of excess. Some arguments have been lifted into other pieces, an entire research project was funded and concluded in the process, and new ideas for other projects have emerged. You could say that the deferred concluding is just a sign of long-windedness and lack of determination. But we will argue that there is more to it than capriciousness. In the prolonged process of writing, we observed something that would probably not have appeared in a less hesitating analysis: the truth about an individual life (and hence about a particle of the possible) is discernible only in the sameness of its varied, often divergent manifestations.

Acknowledgments

The authors would like to thank the participants of the workshop "Time and the Field," which was held at the August 2009 Megaseminar of the Danish Research School of Anthropology and Ethnography, as well as Susanne Højlund and Lotte Meinert for their constructive comments on an earlier version of the text. Morten Axel Pedersen provided valuable suggestions during the finishing process. This chapter, to which both authors have contributed equally, has been written as a tribute to our mutual friend Marie Højlund Bræmer.

Anne Line Dalsgaard is an Associate Professor at Aarhus University. Based on extensive fieldwork in Northeast Brazil since 1997, she has published several articles on motherhood, youth, violence, and temporality. Her book *Matters of Life and Longing: Female Sterilisation in Northeast Brazil* (2004) has been translated into Portuguese and was awarded an Honorable Mention by the Eileen Basker Memorial Prize committee of the American Anthropological Association in 2004.

Martin Demant Frederiksen holds a doctorate in Anthropology and is an Assistant Professor in the Department of Cross-Cultural and Regional Studies at the University of Copenhagen. He has conducted long-term fieldwork studies in the Republic of Georgia since 2006 and in Bulgaria since 2015 and has published on issues such as urban planning, hope, youth, crime, temporality, and ethnographic writing. His current research concerns the role of meaninglessness in social life. He is the author of *Young Men, Time, and Boredom in the Republic of Georgia* (2013) and co-editor of the anthology *Ethnographies of Grey Zones in Eastern Europe: Borders, Relations and Invisibilities* (2015).

References

Arendt, Hannah. [1958] 1998. *The Human Condition*. 2nd ed. Chicago: University of Chicago Press.
Berger, John. 1982. "Stories." Pp. 277–291 in *Another Way of Telling*, ed. John Berger and Jean Mohr. London: Writers and Readers.
Birth, Kevin. 2008. "The Creation of Coevalness and the Danger of Homochronism." *Journal of the Royal Anthropological Institute* 14, no. 1: 3–20.
Boissevain, Jeremy. 1992. "On Predicting the Future: Parish Rituals and Patronage in Malta." Pp. 68–80 in *Contemporary Futures: Perspectives from Social Anthropology*, ed. Sandra Wallman. London: Routledge.
Cohen, Anthony P. 1992. "Post-fieldwork Fieldwork." *Journal of Anthropological Research* 48, no. 4: 339–354.
Crapanzano, Vincent. 2006. *Imaginative Horizons: An Essay in Literary-Philosophical Anthropology*. Chicago: University of Chicago Press.

Dalsgaard, Anne Line. 2004. *Matters of Life and Longing: Female Sterilization in Northeast Brazil.* Copenhagen: Museum Tusculanum Press.

Dalsgaard, Anne Line. 2013. "Being a Montage." Pp. 100–105 in *Transcultural Montage,* ed. Christian Suhr and Rane Willerslev. New York: Berghahn Books.

Dalsgaard, Anne Line, Mónica Franch, and Russell P. Scott. 2008. "Dominant Ideas, Uncertain Lives: The Meaning of Youth in Recife." Pp. 49–73 in *Youth and the City in the Global South,* ed. Karen T. Hansen in collaboration with Anne Line Dalsgaard, Katherine V. Gough, Ulla A. Madsen, Karen Valentin, and Norbert Wildermuth. Bloomington: Indiana University Press.

Eisenstein, Sergej. 1972. *Udvalgte Skrifter.* Holstebro: Odin Teatrets Forlag.

Fabian, Johannes. 1983. *Time and the Other: How Anthropology Makes Its Object.* New York: Columbia University Press.

Frederiksen, Martin Demant. 2011. "Good Hearts or Big Bellies: *Dzmak'atsoba* and Images of Masculinity in the Republic of Georgia." Pp. 165–187 in *Young Men in Uncertain Times,* ed. Vered Amit and Noel Dyck. New York: Berghahn Books.

Frederiksen, Martin Demant. 2013. *Young Men, Time, and Boredom in the Republic of Georgia.* Philadelphia, PA: Temple University Press.

Good, Byron J., and Mary-Jo Del Vecchio Good. 1994. "In the Subjunctive Mode: Epilepsy Narratives in Turkey." *Social Science & Medicine* 38, no. 6: 835–842.

Hage, Ghassan. 2003. *Against Paranoid Nationalism: Searching for Hope in a Shrinking Society.* Sydney: Pluto Press.

Jackson, Michael. 1998. *Minima Ethnographica: Intersubjectivity and the Anthropological Project.* Chicago: University of Chicago Press.

Jackson, Michael. 2005. *Existential Anthropology: Events, Exigencies, and Effects.* New York: Berghahn Books.

Jeffrey, Craig. 2010. *Timepass: Youth, Class, and the Politics of Waiting in India.* Stanford, CA: Stanford University Press.

Jenkins, Richard, Hanne Jessen, and Vibeke Steffen. 2005. "Matters of Life and Death." Pp. 9–30 in Steffen et al. 2005.

Johnson-Hanks, Jennifer. 2002. "On the Limits of the Life Cycle in Ethnography: Toward a Theory of Vital Conjunctures." *American Anthropologist* 104, no. 3: 865–880.

Johnson-Hanks, Jennifer. 2005. "When the Future Decides: Uncertainty and Intentional Action in Contemporary Cameroon." *Current Anthropology* 46, no. 3: 363–385.

Miyazaki, Hirokazu. 2004. *The Method of Hope: Anthropology, Philosophy, and Fijian Knowledge.* Stanford, CA: Stanford University Press.

Miyazaki, Hirokazu. 2006. "Economy of Dreams: Hope in Global Capitalism and Its Critiques." *Cultural Anthropology* 21, no. 2: 147–172.

Moltmann, Jürgen. 2004. *In the End—the Beginning: The Life of Hope.* Trans. Margaret Kohl. Minneapolis, MN: Fortress Press.

Muzzetto, Luigi. 2006. "Time and Meaning in Alfred Schütz." *Time & Society* 15, no. 1: 5–31.

Pedersen, Morten A. 2012. "A Day in the Cadillac: The Work of Hope in Urban Mongolia." *Social Analysis* 56, no. 2: 136–151.

Rapport, Nigel. 2003. *I Am Dynamite: An Alternative Anthropology of Power.* London: Routledge.

Rapport, Nigel. 2010. "Apprehending *Anyone*: the Non-indexical, Post-cultural, and Cosmopolitan Human Actor." *Journal of the Royal Anthropological Institute* 16, no. 1: 84–101.

Rosaldo, Renato. 2004. "Grief and a Headhunter's Rage." 3rd ed. Pp. 579–593 in *Anthropological Theory: An Introductory History,* ed. R. Jon McGee and Richard L. Warms. New York: McGraw-Hill.

Steffen, Vibeke, Hanne Jessen, and Richard Jenkins, eds. 2005. *Managing Uncertainty: Ethnographic Studies of Illness, Risk and the Struggle for Control.* Copenhagen: Museum Tusculanum Press.

Whyte, Susan R. 1997. *Questioning Misfortune: The Pragmatics of Uncertainty in Eastern Uganda.* Cambridge: Cambridge University Press.

Wilk, Richard. 2009. "The Edge of Agency: Routines, Habits and Volition." Pp. 143–157 in *Time, Consumption and Everyday Life: Practice, Materiality and Culture,* ed. Elizabeth Shove, Frank Trentmann, and Richard Wilk. Oxford: Berg.

Zigon, Jarrett. 2009. "Hope Dies Last: Two Aspects of Hope in Contemporary Moscow." *Anthropological Theory* 9, no. 3: 253–271.

Chapter 4

TIMES OF THE OTHER
The Temporalities of Ethnographic Fieldwork

Ton Otto

The rise of modern ethnographic fieldwork is rooted in a paradox. The key methodological move as formulated by Malinowski was to 'put one's tent among the natives' and thus to share their time and lives, but the intellectual drive, as Johannes Fabian has argued, was to study people who were assumed to live in another time than our own. According to Fabian (1983: 31), anthropology has been characterized by a consistent and pernicious "denial of coevalness" to the people who were the subjects of the discipline. By this he means "a persistent and systematic tendency to place the referent(s) of anthropology in a Time other than the present of the producer of anthropological discourse" (ibid.). The paradox, then, is that this creation of another, non-coeval time is based on the actual sharing of real time. In this chapter I will argue that this paradox

Notes for this chapter are located on page 77.

is not as devastating for the anthropological endeavor as Fabian wants us to believe. Even though I fully agree that temporal stereotypes stand in the way of ethnographic understanding, I maintain that the sharing of time in the present also reveals differences of temporal orientation co-existing in the present and reflecting different pasts. Thus, one could argue that in this sense people do live in different times while sharing the present. Because of its focus on direct experience and participation, ethnographic fieldwork is a key method to make these differences in time orientation or temporality visible.

Fabian's exposition of the temporal interpretations of anthropological encounters, leading to the placement of the Other in another time than the present, may be a specific Western example of a widespread human practice that occurs when people meet people from a different culture. Take, for example, the reaction of Papua New Guinea Highlanders to the first white people patrolling into their country. They saw the strange white beings as travelers from the sky—a cosmological place populated with spirit beings—or as their returned ancestors, that is, as people from the past (Gammage 1998). Thus, temporal speculations appear to be part of intercultural encounters generally and not only of the ethnographic endeavor.

The editors of this volume have to be congratulated for putting time at the center of reflection about fieldwork. As the term 'fieldwork' itself already indicates, our understanding of doing ethnographic research is dominated by spatial metaphors: we go to a specific geographical location, we cross political and cultural boundaries, we travel to our 'field' (Clifford 1997; Gupta and Ferguson 1997; Olwig and Hastrup 1997). Recently, there has been a critical revision of the idea that the field is one particular place, but still the focus appears to be on how a virtual field can be constructed in spite of this. George Marcus's (1995) useful concept of 'multi-sited' fieldwork captures this very well. The phenomena that we study are not, or no longer, localized in particular places but have to be identified by tracking them across different field sites. Marcus's concept is no doubt an apt characterization of how most modern fieldwork is conducted, but the spatial orientation still lingers. In line with the editors (see the introduction), I suggest that we give equal value to the dimension of time when defining both our fieldwork and the subjects we study.

I. Sharing the Present

The topics that anthropologists study—human social activity, social relations, cultural continuity and change—are all temporal phenomena, just as much as they have a relationship to space. Therefore, it is of the utmost importance to understand how these phenomena are constituted in time and how our research can provide access to their temporal dimension. Time for human beings minimally involves a past, a present, and a future. These dimensions of time are embedded in the grammatical structures of human languages and have been the object of much religious and philosophical thought. Social time is both created through human activities and objectified in mechanic measurement and theoretical reflection. Philosophical speculation about time, especially in the twentieth century, has been extensive and overwhelming, in particular in the currents of thought that are defined as pragmatism, phenomenology, and existentialism (Mead, Bergson, Husserl, Heidegger, Schutz, Deleuze). I suggest that it will be a major task for anthropological theory to catch up with these theoretical ideas and speculations and investigate their leverage in intercultural research. In spite of a corpus of very interesting and relevant anthropological work, it is generally felt that an anthropology of time is still in its infancy (cf. Adam [1994] 2002; Gell 1992; Hodges 2008; Munn 1992).

For the present chapter, I have been inspired by the pragmatist philosopher George Herbert Mead, in particular his posthumously published *The Philosophy of the Present* ([1932] 2002).[1] I find that Mead's focus on how human reality, including consciousness, emerges in action is very relevant to the empirical perspective of anthropologists. One of the core ideas of Mead's book is that the present is the locus of reality or, in other words, that existence happens in the present. In a strict sense, only the present exists, which is always emerging from a previous present and becoming a new one. Mead does not deny the existence of a past—a time gone by that is irrevocable—but this past is accessible only as far as it is present in the present. As present interests and categories change, so does our knowledge of the past, which is continuously constructed from the present and therefore revocable. The past is thus simultaneously irrevocable and revocable, but it is only the latter, revocable form that we can deal with. In the same vein, the future is based in the present as hypothetical and revocable. Hence, both past and future exist for human action only as dimensions of the present.

Mead's insight is of critical relevance for understanding anthropological fieldwork. Since human action always—necessarily—happens in the present, anthropologists doing ethnographic fieldwork enter a real time interaction with coeval human beings. This interaction in the present is the basis for emerging knowledge, derived from participating in the same events. Therefore, I see the sharing of real time as the rock bottom of ethnographic fieldwork. But the sharing of the present does not mean that one shares the other actors' conceptualizations of past and future. Nor does one necessarily share their habitual time orientations and modes of 'time reckoning' (Munn 1992), with the result that the interaction lacks 'synchronization'.[2] Every field anthropologist will have stories to tell about the often comic and sometimes distressing miscommunications of time expectations that characterize the early stages of fieldwork in a different cultural environment. When Western anthropologists go to remote places in Africa or Melanesia, for example, the contrast between clock time dispositions and event time orientations is often felt as disturbing and even physically discomforting, as it can be part of an experience of culture shock where one loses control of the minutiae of one's daily life. In these non-Western places, clock time is not—or no longer—absent but often has a different function or meaning as a marker of special value (Otto 1992a; Schieffelin 2002).

When anthropologists go to a culturally different place, they go in some sense to a different time—even though existing in the same present—because they interact with people with whom they do not share a culturally common past.[3] The absence of this common experience of shared time creates a strong likelihood of miscommunication and alienation because anticipations of future events—based in the present—are easily frustrated. In his writings on time and timing, Pierre Bourdieu (1977, 1990, 2000) provides an excellent conceptual framework for explaining what is happening. According to Bourdieu (2000: 206), human practice is not *in* time but actually *makes* time. Human time is based on the interest of actors in the 'game' they are involved in that gives sense—both meaning and direction—to their activities, which anticipate their future chances or "lusiones" (ibid.: 207). In his famous shorthand, Bourdieu summarizes the core of the process as follows: "Habitus is that presence of the past in the present which makes possible the presence in the present of the forth-coming" (ibid.: 210). On the basis of their previous participation in the game, actors have acquired a habitus—a set of dispositions—that gives shape, both consciously and unconsciously, to their anticipations of the near future and thus guides their actions in the present. This is a good way to understand how past and future are both part of the present, which, according to Mead, is the only locus of reality.

When we try to participate in another game, which is the central epistemological move of ethnographic fieldwork, we do not have the habitus necessary for making sense of the immediate future. We try to apply whatever categories and anticipations we normally use, but many of these will cause us to miscalculate or react inappropriately. The resulting 'breakdowns' are the building stones of anthropological understanding (Agar 1986), as they force us to become aware of and formulate what it is that creates these differences. We thus translate habitus into explicit rules, values, and norms in order to provide a cultural context for understanding different human behavior. Bourdieu (2000: 208) further elaborates on the experience of time: when there is a good fit between habitus and the world, between expectations and chances, actors tend not to experience time in a very conscious way even though human time is created by the practices they are involved in. The conscious experience of time is foregrounded only when this tacit correspondence is broken, resulting in feelings of waiting, impatience, regret, boredom, and the like. Thus, according to Bourdieu, time becomes clearly visible only in the discrepancy between anticipation and outcome, habitus and world.

Of course, people work in and with time all the time in their daily lives: they make plans for the future and communicate this in language, they structure the activities of the day using clock time (or other ways of time measurement), and they use different forms of seasonal calendars to plan events further ahead. Thus, one could argue that there are many cultural means to deal with time in a more or less conscious way. What Bourdieu highlights is that this making and reckoning of time, although it involves human consciousness, nevertheless becomes habitual when the expectations generated by habitus neatly fit with real chances in the world. It is only when there is a discontinuity between expectations and events that time inescapably imposes itself on human consciousness as a problem connected with strong feelings about its passing, such as boredom, impatience, and regret. This means that ethnographic field research, with its inbuilt discrepancy between the fieldworkers and their field, is a strong method to make time visible, since the fieldworker is cast out into experiences of confusion, waiting, and frustration. The resolution of this situation of misfit between implicit anticipation and the social world is the work of making time differences explicit, in other words, 'cultural interpretation'.

Michael Young (1988) has also written extensively about the relation between the experience of time and the effect of what he calls "habit" (ibid.: 79). He formulates a "law of the disappearing cycle" (ibid.: 87). When events become recurrent and thus habitual, they become less noticed and remembered by human actors: "As memory fades, habit takes over. If nature adores cycles, the conscious mind abhors them. The mind adores difference, especially the kind of small variations from moment to moment that keep people alert" (ibid.). People experience time and remember events when these do not follow the pattern anticipated by their habits. This is why it is so difficult to interview people about their culture—because culture basically is the routine behavior that no one really remembers and is able to formulate, unless it is challenged or changing. The temporary but extended presence of anthropologists can be part of such a challenge to their interlocutors, as the anthropologist lacks the habits that represent a common past. The communicative negotiations following from this constitute the process in which collaborators and anthropologist alike become aware of and formulate their differences and thus their cultural contexts. It is a process of trial and error and also of premature assumptions and conclusions about a mutual basis for comprehension. But the sharing of time will create the opportunity for continuous checking and for serendipitous occurrences that can reveal still hidden differences.

Let me conclude this section by providing an example of how crucial the sharing of time is for differences in temporality to become visible. The case is from Baluan Island, Papua New Guinea, where I conducted my first ethnographic research from 1986 to 1988. After the usual adaptations to the conspicuous differences in temporality between myself and the people whose culture I had come to study, I became settled in some work routines on the island. I had become used to the uncertainties of work agreements and was less frustrated on the occasions when my language assistant did not turn up because other people had made claims on his time. I had accepted that money value did not carry as much weight as family obligations. An important way for me to create systematic data, as well as to structure my time, was to conduct a census of all households in the village where I was living. This was in line with people's expectations of white men's activities on the island, but they still made jokes about my interest in the number of marriages people had had and their offspring from these separate marriages, as I apparently was much more inquisitive than the patrol officers they had known. Of course, people would not always be at home when I tried to visit them, so I would just go to their neighbors to fill out my questionnaires with them. There would always be someone at home whom I had not interviewed yet, and that meant one to several hours of work. Furthermore, whenever there was an exchange ceremony in 'my' village or an adjoining one, I would go to attend it. Most of the time people let me know about these events or came to collect me for the occasion. It had clearly been communicated by the local leaders that I was there to learn about *kastam* (tradition), and therefore *kastamwok* (ceremonies) had become established as a common field of interest for the Baluan people and their anthropologist.

I did my best to make sense of the complex exchanges, and because I was not yet able to understand most of what was being said during the long speeches that were part and parcel of the ceremonies, I relied to a large extent on interviews in Tok Pisin to reconstruct the events and their meaning.[4] An important field of my investigations concerned religious beliefs and practices, as I happened to attend a considerable number of funerals during the early days of my fieldwork. Funerals and their aftermath were about restoring the social fabric that was broken because of the demise of a person, a node in the social network, but they were also about beliefs in life after death and the agency of the spirits. Early on during the interviews I was asked about my own beliefs, and soon my informants and I had established each other's orientations in the religious domain. I had been raised in the Catholic faith, as had the majority of my informants in the village, and this provided a common backdrop or cultural past for our discussions. Although I had long ago left the certainty of the Catholic belief, I could still share with my informants a universe in which spirits of the dead existed in the present of the living but at a safe distance from them. At least, that was my perspective on the shared temporality concerning death and the afterlife based on the discussions we had. But an unexpected event proved me fundamentally wrong.

A relatively young man, the father of three children, had died after medical examinations in the hospital on the mainland had not been able to determine the cause of his illness. Later I was to learn that he had passed away because of a serious conflict with his adoptive father about where he was to live and whose property he was to guard. The old man had been unforgiving, and the adopted son died on the island after a short illness. It was a most dramatic event, which became even more so when the old man nearly drowned on his way back to the island to attend the unexpected funeral. The funeral was deeply moving, and the grave was beautifully decorated. I took some pictures but was not able to get a good shot of the decorated grave because of the mass of people attending the funeral. Therefore, I decided to go back later in the afternoon when everyone had returned home. This visit to take some photographs was a turning point, because I realized straightaway on my return to the village that something was wrong. As usual, people asked me where I had been, and when I answered truthfully that I had visited the grave, they had difficulty hiding their astonishment. Later that evening, some people who were willing to talk about the event gave me a completely new insight into the time and space of the dead.

I noticed that my visitors had brought light with them, whereas people would usually walk about at night without it, and that they were anxious to be outside of their houses. The reason was, as I learned later that evening, that the spirits of the dead are believed to be roaming around immediately after the funeral of their deceased bodies and can be dangerous. This was especially the case with this young man, who died before his time and had probably become an angry spirit as a result. It was believed that he might want to take another life to get revenge on the living, and it became suddenly clear to me that, in the eyes of the Baluan people, I had risked my life by returning to the grave all by myself. The restrained reaction that I had sensed was caused by their uncertainty about me. Was I just stupid or was I perhaps rather the reverse, a very powerful man who knew how to deal with the dead? The people who confided in me were struggling with their own fear and wanted to know my reaction. As a result of this event, I suddenly gained new insight into the temporal and spatial universe of the Baluan people, which included the spirits of the dead as powerful agents in the present—something that no one had volunteered to tell me before during numerous discussions about funerals and the afterlife. In the conversations that followed about my unexpected experience, the details of a different worldview were revealed. The angry spirit of the deceased was believed to be hovering close to his grave and roaming around the edge of the village at night, thus constituting a real danger to the living. Only after the lapse of considerable time and the execution of divination ceremonies within the deceased's family to establish guilt and proper compensation would the spirit come to rest. But he would still be around for several generations, not so much as a dangerous spirit, but rather as a protector and moral guardian of his descendants. After this, the spirit would gradually become less active in human affairs and eventually disappear into oblivion (cf. Fortune [1935] 1965).

This vignette shows how a period of time shared by an anthropologist and his collocutors revealed this fundamental difference in understanding the present and its temporal and spatial dimensions, which resulted in the breakdown in communication that was necessary for both parties to discover that their previous assumptions about mutual understanding had been flawed.

II. Different Timescapes

After having established that the time of the Other can be different even though it is part of the same present and thus coeval to that of the anthropologist, it is important to steer clear of the simple and pernicious dichotomization between 'us' and 'the others' that has so often characterized anthropological writing about time (Adam [1994] 2002; Fabian 1983). Examples abound: modern versus traditional, lineal versus cyclical, clock time versus natural time, quantitative time versus qualitative time, hot societies versus cold societies, history versus tradition, developed versus primordial, forged versus authentic. These dichotomies can be useful in determining different modalities of time, but they become pernicious when they are used to characterize whole societies. This kind of classification reduces the actual complexity of existing societies and essentializes certain aspects of them as defining characteristics. Barbara Adam ([1994] 2002: 505) argues that these dichotomies are often based upon unquestioned and stereotypical assumptions about Western time, defined in contrast to that of the others. She demonstrates that these modalities of time, such as linearity versus cyclicity or quality versus measurement, can be found in most societies and calls for greater reflection and analysis of Western notions of time, which form the invisible backdrop of anthropological analyses of the times of the other.

I fully agree with Adam's analysis, and, in complement to her focus on Western notions of time, I want to plea for a much greater openness regarding diversity of temporalities in non-Western societies. The often reiterated dichotomies not only reaffirm unquestioned stereotypes about Western notions of time but also hinder an open-minded investigation of the temporal categories of other societies. Hirsch and Stewart (2005) usefully argue for the employment of the term 'historicity' to break away from implicit notions of chronology and linearity that are linked to the Western notion of history. Historicity refers to the ongoing construction of pasts and futures in relation to the present. It highlights that the nexus past-present-future is culturally variable and developing and that researchers have to become reflexively aware of the premises of their own time frames when analyzing the historicities of other societies.

In his contribution to the anthology *The Qualities of Time* (James and Mills 2005), Roy Dilley articulates an insight that has also emerged independently in the analysis of my own data on Baluan Island, as I will elaborate below. Inspired by the editors of the anthology, Dilley (2005: 235) uses the term 'time-shape' to refer to the "types of concern encompassed by the conventional concept of cultural representation of time and history: within different cultures the notion of time and a sense of the past can take on different shapes or be represented by specific forms that are particular to a social community." His particular contribution consists in emphasizing that different time-shapes can exist side by side in the same society. On the basis of his ethnography of musicians and blacksmiths among the Haalpulaaren from northern Senegal, Dilley shows that these groups can employ different time orientations, including the cyclical and repetitive Muslim calendar, genealogical time, and also 'collapsed' chronological time. These different time-shapes are closely linked to cultural notions of agency and personhood (ibid.: 235–236).

From my first attempts to analyze Baluan culture, I was struck by the absence of an encompassing cultural system. I found instead different 'universes of practice and discourse' or 'institutional and semantic domains' that informed the actions of the Baluan people (Otto 1991, 1992c). Later (Otto 2005), I became greatly inspired by Barth's (1993, 2002) concept of 'knowledge traditions', which highlighted in a similar way the cultural diversity existing within the same society. Barth even talks about a surfeit of culture in Balinese society. I have recently begun to focus more on how these different domains/spheres/knowledge traditions also incorporate different orientations in time and history and how this is linked to different notions of agency. Obviously, ideas about whether and how humans can act on their environment involve notions about time and change. Different historicities are therefore intimately intertwined with different concepts of personhood and human agency. To capture this temporal orientation, I suggest using the term 'timescape', rather than 'time-shape', in analogy to terms such as 'landscape', 'ethnoscape', 'mediascape', 'technoscape', and so forth (Appadurai 1990). I prefer the suffix '-scape' over '-shape' because—based on the root metaphor of the word 'landscape'—it better articulates the perspectival dimension of these cultural constructs. Timescape refers to the details of the temporal orientation of a specific group of actors—their use of means of time reckoning, their temporal valuations and anticipations. Although the term derives its meaning from a spatial metaphor, I find it a useful way to conceptualize the temporal 'mapping' that it aims to indicate: one should replace the spatial coordinates of the concept of landscape with temporal ones from the perspective of subjects moving through time and anticipating events to come by remembering and acting on events gone by.

Modern Baluan society is characterized by a complex 'temporal landscape', or, rather, by a variety of timescapes. In the remainder of this chapter, I sketch two different timescapes (I have identified more) and emphasize their emergence and mutual articulation. I will describe one major event on the island during which the different timescapes became apparent, I argue, in the practices and representations of the participants. This event was the Balopa Cultural Festival, which took place from 27 December 2006 to 1 January 2007. It was planned as the largest festival ever to be organized on the island, and groups from neighboring islands were invited to participate. The main organizers were returned expatriate workers with extensive experience away from the island. They were able to get substantial financial support for the event, in particular from the governor of Manus Province. They had invited me, as the long-term ethnographer of Baluan, and a film crew to make a documentary of the festival, and we were also asked to help raise support, which we did. The festival ran over six days and attracted many officials from Manus, including the governor, and participants from other islands and even the Manus mainland. It was probably the largest public event to have taken place on the island, reckoned in size, financial support, and number of participants.[5]

The festival began with a grandiose opening ceremony in which all traditional dancing groups took part. A traditional leader performed a spectacular dance on a *sinal*, a typical Manus dancing beam, and welcomed all the officials and participants. The following days were filled with various kinds of performances: traditional dancing and songs, string band music, choir singing, drama performances, the display of traditional houses, canoe races, and the very popular 'queen quest'—a kind of beauty contest in which young girls in traditional dress performed a traditional dance, did a presentation of their dress like models on a catwalk, and gave a speech. The festival was concluded with the distribution of 'prize money' as all performances had been carried out competitively within the various categories, with jury members giving their assessment in the form a 10-point marking system. Interestingly, all participants got a prize: if they had not won the first, second, or third prize, they would still receive a so-called consolation prize, which was only slightly less in value than the top prizes. In this way, the festival was reminiscent of the distributions made during traditional ceremonies in which it was important to give a fair share to all relevant groups.

The organizers had chosen the following motto for the festival: *unity thru kalsa* (unity through culture). This was a very significant innovation, as I see it, because existing concepts of culture were linked more to diversity. Baluan language has a number of words that refer to that which is typical for a person or group, such as *nurun* (focusing on the things that belong to the group, their material and immaterial possessions), *arona* (focusing on the characteristic, habitual activities of the group), and *mamarou* (focusing on the knowledge and skills of the group). The Tok Pisin term *kastam*, which had become very central during the past decades (Otto 1992c, 2011), was also linked to cultural traits that distinguished groups rather than united them. For example, every descent group of some importance on Baluan had their own *kastam* property, which included body decorations, names for important objects, and special ways to carry out their ceremonies. Thus, *kalsa* was intentionally chosen as the motto for the festival as an alternative to *kastam*, indicating a different view on culture.

The central organizer, Soanin Kilangit, had a background as a social worker and a lecturer at a college for public servants. He saw culture as a way to create development in rural areas by motivating people to take their destiny into their own hands. A cultural show could motivate young and old alike into collective activities and create a sense of unity and belonging that extended beyond local descent groups, villages, and even islands. The term 'Balopa' was an acronym for Baluan, Lou, and Pam, three islands that formed one administrative and electoral district in Manus Province. Tourism was seen as an important aspect of the developmental capacity of culture: by performing their 'unique culture', the people of Balopa expected to be able to attract international tourists. Kilangit had some experience leading a dancing group that had toured Australia and several European and Asian countries, and he had become aware of the unique quality of Manus dances. A combination of cultural tourism and ecotourism was envisaged as a viable way of development for the islands. At the time of the festival, this was more a vision than a reality, as there were no tourists present.[6] The only foreigners were myself, the film team, a group of archaeologists who were sponsored as part of the same field project, and one ethnomusicologist doing research on *garamut* (log drum) drumming on the island. But the invitation to the film team was part of the strategy to make Balopa culture known to the world.

Thus, culture (*kalsa*) was linked to expectations concerning the near future. It was anticipated that culture would create greater unity at home and attract foreigners who would bring in money and foster economic development in the region. Some, in particular the chairman of the provincial tourism board, even used modern economic terminology to describe this development, for example, calling the Cultural Festival a 'tourism product' to attract visitors and portraying tourism as 'a way of life' that had to be supported by a strong local culture. This commoditized view of culture was in line with a new temporality introduced by the recently returned migrants. Not only had the speed of dancing been increased to make it more attractive to the public, but the performances were timed by the jury, who would deduct points if the dancers used more time than allowed. Especially among the group of leaders involved in organizing and managing the festival, there was a strong sense that they were involved in giving shape to the future, and the word 'future' was frequently used in their discussions.[7]

In contrast, there was a group of traditional leaders who were critical of these developments. One of their central objections was that *kalsa* (culture) was not the same as *kastam* (tradition). They would argue that the drum beats and dances performed at the festival did not follow the Baluan tradition but instead included innovations as well as elements imported from elsewhere. Although change as such was not condemned, these people feared that their traditional culture was in the process of being lost. They also found that the manner in which the festival was organized violated some traditional norms and values, for example, concerning the consultation and involvement of local leaders. These disputes had real consequences for the people involved. For example, a respected village elder had, against the advice of some other traditional leaders, participated during the first day of the festival by carrying out a small traditional ceremony that involved the distribution of a bunch of betel nuts. When, on the following day, he fell and hurt his knee, he saw this as a punishment from the ancestors that was caused by the disagreement with his peers. Even Kilangit, the main leader of the festival, did not escape from the power of the traditional leaders when he violated a customary rule by hitting an important guest in the face in an outburst of anger and frustration. Being at risk of creating a major fight and the potential walk-out of a large group of participants, he had to submit to a mediation ceremony led by traditional leaders, during which he humbly offered his apologies and presented a substantial gift to the insulted party (Dalsgaard and Otto 2011).

The time orientation of these traditional leaders was very distinct from those of the festival leaders. The traditional leaders looked toward the past to define the key values that should guide the contemporary practices on the island. This included the characteristics of good leadership, respectful behavior, and mutual obligations. They preferred *kastam* over *kalsa*, as the latter caused ambivalences concerning ownership and knowledge of traditional practices. The ownership of *kastam* objects and activities was more clearly defined and managed by descent groups and their traditional leaders, who received their status from the execution of these practices. *Kastam* activities were also intertwined with the ownership of other resources, such as land, trees, and products of the sea. The discussion about the ownership of these resources invoked a particular timescape that was based on the remembrance of genealogies, past exchanges, ceremonies, and migrations. In short, a continuously reproduced history of reciprocal exchanges and obligations directed actions in the present. In contrast, the festival leaders were less concerned with these traditional claims, even admitting ignorance of parts of the traditional lore, and were more interested in the potential of culture for the future. Their articulation of the concept of *kalsa* instead of *kastam* reflected this future orientation.

In this short description I have focused on the actors who took a lead in the developments: the organizers of the Balopa Cultural Festival, who were mostly returned migrants with extensive experience as highly trained employees away from the island, and the traditional leaders, who chose not to support the festival and who had less experience outside of the island. It thus appears that the emerging contrast in timescapes was linked to exposure to and internalization of Western ways. Although I find that this generally was the case, the situation was more complicated than my short exposé can account for. For example, the difference was not simply a generational one, as some of the traditional leaders critical of *kalsa* development were younger than the organizers of the festival. Among the youth on the island, opinions were divided, with a great number supporting the idea of promoting tourism through culture, but others being aware of the risk of losing their autonomy. This qualification of the supporters of the different notions, however, does not affect my general conclusion— namely, that *kalsa* and *kastam* and their corresponding timescapes emerged as separate domains of Baluan culture in mutual definition and delineation spurred by the activities and discourse of interested actors.

III. Change and Agency

My brief case study shows how different timescapes developed and co-existed in the same society. Elsewhere I have discussed how the concept of 'the New Way' arose in the 1950s as part of the efforts of the Paliau Movement to change their colonial present, which was experienced as very unequal and unjust (Otto 1992b). The New Way contained a timescape that favored change and demanded a radical break with the traditional practices of the past, in particular the large ceremonial exchanges. One could argue that this new timescape implied a concept of tradition as a negative category, something to be abolished and superseded by a new cultural order. A countermovement started in the 1960s that led to the gradual reversal of the negative valuation of tradition and to the establishment of *kastam* as a central positive value for the present (Otto 1992c, 2011). Thus, there appears to be a serial connection between the different timescapes that have evolved over the years in Baluan, both in contrast to each other and in line with the interests and potentialities for action of the people involved in the historical changes.

In the case study sketched above, the articulation of a new contrast arose from different experiences and social trajectories, primarily between those who had stayed most of their life on the island and those who had spent most of their adult life away from it to work in urban centers. As mentioned, this opposition was not absolute and depended also on individual biographies and idiosyncrasies: a large number of island residents were in favor of *kalsa*, and *kastam* was defended by some returnees from city life. It is clear, though, that the promoters of the festival saw themselves as the bearers of a new future, as the agents of cultural change that was considered unavoidable but had to be steered in a manner that was beneficial to the Baluan people. In the process of organizing the new activities, geared toward the anticipated future, a new concept of culture (*kalsa*) crystallized in opposition to the notion of *kastam*, which had been dominant for almost three decades. This emergent concept was linked to a new temporal orientation, directed toward gradual change on the basis of creating a strong cultural heritage and involving a greater emphasis on clock time. The resulting opposition between temporalities and anticipated futures created the specific dynamics of the Baluan present. Thus, this case study illustrates what I believe to hold general validity, namely, that societies normally are characterized by a plurality of evolving timescapes and that this plurality is an important aspect of the way that human beings react to and create social change.

Although I have not elaborated upon this point, it may be apparent from my case study that the various timescapes are closely related to human agency. The festival leaders saw a role for themselves in directing social change, which they believed was both necessary and manageable. The traditional leaders considered it their duty to warn against some of the changes and to safeguard the continued adherence to traditional values and rules. Timescapes involve notions about changeability and causality, and it is through their connection to agency that timescapes become a factor of social action in the present.

Also, the agency of anthropologists is informed by their temporal orientation. I have argued that doing fieldwork means engaging with people in the present in such a way that differences in timescapes can be revealed and articulated. This requires the fieldworker to get involved in local events and to maintain a crucial sensitivity to contrasts in people's perspectives, which are partly invisible but can become manifest in and through disputes and conflicts, often the result of serendipitous circumstances. The times of the Other can only be accessed through real time involvement in the present. The ethnographic field is thus a temporally defined entity as much as it involves encounters in space.

Acknowledgments

For inspiration I thank the organizers and participants of the workshop "Time and the Field," held at the August 2009 Megaseminar of the Danish Research School of Anthropology and Ethnography, and in particular Marilyn Strathern, who acted as a discussant. In addition, I am grateful to Steffen Dalsgaard, Pia Schurtenberger, Borut Telban, and Dineke Schokkin for stimulating discussions and useful comments on a draft version of this chapter. I also thank two anonymous reviewers for their very useful and thorough critique. All remaining flaws are solely my responsibility. As always, I wish to acknowledge my debt to the people of Baluan, who adopted me into their lives and times.

Ton Otto is a Professor of Anthropology and Ethnography at Aarhus University and a Professor and Research Leader at James Cook University. He is also currently Head of the Ethnographic Collections at the new Moesgaard Museum of Aarhus. Since 1986 he has conducted ethnographic field research in Papua New Guinea and published widely on issues of social and cultural change. He has a strong interest in the epistemology and methodology of ethnographic research and its relationship to innovation, intervention, and design. Recent publications include the co-edited volumes *Experiments in Holism: Theory and Practice in Contemporary Anthropology* (2010, with Nils Bubandt) and *Design Anthropology: Theory and Practice* (2013, with Wendy Gunn and Rachel Smith). He also co-directed the films *Ngat Is Dead: Studying Mortuary Traditions* (2009, with Christian Suhr and Steffen Dalsgaard) and *Unity Through Culture* (2012, with Christian Suhr).

Notes

1. Adam (1990: 37ff.) remarks that Mead is often referred to but that the body of his thought has not really been taken on board by social theorists and that it could alter the way social reality is understood, once properly appropriated and digested.
2. I thank one of the anonymous reviewers for suggesting this term.
3. I am grateful to Borut Telban for articulating the problem in this way (pers. comm.).
4. Tok Pisin is a creole language spoken widely in Papua New Guinea. On Baluan, everyone is fluent in this language, and it is often used at public occasions (church services, exchange ceremonies), in particular when people from outside the island are present. A number of migrants to the island use Tok Pisin for daily conversation (as their mother tongues are not understood), but they understand the Baluan language passively.
5. This is difficult to establish with certainty because Paliau Maloat, a great Manus leader originating from the island, had organized major events, and his funeral on the island had also attracted many people. It is impossible to get an accurate picture of the size of these events on the basis of oral accounts. After the Cultural Festival took place, a large traditional ceremony was held on Baluan that possibly exceeded the festival in terms of money spent.
6. Baluan had had some tourists on occasion, in particular from cruise ships on short stops.
7. It is interesting to observe how the temporal changes in the dance reflected some of the major changes involved in the timescape of *kalsa*, supported by those who wished to promote tourism as well as cultural unity. See J. M. Taylor (1982) for a comparable debate about how the aesthetics of a dance involved political interests and had political consequences, but in a very different cultural and political setting— in this case, Brazilian carnival.

References

Adam, Barbara. 1990. *Time and Social Theory*. Cambridge: Polity Press.

Adam, Barbara. [1994] 2002. "Perceptions of Time." Pp. 503–526 in *Companion Encyclopedia of Anthropology*, ed. Tim Ingold. London: Routledge.

Agar, Michael H. 1986. *Speaking of Ethnography*. Qualitative Research Methods Series 2. Newbury Park, CA: Sage.

Appadurai, Arjun. 1990. "Disjuncture and Difference in the Global Cultural Economy." *Public Culture* 2, no. 2: 1–24.

Barth, Fredrik. 1993. *Balinese Worlds*. Chicago: University of Chicago Press.

Barth, Fredrik. 2002. "An Anthropology of Knowledge." *Current Anthropology* 43, no. 1: 1–18.

Bourdieu, Pierre. 1977. *Outline of a Theory of Practice*. Trans. Richard Nice. Cambridge: Cambridge University Press.

Bourdieu, Pierre. 1990. *The Logic of Practice*. Trans. Richard Nice. Stanford, CA: Stanford University Press.

Bourdieu, Pierre. 2000. *Pascalian Meditations*. Trans. Richard Nice. Cambridge: Polity Press.

Clifford, James. 1997. *Routes: Travel and Translation in the Late Twentieth Century*. Cambridge, MA: Harvard University Press.

Dalsgaard, Steffen, and Ton Otto. 2011. "From *Kastam* to *Kalsa*? Leadership, Cultural Heritage and Modernization in Manus Province, Papua New Guinea." Pp. 141–160 in *Made in Oceania: Social Movements, Cultural Heritage and the State in the Pacific*, ed. Edvard Hviding and Knut M. Rio. Oxford: Sean Kingston.

Dilley, Roy. 2005. "Time-Shapes and Cultural Agency among West African Craft Specialists." Pp. 235–248 in James and Mills 2005.

Fabian, Johannes. 1983. *Time and the Other: How Anthropology Makes Its Object*. New York: Columbia University Press.

Fortune, Reo F. [1935] 1965. *Manus Religion: An Ethnological Study of the Manus Natives of the Admiralty Islands*. Lincoln: University of Nebraska Press.

Gammage, Bill. 1998. *The Sky Travellers: Journeys in New Guinea 1938–1939*. Melbourne: Melbourne University Press.

Gell, Alfred. 1992. *The Anthropology of Time: Cultural Constructions of Temporal Maps and Images*. Oxford: Berg.

Gupta, Akhil, and James Ferguson, eds. 1997. *Anthropological Locations: Boundaries and Grounds of a Field Science*. Berkeley: University of California Press.

Hirsch, Eric, and Charles Stewart. 2005. "Introduction: Ethnographies of Historicity." *History and Anthropology* 16, no. 3: 261–274. Special issue titled *Ethnographies of Historicity*, ed. Eric Hirsch and Charles Stewart.

Hodges, Matt. 2008. "Rethinking Time's Arrow." *Anthropological Theory* 8, no. 4: 399–429.

James, Wendy, and David Mills, eds. 2005. *The Qualities of Time: Anthropological Approaches*. Oxford: Berg.

Marcus, George E. 1995. "Ethnography in/of the World System: The Emergence of Multi-sited Ethnography." *Annual Review of Anthropology* 24: 95–117.

Mead, George H. [1932] 2002. *The Philosophy of the Present*. Amherst, NY: Prometheus Books.

Munn, Nancy D. 1992. "The Cultural Anthropology of Time: A Critical Essay." *Annual Review of Anthropology* 21: 93–123.

Olwig, Karen F., and Kirsten Hastrup, eds. 1997. *Siting Culture: The Shifting Anthropological Object*. London: Routledge.

Otto, Ton. 1991. *The Politics of Tradition in Baluan: Social Change and the Construction of the Past in a Manus Society*. Nijmegen: Centre for Pacific Studies.

Otto, Ton. 1992a. "From Paliau Movement to Makasol: The Politics of Representation." *Canberra Anthropology* 15, no. 2: 49–68.

Otto, Ton. 1992b. "The Paliau Movement in Manus and the Objectification of Tradition." *History and Anthropology* 5, no. 3: 427–454.

Otto, Ton. 1992c. "The Ways of *Kastam*: Tradition as Category and Practice in a Manus Village." *Oceania* 62, no. 4: 264–283.

Otto, Ton. 2005. "Concern, Norms and Social Action: Notes on Fredrik Barth's Analytical Model." *FOLK: Journal of the Danish Ethnographic Society* 46/47: 143–157.

Otto, Ton. 2011. "Inventing Traditions and Remembering the Past in Manus." Pp. 157–173 in *Changing Contexts, Shifting Meanings: Transformations of Cultural Traditions in Oceania,* ed. Elfriede Hermann. Honolulu: University of Hawaii Press.

Schieffelin, Bambi B. 2002. "Marking Time: The Dichotomizing Discourse of Multiple Temporalities." *Current Anthropology* (supp.) 43: S5–S17.

Taylor, J. M. 1982. "The Politics of Aesthetic Debate: The Case of Brazilian Carnival." *Ethnology* 21, no. 4: 301–311.

Young, Michael. 1988. *The Metronomic Society: Natural Rhythms and Human Timetables.* Cambridge, MA: Harvard University Press.

Chapter 5

SURFACING MOVES
Spatial-Timings of Senior Home Care

Peter A. Lutz

Time thoroughly intra-weaves the field of senior home care in Sweden.[1] Scheduling and coordination depend on present and past knowledge of what works. Time-worn bodies and fading memories mix with present concerns about aging and well-being. In turn, these entangle hardships and inevitable mortality. Declining fertility rates combined with increasing life expectancies have spawned broader concerns about the demographic challenge of population aging and health care. People over the age of 60 are the fastest-growing group in most countries (WHO 2012). Along with other future challenges—including climate change, water and food shortages, peak oil, and poverty—most countries face important questions about who will perform and pay for senior care and what new infrastructures must be put in place.

Time management is increasingly engaged in strategic health-care planning and senior home-care delivery. In turn, this links with a range of policies to

Notes for this chapter begin on page 91.

reduce expenditures as well as improve the accountability and efficiency of welfare services. In the 1970s, with the introduction of 'Taylorization' into the Swedish public sector, senior home care was reconfigured into manageable products and services (Szebehely 2007). As in many other countries, these market-inspired reforms have intensified in recent decades, along with the privatization of senior home care (Szebehely and Trydegård 2012). Many welfare scholars identify this trend as 'new public management' or NPM (cf. Dahl 2009; Pollitt and Bouckaert 2004; Rose 1999). This includes not only the shift toward customer choice, found in Sweden since the 1990s (Trydegård 2000), but also the specification and standardization of activities of daily living (ADLs) as distinct tasks. In turn, administrators use 'clocked time', scheduled in minutes, to standardize and control senior home care. For instance, a Swedish municipality's guidelines for needs assessment and care allocates 15 minutes to prepare a meal, 30 minutes to clean a two-room flat twice a month, and 83 minutes for upper body washing supervision and preparation per month.[2] The managerial assumption behind such arrangements is, of course, that senior home care conforms to specific tasks and specific units of time, which are then generalizable across a variety of different situations.

Those on the ground of senior home care, so to speak, often contest such managerial attitudes toward time. Scholars have analyzed these tensions as competing perspectives, for example, between management and staff (cf. Green-Pedersen 2002; Szebehely 2007; Vabø 2006). These conflicting views have given rise to what some have termed the 'politics of time' (cf. Bryson 2007; Dahl 2009; Ellingsæter 2007) and are again related to the 'objective' and 'subjective' figuring of time. Recent headlines in the Swedish news media also echo these frictions: "Elderly Get Too Little Time" (Sveriges Radio 2005), "Give Us More Time for the Old" (Eriksson 2009), "Short of Time in Elderly Care" (Sveriges Television 2009), and "Time for the Elderly Shrinks—Stress Grows" (Hernadi and Olsson 2010). Hence, efforts to cut costs and increase the efficiency of care by saving time conflict with deep-seated ideas that quality care requires the taking of time. This links as well with competing temporal-economic notions of time as money and time as not money (Kaufman-Scarborough 2006). Time in Swedish senior home care has clearly shifted from a 'matter of fact' to a 'matter of concern' (Latour 2004)—or, more to the point, a 'matter of care' (Puig de la Bellacasa 2011).

As the literature on the social analysis of time suggests, the recognition of objective versus subjective time is the first step toward considering the possibility of spatial-temporal differences (cf. Evans 2004; Nowotny 1992; Orlikowski and Yates 2002). This often takes the form of different dichotomous guises: absolute-situational, quantitative-qualitative, clock-event, material-social, and so on.[3] Vyvyan Evans (2004: 4), for instance, notes: "On the one hand, we have the common-place view and the view of modern physics which has built a theoretical edifice on the foundational axiom of the reality of time. Yet, on the other hand, time is 'elusive', 'intangible', 'stealthy' and 'imperceptible'." Meanwhile, Ramón Ramos Torre (2007: 158) concludes that "this is a broad field of research, often oscillating between two futile extremes ... Time in sociological research is often caught in this bind, between triviality and obscurity."

Anthropologists writing about time often acknowledge similar challenges. Some see this dilemma as a Western phenomenon and one that serves to generate ethnographic knowledge. Tim Ingold (2000) claims, for instance, that the apparent incommensurability of Western 'clock time' and non-Western 'event time' has sustained much anthropology. He roots this tension in historical transitions that include capitalism and industrial manufacturing.[4] Meanwhile, drawing on a range of philosophers including McTaggart and Mellor,[5] Alfred Gell (1992) points to an 'A-series time' that encompasses the subjective human experience of temporal change as past, present, and future. This is in contrast with 'B-series time', which is objective and real—that is, "it reflects the temporal relationships between events as they really are, out there" (ibid.: 165). Once again, we find the objective-subjective distinction in play.

Rather than pursuing a solely temporal analysis that pits objective time against subjective time, this chapter explores how relational movements surface different 'spatial-timings' of care in practice. This approach joins others that posit the inseparability of time and space and their comingling in a relational field (cf. Munn 1992). In his article "Trains of Thought," Bruno Latour (1997) takes a similar stance by directing attention to the flux in the world and the relational differences that precede distinct notions of space and time. He writes: "We never encounter time and space, but a multiplicity of interactions with actants that have their own timing, spacing, goals, means and ends ... Long before we can talk of space and time, it is these sorts of connections, short circuits, translations, associations, and mediations that we encounter, daily" (ibid.: 182–183). I propose that such realizations are essential for refiguring senior home-care management strategies to better accommodate spatial-temporal differences.

In turn, this chapter adapts Latour's approach to trace relational movements and the ways they underpin different spatial-timings of senior home care. This includes how care times emerge as spaced or situated, made and unmade, present or absent, visible and invisible. Furthermore, I employ the ethnographic heuristic 'surfacing', borrowing from Janelle Taylor's (2005) article "Surfacing the Body Interior." Drawing on anthropological accounts of 'body work', Taylor argues that surfacing is one way to bring the creative ethnographic exploration of 'messy' worlds—their 'busy intersections' (Renato Rosaldo) and 'awkward scales' (Jean and John Comaroff)—into the discipline of anthropology (ibid.: 741). Indeed, Taylor employs surfacing to question overly medicalized notions of the body in medical anthropology. In contrast, I use the heuristic 'surfacing' to reconsider subjective-objective distinctions and how relational movements of senior home care generate different spatial-timings in practice.

Talyor (2005: 747) suggests that surfacing shifts the analytical focus from the 'thing' to 'thing-ing'. In addition, with regard to more frequently used terms like 'emerging', I suggest that surfacing offers a stronger material connotation. The *Oxford English Dictionary* explains that 'surfacing' is the action or process of giving a surface or coating to something, such as a body. Entities may thus achieve 'surface' as an additive practice, for example, when roads are paved (Taylor 2005) or tables are set for dinner. It also stands to reason that things *lose* surface through (violent) subtraction, as when an animal is skinned or a log is planed. Seen in this way, the association with transformation is clear. As such, surfacing offers a way to think along the ephemeral 'intra-actions' (Barad 2007) of making/unmaking in motion. Similarly, surfacing helps to imply the various intensities or 'frictions' (Tsing 2005) between pushing and pulling, as when pumping water from a well or when giving birth. Combined, these points ground my proposal for surfacing as an ethnographic heuristic to explore the 'thing-ing' of spatial-temporal differences. Here Latour is particularly useful. In conversation with Latour's article "Trains of Thought," the following sections present a series of ethnographic stories about the relational surfacing of spatial-temporal differences in Swedish senior home care. I collected these accounts during stints of fieldwork between 2008 and 2010. The chapter closes by dis-cussing the heuristic implications of surfacing for the fields and desks of both senior home care and ethnography.

Eva's Surfacing

It is early, around 7:00 AM. Eva, a widow in her late eighties, is secured in her stairlift chair. Together with her care workers, she uses it to move from her bedroom upstairs to the bathroom downstairs. It had taken several minutes for the workers to get her frail body from her bed to her wheelchair and then into the lift. Now they suggest that she try the controls herself. Eva attempts to grasp the small control knob, but tremors force her hands to shake, and her fingers slip off the smooth metal side of the knob. We wait, patiently. The care workers have a schedule to keep, but they continue to encourage her: "Not that way Eva, this way." The care worker takes Eva's fingers into her own hand, and together they push the knob to the left to start the lift. They do this col-lectively—knob, fingers, hands, lift. Success! As Eva glides downstairs, I catch a brief smile across her face. One care worker has gone ahead to prepare Eva's shower. I stay upstairs with the other worker, busy now changing Eva's bed linens. When she finishes, she will follow after to help transport Eva from the lift to the shower. I ask her about the timing of care tasks, and she explains: "Our manager wants us to brush their teeth while they're on the toilet to save time, but we don't want to do that. We think it's just wrong."

In "Trains of Thought," Latour (1997: 172) illustrates his argument with an anecdote that he calls "the paradox of the twin travelers." This is a tale about a hypothetical brother and sister, each pursuing different modes of travel.[6] The twin brother is effortlessly speeding in a train, made possible by the arrange-ment of invisible entities or 'intermediaries' that generate what Latour terms "displacement without transformation" (ibid.: 178). These entities include both human and non-human actors, from the engineers and train companies to the miles of aligned steel tracks with their atoms, switches, and signals. Mean-while, the twin sister fights her way along a jungle path obstructed by thick tangled roots, snakes, and trees. Latour argues that, through her relational moves, these entities become 'mediators' that effect transformations across her body in the form of sweat, cuts, and bruises. In other words, rather than being invisible or submerged, these entities surface with their own agential, mediating presence. They become visible with the attention they draw to themselves as they interfere with her passage. As mediators, these entities alter the ratio of transportation-transformation. In turn, Latour argues that this high ratio of mediators produces a unique space-time that displaces the subjective-objective distinction. I suggest we figure this as the surfacing of different spatial-timings.

Eva's story, together with her care workers and the stairlift, shows how surfacing frictions between transportation and transformation produce spatial-temporal differences in senior home care practice. At the top of the stairs, Eva and her body tremors surface as visible mediators in the care workers' paths. Eva's uncontrolled body produces 'messy' movements that are misaligned with the workers' efforts. They emerge as surfacing mediators with their own agency that cause the care workers to stop and take notice. With their training and skill, the workers focus on Eva and her body, taking the space-time to urge Eva to operate the stairlift. Since she spends most of her days in bed or sitting in her wheelchair, they know instinctively that her cooperation with the lift could potentially surface both a smile and a spatial-timing of care. The collective knob-fingers-hands-lift submerged the care schedule, surfacing in its place a specific spatial-timing. Without this collective 'tinkering' (Mol 2008; Mol et al. 2010), I proffer that the minute-by minute schedule, based on desk work, would have surfaced a different spatial-timing.

Then, like Latour's example of the twin brother speeding effortlessly along in the train, the machine carefully lifts and transports Eva downstairs. Eva and her tremulous body have literally been strapped down for her 'speedy' ride (relatively speaking). Mediators become intermediaries: the aging body, the staircase construction, the electrical wiring, and the machine. Eva becomes an intermediary, safely tucked away out of sight while the care workers attend to other mediators: the shower, the bed linens, and so on. Following Latour's argument, this new arrangement suggests the surfacing of yet another space-time. One could trace additional events of Eva's home care as different spatial-timings strung together in a series of surfacings. We might consider, for instance, the specificity of surfacing 'washing time' (cf. Pols 2006) or 'teeth-brushing' time, overlapping here as a site of both resistance and care. My point is that these different mediator-intermediary collective ratios potentially surface multiple spatial-temporal differences of senior home care. This in turn challenges the notion that home-care practice resides simply in subjective or objective temporal modes.

Scheduler's Surfacing

I am with a home-care unit that specializes in dementia care. The unit is participating in a scheduling software pilot study to investigate improved efficiency.[7] The scheduler/controller has worked previously as a care worker and now operates the program skillfully. She explains: "The purpose of the system is to collect data for planning ahead, perhaps a week, and figure out how many employees we need. We can also plan further, say a month, as well as look back at how many employees we used. For example, we know how many we need next Wednesday when three clients have doctor's appointments instead of arriving in the morning and realizing, 'Oh my God, we need more people because we have so much to do!'"

Latour (1997: 175ff.) proposes that as entities become invisible intermediaries and the speed of transportation intensifies, space and time merge as a form. This falls clearly in line with the making of senior home care schedules. Here, this scheduling care collective shapes many different home-care times and spaces into surfacing colored blocks. The fingers-mouse collective then effortlessly move these around, ordering them into neatly ordered rows and columns. However, this formalization of space-time would be difficult without first transforming people and things into obedient intermediaries: the scheduler's own work experience, the workers' careful notes about the specificities of home-care client needs, the paper archives with printed records of past schedules. According to Latour, however, this invisible work of formalizing space-time entails a certain risk or "professional hazard" (ibid.: 187). This concerns the displacement of knowledge about what makes the world tick, that is, the intricate surfacing of different space-times. He writes: "'Objective' time and 'subjective' time are like taxes exacted from what peoples the world, they are not all that these multitudes do and see and mean and want" (ibid.: 172).

The scheduler continues to demonstrate how the program works. She explains how the data controllers have previously entered the workers' names and qualifications into the program's database. The program now presents this information vertically down the left side of the screen in a row of names. At the top of the screen, it displays the work hours, from 7:00 AM to 11:00 PM. Controllers have also previously entered the clients' standardized care tasks, allocated in minutes. These now appear as a pile of cluttered blocks just below the timeline of work hours. It is the scheduler's job to link each block with a care worker. This she does by dragging the blocks into the appropriate square with the mouse. With this move, the program simultaneously encodes each block with the worker's predesignated 'team' color. As mentioned, however, she does not achieve this by digital means alone. First, she must consult a messy pile of handwritten notes produced by her team of care workers. These include amendments to client routines and workers' vacation days. She must also juggle staff meetings, doctor's appointments, and changes due to new clients, hospital transfers, or deaths. The software is unable to cope with many of these exceptions. Hence, constant manual overrides and tinkering with space-time exceptions are necessary to make things 'fit' inside the digitized spatial-temporal boxes.

While the scheduler expresses pride about her work, she also notes some frustration, linked partly with the need to tinker with the system. In addition, some care workers complained that the continuity of their clients' care had worsened since the introduction of the system.[8] The scheduler remained convinced, however, that the system had scheduled the best possible arrangement. While sitting at her desk, she gestured to the multiple colored boxes neatly arranged in rows as proof.

I suggest such frictions are easily exacerbated by the professional hazard Latour warns us about—a blindness generated by the space-time forms created with relative smoothness from the 'desk' frame of reference. In other words, the scheduling collective of formalized space-time produces an inherent mismatch between the many spatial-temporal differences of care in practice. However, this is not as a question of objective versus subjective time but rather as a question of agential arrangements, positions, and relative efforts. Here, the increased intensity of formalization and speed surface over and render invisible the very spatial-temporal intricacies inherent in, and necessary for, the performance of senior home care.

Inga's Surfacing

Inga is an 80-something-year-old woman who suffered a stroke some years back. I am sitting with her at her kitchen table, waiting[9] for the care workers to deliver lunch. They should have been here by now. She asks me for a glass of water, and I place it on the otherwise smooth surface in front of her. She is in good spirits, but the waiting is beginning to take its toll. The grandfather clock standing in the hallway diligently calls out the seconds. Inga notes that she is accustomed to waiting. She explains that she fills many hours watching people, both neighbors and strangers, from her ground-floor window. She reminds me of a train passenger, silhouetted by the window as people pass by. I consider posing some questions, but talk has been difficult for her since the stroke. I resign myself to sitting and waiting too.

Abruptly, the doorbell rings. It surprises us with its suddenness, although we had been anticipating it. Two care workers let themselves in with their own keys, an arrangement made previously. The wall separating the hallway from the kitchen partially veils their presence, but I overhear them discussing a previous client. The care schedule must have displaced the spatial-timing of their car discussion, surfacing it into Inga's hallway. I wonder if they even realize their own arrival. Eventually, they move into view, holding packets of warm food in various assortments of tin and plastic containers. After a brief greeting, their attention shifts to the food preparation. This consists of opening each packet and spilling the contents onto a plate. Their polite etiquette floats on top like a thin film, but it helps call up the spatial-temporal surfacing of Inga's meal. They have known Inga for several years, which affords some informality, but they are obviously in a hurry. The home-care schedule, most probably shoved into a jacket pocket, is still obvious in their rushed efforts. A plate of food, aluminum containers, and utensils now clutter the table's surface. "Do you want all of the potatoes?" a care worker asks, standing with a ready spoon. Inga replies, "I can take two and some salad." A few moments later, the workers pack their things and say goodbye, disappearing where they had surfaced only a few minutes earlier. There is now relative quiet, excluding Inga's efforts to chew and swallow her food. Some salad gets stuck in her throat, and she coughs. My heart skips a beat. I quickly hand her some water to wash it down.[10] I feel lucky to be there and wonder how she would have managed otherwise. As Inga finishes, the clock steals my attention. I realize that it marks the disappearance of the meal's spatial-timing. I remove the dishes and resurface the tabletop. Inga disappears for her afternoon nap.

Inga's story illustrates further how different socio-material relations make and unmake different spatial-temporal surfacings. Among others, this includes bodies, food packets, clocks, schedules, the tabletop, a parched throat, and a water glass. Consider, for instance, the transportation-transformation of food. It surfaces and disappears—from car to table to mouth to throat to stomach—thereby participating in a spatial-temporal articulation. This is no smooth move, though. Food resists in Inga's dry mouth. Only with the lubricating glass of water can food transform from visible mediator to invisible (digestible) intermediary. My point is that senior home care, as a moving collective of relations, diffracts endless spatial-temporal differences, exemplified here as nap-time surfacing meal-time surfacing wait-time. Again, this is not a question of objective or subjective time but rather overlapping spatial-timings—folding, unfolding, and refolding—generated by moving networked entities.[11]

One last point I wish to make concerns how Inga's waiting and window watching compares, albeit inversely, to Latour's anecdote about the speeding twin train traveler. This inside-outside relationship produces the presence of movement and stillness. In both instances, the human emerges as a fulcrum-like position where mobility and immobility co-exist. One might even argue that this position reasserts the bifurcation between subjective (relative) and objective (absolute) time. However, this is where Latour's thinking is instructive. A distinction between subjective and objective time would simply overlook the infrastructural relation that produces such effects, namely, moving while *still*. However, unlike the train-traveling brother, the important difference here is that Inga has little choice in the matter. She does her best to transform waiting into watching, but this is negotiated in relation to her other mediators—her stroke, the ticking clock, the care workers' schedule, and so on.

Careful Surfacing

It is early, about 6:00 AM, and coffee is brewing. I am in a small rural town with a care team of four workers prepping for their morning rounds. A wooden kitchen table, similar to Inga's, provides the nexus of activity. It is the team's desk for coming together and discussing care work. Its cluttered surface contains coffee cups, a potted plant, and a bowl of fruit. Seniors' home care schedules in a semi-transparent folder join this collective. Remarkably, the schedules remain folded, unopened, during the discussion. Eventually, the conversation shifts from general gossip to their clients. The workers service the town and two adjacent villages. I interrupt to ask how they decide who does what. One of them replies, "We have a schedule, but generally we don't use it. We know all the clients. We tend to reach an agreement among ourselves. Also, we don't make the same rounds every time. We switch villages every other Sunday and on main holidays so we can know everything. We have so many clients now. We try to vary ourselves. Otherwise, we have no real perspective."

In "Trains of Thought," Latour (1997) presents two additional travelers besides the twins: a sailboarder and a train engineer. He describes how the sailboarder enjoys the morning excitement of navigating across a windy lake, experimenting with speeds, directions, winds, and angles. Latour argues that this is beyond the objective-subjective distinction—terms that do not capture the sailboarder's display of work, skill, and movement: "He is not adding a subjective morning to real mornings; subjective lakes to real lakes. He explores the multiplicity of ways of being, he goes from some to many, from a little wind to a fierce gale, from a lower to a higher intensity" (ibid.: 171–172). This movement between positions within positions—'more than one and less than many' (Mol 2002; Strathern 1991)—offers multiple frames of reference and different spatial-temporal intensities.

The fourth traveler, the train engineer, enacts similar positional movements. Like the sailboarder, the engineer is aware of the labor needed to produce calculations and alternative references. Furthermore, he invests his energy in "making sure that the routine institutions on which transportation depends are running 'like clockwork'" (Latour 1997: 176). This relies on figuring the "subversion, disjunction, displacement, rescaling, and crossing-over of relations between spatial, actorial, and temporal features" (ibid.: 184).

There is a striking similarity here between sailboarding/engineering and the care workers' surfacing of different spatial-timings. Like sailing or running a train, care work entails testing and tinkering (Mol 2008) with the multiple spatial-temporal surfacings. Care workers congregate with one another on a daily basis, tweaking their frames of reference, shifting positions up and down within the institutions of senior home care. They criss-cross between check-ups and check-ins with clients, support staff, administrators, doctors, and nurses. Like the partially transparent present-absent schedules, care workers operate in the middles: between mediator-intermediary, transportation-transformation, home and care. They traverse not only oscillations between objective-subjective but also stair times, wait times, mealtimes, and countless other spatial-timings. They tinker with their movements and perspectives. They must find ways to marry the spatial-temporal forms created by schedulers with the multiple spatial-timings of their clients. My point is that good senior home care work involves not only knowledge and experience but also flexible practices or possibilities for tinkering that far exceed the objective-subjective temporal divide on which NPM strategies depend.

Surfacing Spatial-Timings between Fields and Desks

Time may 'pass like nothing' inside a Swiss train compartment, but a good test of this notion's validity outside the train might be to jump off the TGV at full speed … Epistemology is a professional hazard of first-class, air-conditioned train travel" Latour (1997: 187, 189).

What more can we conclude from these stories about surfacing spatial-temporal differences? First, I wish to reiterate the utility of Latour's ideas. For Latour (1997), spatial-temporal differences map onto continua of transformation-transportation and visible-invisible. This in turn suggests multiple conceptual paths out of the Newtonian objective-subjective, space-time deadlock: "[I]nstead of a single space-time, we will generate as many spaces and times as there are types of relations. Thus, progressing along jungle trails will not produce the same space-times as moving smoothly along networks. It makes an enormous difference if that body is a suffering body among other suffering bodies or a relaxed air-conditioned [body] on a bullet train" (ibid.: 174). Here Latour demonstrates that objective or subjective time and space are not a priori. Instead, they are merely a few of the many differences that mediator-intermediary ratios surface in and out of attention. This is an important conceptual move to make in the field of senior home care, which is increasingly populated by managerial desk-based (epistemological) assertions about objective time employed to enfold (formalize or standardize) many surfacing spatial-temporalities.

A second and related point is how different 'contingent configurations' (Taylor 2005) surface in different spatial-timings between transportation-transformation and visibility-invisibility, or presence-absence. Consider, for instance, how the care workers' attentions shifted during Eva's 'fast' transportation down the stairs. Consider also how this shifted their work from a hands-on to a hands-off presence. Here I tentatively suggest that Latour's ideas might be used to establish a socio-material ethics of care based on speed. We have speed limits on our roads and highways. Why not put up speed limits for surfacing care? We slow traffic in school zones. Why not slow care in home zones? The Slow Food movement aims to overcome the health risks of fast food. Why not a Slow Care movement? Inga would surely have appreciated a more relaxed mealtime—one that would not risk her choking alone. The care workers surfaced care efficiency and coordination during their slow table talk, yet such efforts signal inefficiency or lack of productivity. I am not advocating 'slow' as a universal standard for home-care policy, design, and management. Certainly, quicker moves are 'good' in emergencies that demand it. However, I do propose greater accountability of the multiple spatial-temporal surfacings, with their rich scales of fluctuations, tones, rhythms, and tempos. This, I suggest, demands further study and tinkering with surfacing care at its optimal speeds.[12]

My closing point concerns the ethnographic heuristic value of surfacing for thinking through not only the transportation-transformation of spatial-temporal differences across the fields and desks of care, but also ethnography. Taylor (2005: 745) contends that the verb 'surfacing' suggests a move from the conceptual stability of things (bodies or objects) toward the instability of the '-ing' (and 'un-ing'), as in embodying/disembodying or the making/unmaking of entities. It is this fertile instability, she argues, that lends surfacing its conceptual power for tracing the objects of our study, be these bodies, spaces, times, and so forth, and not merely texts or subjectivities—"but rather ... a contingent configuration, a surface that is made but never in a static or permanent form ... [S]urfacing remains unstable, its resolution never entirely predictable. Indeed, its very instability renders dynamics of revelation and concealment interesting and productive, for social actors and social analysts alike" (ibid.: 747, 748).

In this way, surfacing offers an analytical means to disturb and intervene more vigorously with our own subject-objects and how we study them. As the bearers and guardians of ethnographic fields and desks, we are co-implicated in their surfacing differences, temporal or otherwise. Marilyn Strathern's insights are instructive. She argues that ethnography has always been co-located in the field-desks of its analysis: "[I]t is a moment of immersement that is simultaneously total and partial" (Strathern 1999: 1).[13] She maintains that the relationships or connections between field and desk, while mutually shaped, remain infinite because the field "consists of the sum of all the possibilities that may be sampled" (Strathern 1991: 596). Hence, surfacing the field-desks of 'thing-ing', I suggest, effectively positions ethnography for making visual the expansive possibilities of spatial-temporal becoming.

Nevertheless, surfacing and submerging, as we have seen, nearly always involve some degree of friction, or what Taylor (2005: 749) terms 'struggles'. Similarly, Latour (1997: 186) postulates that transportation is never without transformation or deformation, except in a few rare cases. This is because transportation is relational and relations take work. Surfacing field-desk frictions may become unruly, leaping up to bite the hand that feeds. They may threaten to become the objective-subjective monster they set out to destroy. Remember Latour's cautions about the professional hazard. Ethnographic surfacing, in my view, requires careful tinkering in its own right to remain open to the multi-sitings (Marcus 1995) of field-desk spatial-timings. This is where attention to the 'messy' scales of surfacing is crucial. Surfacing is something of a multi-scaling that entangles intricate and seemingly small or insignificant material entities: tabletops, computer screens, control knobs, or a small leaf of lettuce. In other words, small is not equivalent to unimportant. As Strathern (2004: xix) aptly proffers, "A 'small' thing can thus be made to say as much as a 'big' thing." Similarly, this chapter has proposed surfacing as an ethnographic heuristic for tracing *small* spatial-temporal distinctions in senior home care that can make *big* differences.

Acknowledgments

I wish to thank all of the people who made this chapter possible, particularly my fellow authors in this volume and the anonymous reviewers. Several other colleagues and friends also offered valuable comments. These people include Annika Capelán, Randi Markussen, Tine Tjørnhøj-Thomsen, and Anna Tsing. I am obliged to Casper Bruun Jensen for recommending Bruno Latour's "Trains of Thought" and Janelle Taylor for bringing her article "Surfacing the Body Interior" to my attention. A PhD Fellowship from the IT University of Copenhagen and a European Commission Marie Curie European Reintegration Grant (ERG) (No. 249322) have financially supported this research.

Peter A. Lutz has a background in anthropology and in science, technology, and society (STS). He has researched the relation between care and technology in senior home care. Based at Lund University, Sweden, he currently works on questions of environmental care and urban design.

Notes

1. Hedman et al. (2007) distinguish two types of home-care services in Sweden: 'home care' (medical treatment) and 'home help' (domestic services). Additional categories employed in Swedish home care found in fieldwork include 'service care', 'general care', and 'self-care'. The point here is simply that home care is a heterogeneous field and not easily defined. For an overview of Swedish senior home care, see, for example, Szebehely (2007).
2. The *handläggare* (handling officer) in Swedish state-run home care allocates minutes in monthly totals depending on the type of care plan. My fieldwork confirms that a care scheduler rations these minutes on a daily or weekly basis after consulting with the care staff, client, and/or guardian. Szebehely (2007) provides a similar example.
3. The social analysis of time has increased significantly since the early 1990s, aided with the inauguration of the journal *Time & Society* in 1992.
4. Ingold (2000) goes on to argue that event time is recognizable in Western societies but that the dominant mode is clock time. See Mumford (1986) for a provocative essay about such developments.
5. I wish to thank an anonymous reviewer for this clarification.
6. Latour's anecdote of the twin travelers bears a striking resemblance to the 'twin paradox' in Einstein's theory of relativity, which was debated between Bergson and Einstein in 1922—a debate that Bergson apparently lost. For a fascinating exposé of the Einstein-Bergson debate, see Canales (2005).
7. The program is sold as Laps Care by Tieto, a software technology company. For more information, see Eveborn et al. (2006) and Tieto's website (http://www.tieto.com/).
8. The term 'continuity' refers to the number of care workers that a client has daily. The ambition is to link a client with only a few care workers, especially in the case

of dementia clients. This was generally recognized as a factor of 'quality' or 'good care' by care managers, staff, and clients alike.

9. For a fascinating study of 'waiting', see Schweizer (2005).
10. The stroke and its medications cause Inga's mouth to be dry, making it difficult to swallow.
11. The association is strong here with the term 'diffraction' as developed by Barad (2007).
12. Indeed, Latour (2005) has argued for slower socio-material analysis. See also Law (2004) and Gad and Jensen (2010).
13. Riles's work expands this argument, most notably in *The Network Inside Out* (2000).

References

Barad, Karen. 2007. *Meeting the Universe Halfway: Quantum Physics and the Entanglement of Matter and Meaning*. Durham, NC: Duke University Press.

Bryson, Valerie. 2007. *Gender and the Politics of Time: Feminist Theory and Contemporary Debates*. Bristol: Policy Press.

Canales, Jimena. 2005. "Einstein, Bergson, and the Experiment That Failed: Intellectual Cooperation at the League of Nations." *MLN* 120, no. 5: 1168–1191.

Dahl, Hanne M. 2009. "New Public Management, Care and Struggles about Recognition." *Critical Social Policy* 29, no. 4: 634–654.

Ellingsæter, Anne L. 2007. "'Old' and 'New' Politics of Time to Care: Three Norwegian Reforms." *Journal of European Social Policy* 17, no. 1: 49–60.

Eriksson, Jenny. 2009. "Ge Oss Mer Tid för de Gamla." [Give Us More Time for the Old.] *Sydsvenskan*, 6 June. http://www.sydsvenskan.se/omkretsen/vellinge/article 435358/Ge-oss-mer-tid-for-de-gamla.html (accessed 10 September 2010).

Evans, Vyvyan. 2004. *The Structure of Time: Language, Meaning, and Temporal Cognition*. Amsterdam: John Benjamins.

Eveborn, Patrik, Patrik Flisberg, and Mikael Rönnqvist. 2006. "Laps Care: An Operational System for Staff Planning of Home Care." *European Journal of Operational Research* 171, no. 3: 962–976.

Gad, Christopher, and Casper B. Jensen. 2010. "On the Consequences of Post-ANT." *Science, Technology, & Human Values* 35, no. 1: 55–80.

Gell, Alfred. 1992. *The Anthropology of Time: Cultural Constructions of Temporal Maps and Images*. Oxford: Berg.

Green-Pedersen, Christoffer. 2002. "New Public Management Reforms of the Danish and Swedish Welfare States: The Role of Different Social Democratic Responses." *Governance* 15, no. 2: 271–294.

Hedman, Nils O., Roine Johannson, and Urban Rosenqvist. 2007. "Clustering and Inertia: Structural Integration of Home Care in Swedish Elderly Care." *International Journal of Integrated Care* 7: 1–9.

Hernadi, Alexandra, and Tobias Olsson. 2010. "Tiden för de Äldre Krymper—Stressen Växer." [Time for the Elderly Shrinks—Stress Grows.] *Svenska Dagbladet*, 15 February. http://www.svd.se/nyheter/inrikes/tiden-for-de-aldre-krymper-stressen-vaxer_4265169.svd (accessed 10 September 2010).

Ingold, Tim. 2000. *The Perception of the Environment: Essays on Livelihood, Dwelling and Skill*. London: Routledge.

Kaufman-Scarborough, Carol. 2006. "Time Use and the Impact of Technology: Examining Workspaces in the Home." *Time & Society* 15, no. 1: 57–80.

Latour, Bruno. 1997. "Trains of Thought: Piaget, Formalism and the Fifth Dimension." *Common Knowledge* 3, no. 6: 170–191.

Latour, Bruno. 2004. "Why Has Critique Run Out of Steam? From Matters of Fact to Matters of Concern." *Critical Inquiry* 30, no. 2: 225–248.

Latour, Bruno. 2005. *Reassembling the Social: An Introduction to Actor-Network-Theory.* Oxford: Oxford University Press.

Law, John. 2004. *After Method: Mess in Social Science Research.* London: Routledge.

Marcus, George E. 1995. "Ethnography in/of the World System: The Emergence of Multi-sited Ethnography." *Annual Review of Anthropology* 24: 95–117.

Mol, Annemarie. 2002. *The Body Multiple: Ontology in Medical Practice.* Durham, NC: Duke University Press.

Mol, Annemarie. 2008. *The Logic of Care and the Problem of Patient Choice.* London: Routledge.

Mol, Annemarie, Ingunn Moser, and Jeannette Pols, eds. 2010. *Care in Practice: On Tinkering in Clinics, Homes and Farms.* Bielefeld: Transcript Verlag.

Mumford, Lewis. 1986. *The Lewis Mumford Reader.* Ed. Donald L. Miller. 1st ed. New York: Pantheon Books.

Munn, Nancy D. 1992. "The Cultural Anthropology of Time: A Critical Essay." *Annual Review of Anthropology* 21: 93–123.

Nowotny, Helga. 1992. "Time and Social Theory: Towards a Social Theory of Time." *Time & Society* 1, no. 3: 421–454.

Orlikowski, Wanda J., and JoAnne Yates. 2002. "It's About Time: Temporal Structuring in Organizations." *Organization Science* 13, no. 6: 684–700.

Pollitt, Christopher, and Geert Bouckaert. 2004. *Public Management Reform: A Comparative Analysis.* 2nd ed. Oxford: Oxford University Press.

Pols, Jeannette. 2006. "Washing the Citizen: Washing, Cleanliness and Citizenship in Mental Health Care." *Culture, Medicine and Psychiatry* 30, no. 1: 77–104.

Puig de la Bellacasa, Maria. 2011. "Matters of Care in Technoscience: Assembling Neglected Things." *Social Studies of Science* 41, no. 1: 85–106.

Riles, Annelise. 2000. *The Network Inside Out.* Ann Arbor: University of Michigan Press.

Rose, Nikolas. 1999. *Powers of Freedom: Reframing Political Thought.* Cambridge: Cambridge University Press.

Schweizer, Harold. 2005. "On Waiting." *University of Toronto Quarterly* 74, no. 3: 777–792.

Strathern, Marilyn. 1991. "Partners and Consumers: Making Relations Visible." *New Literary History* 22, no. 3: 581–601.

Strathern, Marilyn. 1999. *Property, Substance and Effect: Anthropological Essays on Persons and Things.* London, New Brunswick: Athlone Press.

Strathern, Marilyn. 2004. *Partial Connections.* Updated ed. Walnut Creek, CA: AltaMira Press.

Sveriges Radio. 2005. "Äldre Får för Lite Tid." [Elderly Get Too Little Time.] *Sveriges Radio*, 30 September. http://sverigesradio.se/sida/artikel.aspx?programid = 99&artikel = 703453 (accessed 10 September 2010).

Sveriges Television. 2009. "Ont om Tid inom Äldreomsorgen." [Short of Time in Elderly Care.] *Sveriges Television*, 19 January. http://www.svt.se/nyheter/sverige/ont-om-tid-inom-aldreomsorgen (accessed 10 September 2010).

Szebehely, Marta. 2007. "Carework in Scandinavia: Organisational Trends and Everyday Realities." Paper presented at the 5th Annual ESPAnet Conference, Vienna, 20–22 September.

Szebehely, Marta, and Gun-Britt Trydegård. 2012. "Home Care for Older People in Sweden: A Universal Model in Transition." *Health and Social Care in the Community* 20, no. 3: 300–309.

Taylor, Janelle S. 2005. "Surfacing the Body Interior." *Annual Review of Anthropology* 34: 741–756.

Torre, Ramón Ramos. 2007. "Time's Social Metaphors: An Empirical Research." *Time & Society* 16, no. 2–3: 157–187.

Trydegård, Gun-Britt. 2000. "From Poorhouse Overseer to Production Manager: One Hundred Years of Old-Age Care in Sweden Reflected in the Development of an Occupation." *Ageing and Society* 20, no. 5: 571–597.

Tsing, Anna L. 2005. *Friction: An Ethnography of Global Connection.* Princeton, NJ: Princeton University Press.

Vabø, Mia. 2006. "Caring for People or Caring for Proxy Consumers?" *European Societies* 8, no. 3: 403–422.

WHO (World Health Organization). 2012. "World Health Statistics." http://www.who.int/whosis/whostat/2011 (accessed 29 January 2012).

Chapter 6

BOREDOM, RHYTHM, AND THE TEMPORALITY OF RITUAL
Recurring Fieldwork in the Brazilian Candomblé

Inger Sjørslev

The ideas about time and the field presented in the following pages are inspired by ritual as the theme of my fieldwork, but also by the fact that I have been returning to the same fieldwork location again and again over a period of 30 years. When I first started, I had never imagined that this would happen, much less planned it. On the contrary, on many occasions I have been sure that this visit would be the last. I have taken the invitation to think about temporality and the field as an incentive to look into the meaning of this long-term relationship with the field. Ritual and recurring field visits will be the starting point for reflections on temporality, social rhythm, and the analytical value of boredom, 'deep hanging out', and other temporal perspectives in the course of fieldwork.

The field I am referring to is a small Brazilian town in the state of Bahia. The African-Brazilian syncretistic religion Candomblé builds on a strong tradition

Notes for this chapter are located on page 108.

and a long history, and it is flourishing in Bahia today, providing both continuity and revival of African traditions brought to Brazil with the slaves. The initial objective of my fieldwork was ritual possession with a focus on the predominance of women in Candomblé. I first arrived in Bahia in late 1979, and after some time I became an initiate of a ritual sisterhood (Sjørslev 1995). Although I have often had to skip participation in the yearly rituals, I have kept going back time and again for the ritual events in my particular *terreiro* (Candomblé house). In 2004, I took part in an *axexé*, a memorial funeral for the spirit of my *mãe-de-santo* Mother Lira, who died in 1997 (Sjørslev 2006). In 2008, I was there in August at the time of the public procession of the Boa Morte, the Sisterhood of the Good Death. On the same occasion I made a sacrificial contribution to the rituals in the Candomblé house that I belong to, which consists of a group of women who are not in the Sisterhood. The people of this house expect me to do so from time to time. They know that I come from far away and that I do not always have the opportunity to be present at ritual occasions, but when I do, they expect me to fulfill my obligations along with the rest of the spiritual community.

Candomblé is based on the veneration of the African Orixás, or saints, who are called upon in rituals to take possession of the initiates. Although an initiate myself, I have never been possessed. My role is more the role of an *ekede*, an assistant priest, whose job is to take care of the possessed and assist in the practical and material matters of the house. Since I am not always there and tend to forget the specificities of the ritual rules and the habitus of the ritual performances when I have not taken part in them for some years, my role has become one of economic supporter by way of *obrigaçoes* (obligations), which are both sacrifices to the Orixás and social celebrations. In 2008, I spent only two weeks in Bahia. I had come to study the public procession of the Sisterhood of the Good Death, and I needed to be in the center of town most of the time to follow public events. However, the people of my Candomblé house obliged me to give a gift to my Orixá and to the Candomblé house and to stay in the house as much as possible. I was not opposed to their wishes, but I had problems with the timing, and so did the people of the house. All this, together with the fact that these recurring field visits have happened over so many years, has brought me to reflect on social obligations, timing, and social rhythm. I had already given some thought to the role of time in ritual, and hours and hours of participant observation in ritual events during earlier and longer periods of fieldwork had stimulated ideas about the role of time and presence when nothing special happens—in ethnographic method sometimes subsumed under the label 'deep hanging out'. There was a significant change in the sense of boredom experienced when waiting for the ritual to begin compared to later stages, when it could hardly be called boredom but should rather be characterized as impatient anticipation, a sentiment I shared with the participants.

Alfred Gell (1996) has suggested that a time-anthropology should begin in the realm of time-geography and time-economics, that is, in concrete empirical settings. The time-geography of the Candomblé ritual is the 'time of actions' (Johansen 1989). The multi-temporal approach (see the introduction to this volume) implied in my recurring field visits has indeed been unintended, but it has proven valuable and, together with the experiences of hanging out at long rituals, has led to reflections on temporality in different forms and scales. I thus want to make two points. First, there is value in boredom and deep hanging out in the field, and this value may be lost in some contemporary fieldwork methods (which may, however, have other advantages). I do not want to denigrate 'fieldwork by appointment', as it is sometimes called, which is the kind of fieldwork that is being conducted in much contemporary anthropology, both at home and abroad. However, I do want to point to the value of a fieldwork temporality that implies boredom and what I term 'unfocused presence', which is how I understand hanging out. Second, if the anthropological endeavor consists in identifying social rhythms by way of personal involvement—and this is pretty much how I see participant observation—then recurring presence in the field is a crucial method. If this is not the case in all types of fields, it certainly is in Candomblé. Together, boredom, deep hanging out, and recurring field visits represent the possibility of identifying social rhythms. These points will be illuminated firstly by looking at ritual rhythm and secondly by analyzing the role of time and rhythm in aesthetic forms, pointing to a general discussion of fieldwork temporality.

While I do touch upon what boredom means to the participants, I do not intend to discuss it in detail or to analyze it as a figure and try to relate it to existential questions or particular social circumstances. In the literature, boredom has been associated with meaninglessness and anxiety (Barbalet 1999) or with insecurities about the future (Frederiksen 2011). It should be distinguished from waiting, which has been associated with processes of modernity and 'surplus of time', such as the chronic waiting experienced by refugees and immigrants (Jeffrey 2008). Boredom is a complex and ambiguous concept (Musharbash 2007) that merits more attention, both as an aspect of temporality within fields of study and as a condition in fieldwork situations. In the present reflections, I deal with it as a sentiment of the fieldworker. I set out from my own experiences of boredom in order to arrive at an understanding of how it differs from the expressed sentiments of the people I have spent time with and in order to discuss temporal perspectives of our relation. I do not see my own boredom as a lack of meaning; rather, it was an impatience related to a certain instrumentality in my conceptions of time. Away from home, friends, and familiar life, I did not want time to be 'wasted' with 'nothing happening', since I was there to use my time well. I was at work—fieldwork, yes, but work none the less. Thus, the reflections I want to present also have to do with the fact that time in fieldwork is sometimes dealt with in a very instrumental way. Time has to be *used*. It does not take a Protestant ethic to see that the mere label of field*work* may have significant implications for how we think about time when doing it.

My sense of boredom occurred mainly in the liminal and stressful phase of the fieldwork period, that is, after I had separated from my familiar world and before I had found my feet and begun to feel at home (Jackson 2010: 41) in the challenging and demanding world of Candomblé. The sense of boredom in my state of inexperienced waiting-while-not-knowing-when-something-was-going-to-happen was supplemented by its opposite, a more or less permanent state of exaggeration and confusion that arose from the strong sensual stimuli in Candomblé and from learning about its awesome and emotionally overwhelming symbols. I used to dream of slaughtered animals, body scars, and heads shaven in initiation, intermixing the symbolic world of Candomblé with my personal anxiety about being unable to manage this whole affair and meet the obligations that came with having received a grant to do the study. I read the most rationalist professional literature I could think of (Karl Popper), which I had brought to the field on the suggestion of a friend, who had wisely proposed it as a counterbalance to the emotional excitement of the spirit world, and I built reflections on some of these sentiments into my work (Sjørslev 1995). When I had talked with my friend about how the world of Candomblé might affect me, there was one thing I had not anticipated—being bored. Yet, in my own liminal phase, while waiting for rituals to begin, I experienced boredom, although it was not shared by the local people. They might be anxiously waiting, but they knew from previous experience that what was coming was worth the wait, and they never expressed sentiments of boredom even if they might express impatience and anticipation. The Brazilian word to describe something as being boring would be *chato*. I never heard anyone referring to the waiting time associated with ritual as *chato*, and, in the course of time, my own sentiments changed as well from boredom to more or less patient anticipation, along with the other participants.

Ritual Rhythm

Candomblé comprises a number of rituals, the key ones being possession rituals, which are performed with an audience and, in theory, in public for those who can find their way to the remote locations of Candomblé houses. Sacrificial rituals, rituals of magic, and bodily and spiritual cleansings are usually performed in semi-secrecy and are open only to initiates. The possession rituals celebrate the Orixás by drumming and singing a series of songs and dancing the sequence of dances for each of the more than 10 Orixás that are venerated and called upon in the Ketu nation, which was the nation of my fieldwork house.[1] Each house has its own individual calendar of rituals, but with some common adaptation to the Catholic religious calendar so that no house 'drums' between Lent and Easter. In the house of Mother Lira, June is the month of heavy ritual activity, supplemented by the *festa de Obaluaé* in August and four days of celebration of the *caboclos*, the Indian spirits, in December. The Gregorian calendar thus determines the overall sequence of rituals, but when it comes to the time of each ritual event, another kind of temporality takes over. When in the beginning I asked when the possession ritual—which takes place at night—would start, either I was not given any answer at all, or, after I persisted, I was told that it would begin *depois da novela*, that is, after the daily soap opera on Globo, the national television network. This is a rather specific time, since the *novela das oito*, which was the one referred to, begins at 8:00 PM and finishes an hour later. The point is, however, that the time indicator given was not clock time but event time, and that if one took the specification of 'after the novela' seriously and arrived at 9:00 PM, nothing was likely to happen for yet some time. Things do not happen according to Greenwich-measured time but according to what is sometimes referred to as 'African time', that is, when people are ready.

This is a well-known logic of much non-Western time conception. It is the time of actions, a temporality defined by actions and the course of events as opposed to the abstract temporality of modern Western time construction.[2] Activities regulate the calendar, not the other way around. The logic of the time of action is that the chronology conforms to activities associated with it. Activities follow their own inherent logic, and things happen when all is ready (Johansen 1989: 94–96). This is certainly the case in Candomblé rituals. People in Mother Lira's house would begin to arrive some time after the *novela,* but it might very well take an hour or more before everybody was ready to begin. The drummers would arrive one by one, usually quite late. Often, a bunch of kids would first be playing around in the ceremonial room and practicing their rudimentary drumming skills, sometimes leading beginners among the audience—including the novice anthropologist—to believe that things were soon to begin, only to be disappointed. Quite often it would take yet another hour or so before all the dancing women had arrived with their packages of clothes and had finished getting dressed up in their eloquent and voluptuous costumes. Meanwhile, those of us who had come to watch would sit on the benches in the ceremonial room, and we would wait. When the dancing finally began, there would be excitement and joy and colorful entertainment. On the most vivid occasions, the drummers would build up to an atmosphere of tension, effervescence, and delight as the Orixás began to arrive and take possession of the dancing initiates and sometimes also spontaneously of people among the audience. I have experienced the most entertaining, stimulating, and densely informative events in Candomblé. But I have also spent a lot of time waiting and—mainly in the beginning—being bored. To tell the truth, I have also on occasions been bored while watching the same dances and hearing the same songs again and again. I say this without any remorse or ethical concern, for I know that the most ardent protagonists of Candomblé have had the same experience. Now and then, they would begin the evening ritual with an unmistakable air of 'here-we-go-again-let's-get-started-and-get-it-over-with'. However, the sentiments that characterized this kind of being bored were not the same as the ones in the beginning, when I had not had enough experiences to be expectative. This was more a feeling of tediousness, which also had some pleasant aspects to it, the pleasure of the familiar. And again, I never heard the people mention the word *chato*—unless it was a really bad performance, but that was rare and another story.

Another aspect of the Candomblé rituals is that they are physically strenuous, most of all for the dancers and drummers, but also for people in the audience, who will often have to stand for many hours in cramped spaces and wait for the entertainment to begin. Then they wait for the Orixás to arrive and take possession of the dancers. When the possessed have been guided away from the public eye to be dressed in their adorned outfits, the audience waits again for them to be escorted back into the space of the dance. This will often be commented upon with sighs and sometimes complaints if the sequential process is not experienced as satisfactory. There is a lot of waiting in Candomblé, yet most of it is part of the rhythm of excitement. Waiting is expectation but also anxiety that the unexpected may happen. People therefore do not speak of waiting as boredom. What will be said is that things are held up—*esta demorando!*

There are thus different types of waiting at stake, but not really boredom, except for the anthropologist, mainly in the liminal phase. Although an expression such as "Ai, Candomblé é só esperar" (Oh, Candomblé is all waiting) may occasionally be heard from a *filha-* or *filho-de-santo*—an initiated daughter or son of a saint (an Orixá)—the word 'boredom' would rarely if ever enter the conversation. Boredom in the sense I am dealing with here is not an emic concept. To identify the way that the people of Candomblé deal with the temporalities of the ritual, one rather has to listen to the chatter and gossip that takes place after a ritual event. This is a significant part of the whole affair. The discussions about what happened—the critical evaluations of a ritual evening—are noteworthy elements for a holistic understanding of Candomblé rituals. In emic terms, *fuxico* would be the term that relates to native evaluations of temporality. *Fuxico* means tinkering, manipulation, actions meant to produce effects (Goldman 2007: 114), and a post-(ritual)-party gossiping evaluation of an event will involve comments, often critical or even sarcastic, on the *fuxico* performed, which may in the present analytical terminology be interpreted as a comment on the successful or unsuccessful temporal conduct of the ritual affairs.

In light of boredom, ritual has been understood as a way of interrupting a certain monotony of village life (Nisbet 1982), and perhaps, in a similar vein, fieldwork may sometimes be an interruption of monotonous life in academia. On the other hand, boredom seems to be correlated more with too few opportunities for action than with monotony, if one is to believe the originator of the famous concept of 'flow', psychologist Mihaly Csikszentmihalyi ([1975] 2000). In his experimental research on anxiety and boredom, Csikszentmihalyi sees boredom related not to a deprivation of flow but rather to restricted opportunities for action—as opposed to anxiety, which may arise when there are too many opportunities (ibid.: 49). In these terms, boredom, as an analytical concept and an experiential one related to the fieldworker, may be regarded as a lack of opportunities for action, including mental ones. If one is not able to know what may be done with one's time, this may cause boredom. If, on the other hand, nothing happening is a sequence within a holistic field of smaller and bigger events that are rising and falling in intensity, it may be experienced not as boredom but rather as waiting in expectation—along with the native participants. With this I want to make an analytical point in distinguishing between boredom as related to the observing fieldworker at work and waiting as part of a social rhythm experienced by a participant who is part of a collective, playful flow of rhythmic intensity. Over time, the fieldworker may become included in this rhythm, and her or his perceptions of time will have changed.

As for ritual, the oscillation between monotony and interruptions connects to Edmund Leach's (1961: 132–136) analysis of the role of festivals in the structuring of time, as eloquently expressed in his text on 'time and false noses'. As an interruption of daily (monotonous) life (Nisbet 1982), ritual creates breaks in social rhythm. In doing so, it raises the awareness of time, which is a precondition for the experience of boredom. Ritual breaks monotony, and within ritual itself repetition and recognizability provide for a temporality that allows peaks to stand out in a flow of rising and falling intensities with expectative waiting in between the peaks. As ritual is a breach in daily life, so ritual is in itself characterized by sequences of a certain monotony alternating with breaches. As such, ritual establishes a potential rhythmic time-space in which repetition, routine, and monotony are the ground upon which the figure of peak events can stand out. In a more contemporary theoretical perspective, the idea of shifting between figure and ground in ritual could be elaborated through the more subtle idea of the 'fold', as conceived by Deleuze (2006). The fold has many modalities, including temporal ones. Time is folded in memory, and the temporality of the fold is also related to continuity and discontinuity. In this regard, deep hanging out may be regarded as waiting until what is folded deep inside unfolds, comes out, becomes visible and felt—as a 'figure' in the more simplistic understanding. 'Ground' would then be the folding back into the hidden, the virtual, awaiting a new temporal appearance.

When I witnessed a Candomblé ritual during my initial fieldwork period, I was not sure what to expect. Later on, after numerous repetitions and with earlier occasions alive in my mind, as well as a better knowledge of the expectations of others, my experience was completely different. The fact that I knew what was likely to happen and that I had the pre-experience of the excitement that would probably occur, the meal that would come after, and the pleasant atmosphere of laughter and talks in the kitchen when the Orixás had left and the dancers had come out of possession, as well as the chance that some funny and entertaining spirits (e.g., the *ere* or child spirit) might arrive and tease the people—all of this made the whole experience positively different. In this respect, the sense of time implies the knowledge of what usually happens, what happened previously, and the delight of familiar repetition, all of which sustain the expectation of what is to come, what is going to happen. Sounds, visual impressions, and smells all contribute to the holistic experience of a delightful ritual, but temporality, which implies knowledge based on former experiences, and expectations based on knowledge of regularities are both fundamental elements in the experience as a whole. This is all incorporated in the social rhythm.

In this respect, ritual can be regarded as a 'temporal gestalt'. Waiting and repetitiveness are essential parts of the whole configuration or gestalt of the ritual event. And that again means that the social rhythm brought forth by common memory and expectation may transform the initial boredom of non-familiarity in fieldwork into anxious waiting and a sense of communality, which rests in the common knowledge that nobody is waiting in an empty time of nothingness. Rather, they are anticipating something to happen, which relates to what happened yesterday or last year and the year before. The delight of waiting in this sense is a combination of familiarity with repetition and the potential of divergence from it.

All this implies that the rhythmic modality of ritual is a modality of sociality that cannot be brought forth in a one-time event. Repetition and iterability—in Derrida's ([1982] 2007) understanding, the potential of newness in repetition—are required in order to comprehend the whole rhythmic modality that is an inherent aspect of ritual. In the same vein, temporal repetition and the knowledge that deviations can occur are inherent aspects of social rhythm. The point in the present context is that this fact can hardly be grasped by the fieldworker during a single visit. It is through repetition—over time and of experiences—that regularity can be distinguished from exceptions and deviances. And this can only be brought about by recurring visits.

Fieldwork Rhythm: Oscillation between Events and Unfocused Presence

I am not sure where the phrase 'deep hanging out' originated, and perhaps it does not matter. Whoever introduced this term into anthropological methodological discourse probably did so with a bit of irony. No doubt there is irony in Clifford Geertz's use of it. Others, who have used this phrasing to be self-critical about the core anthropological method of participant observation, have also used it with a self-critical—or at least a self-reflexive—touch, pointing to the vagueness of the precise merit of long-term fieldwork participant observation. 'Deep' must refer to Geertz's (1972) thick description and his analysis of 'deep play' in the Balinese cockfight, and the phrase was perhaps coined by Geertz himself. He did use it as the headline of an article in the *New York Review of Books* in which he discussed the current methodological state of affairs in the anthropological discipline on the basis of a critical reading of two ethnographic books: *Chronicle of the Guayaki Indians* by Pierre Clastres (1998) and *Routes: Travel and Translation in the Late Twentieth Century* by James Clifford (1997). In this article, Geertz (1998: 69) referred to deep hanging out as "the value, the feasibility, the legitimacy, and thus the future of localized, long-term, close-in, vernacular field research." Deep hanging out is an intrinsic part of classical anthropological fieldwork, and it is, according to Geertz (and to me), a threatened species in much contemporary ethnography.

On the basis of my experiences in ritual, I would define the term 'deep hanging out' as an unfocused presence within the context one sees as the field. 'Deep' would then refer to the analytical value of being there when nothing happens. But what, more precisely, does 'nothing' mean? What happens when nothing happens? Nothing happening is precisely what is often associated with boredom in everyday life. In a short piece on boredom, sociologist Robert Nisbet (1982) spoke of it as the monotony of life in the village, which had made people break up and migrate, start a festival, or go to war. But there is not much to be found in ethnographic literature on the issue of what I refer to as unfocused presence.

Boredom is sometimes defined as 'empty time', the kind of time you want to 'kill'. In my perspective, however, I should like to add another value to this state of mind—aside from the fact that boredom can be closely related to expectation, which takes away the negative connotation and replaces it with waiting for something thrilling to happen, as indicated above. Boredom in a sense implies a critique of what is going on (Svendsen 2001). It may lead to reflection by way of the lack of self-evidence that a state of boredom inherently creates. Signifying emptiness of time, boredom can be understood as leading to emptiness of meaning (cf. Barbalet 1999) and then again to reflection on meaning as such, perhaps leading to a critique of the accepted meaning. Empty or open time may thus be seen in a positive critical light as the lack of self-evidence, which is a significant element in the anthropological endeavor.

In relation to ritual, pre-codedness is what may lead to boredom, but the openness and flexibility in ritual—its *per*formativeness in the sense of creating through practice, or, as it has been termed, its 'creation of presence' (Schieffelin 1985)—can only take place on the basis of some amount of pre-codedness. The part of ritual that may lead to boredom is thus also the precondition for ritual being the opposite. Pre-codedness—or the monotonous—is the ground upon which the figures of the unexpected, the improvised, the deviance from well-known repetition, and, in a wider sense, social play take place.

If deep hanging out were to be theorized further, it would imply speculating about uneventfulness and asking about the role of monotony or boredom in interpretative work. Marilyn Strathern (2004) has pointed to the complexity of interpretation that arises from a figure-ground reversal. Such a reversal, she says, results in an "oscillation between perspectives that appear to summon quite different approaches to the world" (ibid.: 88). Each new contextualization presents "a fresh configuration of figure and ground for attention," and such interpretative procedures give "depth to ethnography" (ibid.: 97). Taking these ideas into the methodological fieldwork realm, and hopefully without oversimplifying Strathern's thoughts, I would say that, applied to the concept of deep hanging out, they give 'deep' its proper meaning—namely, that only through the oscillation between unfocused presence (ground) and focused event (figure) can ethnographic depth be achieved. Hanging out is the ground upon which events stand out as figures, and figures (events, such as ritual) may shift to ground for other figures within it (like deviance from normal regularity). In a temporal perspective, hanging out may thus be seen as the ground that is a prerequisite for identifying certain figures. Furthermore, shifts can be made between ground and figure, such as when repetitive presence enables recognition of the significance of expectation and former experiences in understanding the temporality and social rhythm of the Candomblé ritual.

I look on unfocused presence as a value because it is staggered, that is, displaced from ordinary life. Taking place within a framework of 'strangeness', it is devoid of the self-evidence that may, in ordinary life, lead to being bored in a common-sense way. Within the context of fieldwork, the lack of self-evidence is—or should be—the constant condition. The situation of waiting, for instance, has to be taken as a condition that should be accompanied by a readiness to shift the focus of attention. In the case of the Candomblé possession rituals, I came to see waiting for the ritual to start as an exercise in understanding social rhythm. The choice of the term 'rhythm' is deliberate and has to do with the character of ritual as well as the character of fieldwork. I want to elaborate on this point by examining the significance of recurring field visits nourished by social obligations and the food of gods.

The Temporality of Participation

I was initiated gradually into the sisterhood of the Candomblé *terreiro* of Mother Lira beginning in 1981, when I hung around, deeply, as a novice and non-initiate. In 1987, I took the *bori*, the sacrifice that establishes the relation between one's head and the Orixá and which is the first step in the sequence of initiation. In the years to follow, I took part in a succession of sacrificial rituals and gifts to the gods, the last being in August 2008. Initiation is a temporal thing in Candomblé. Initiates move up in the spiritual hierarchy through successive ritual steps over many years (Goldman 2007). The fact that I have come back again and again is no doubt interpreted by my ritual sisters as attached to this gradual rise in the cult, as well as to the need to take care of my Orixá and reiterate the performance of sacrificial duties in order to strengthen my spiritual bond. In my own understanding, I have seen the need to come back again and again as related to the sociality of the sisterhood and my relations with the people. It certainly has to do with a wish to follow their lives, but there is also a sense of obligation, one that applies to the people as much as to the gods. Or perhaps, in the spirit of Durkheim, people and gods cannot be separated.

I had decided to make sacrifices to the Orixás as a way to access information through practice and also to gain a role in the Candomblé house that made sense to the people I hoped would be my interlocutors. Or perhaps the decision was made for me. Certainly, in Candomblé the Orixás are the ones who select individuals for initiation, just as the stone that represents (or 'is') my (initiated) head and connects me to my Orixá itself decided (by way of Mother Lira's discreet interference) that it would be 'my' stone. In any case, it is not easy to study Candomblé without personal involvement, and there has indeed been a high degree of 'going native' in the studies of this religion (Bastide 1983; Dion 1998; Dos Santos 1977; Serra 1995). There is surely more than one reason for this, but the fact remains that since Candomblé is a religion considerably sustained by practice, it is virtually impossible to find a role and live with the people through the rituals without having a position of one's own in the ritual. Mother Lira, the renowned and respected *mãe-de-santo* who took me into her house, did not demand anything from me directly, but she demonstrated by subtle means and with much assistance from her strong Orixá, Iemanjá-Ogum-te, the kind of position that she wanted me to have—or, rather, to work for, because it could not be acquired all at once. Since it would take time, this implied the need for me to return again and again. As a consequence of my presence and my respect for Mother Lira, I was eventually drawn into the ritual hierarchy with implications of spiritual, material, and social obligations to gods as well as people in a long-term relationship. The temporality of my participation was determined by the time-geography of the field itself in the sense that my involvement in Candomblé became the basis for my recurring presence in the field, as Candomblé ritual obligations are dependent upon yearly repetition.

I want to touch on the character of the temporality in ritual before returning to the significance of recurring presence in the field. The particular temporality of the Candomblé ritual field led to analytical results that I believe could not have been achieved if other kinds of temporality had been at play. I propose to elaborate this point by way of rhythm and aesthetics, and I have found inspiration for ideas about rhythm in a comparison of Susanne Langer's and John Dewey's differences and likenesses in their respective understandings of how rhythms shape and constitute aesthetic forms. Although from different philosophic traditions—Dewey being a pragmatist and Langer working within the tradition of symbolic forms—both link rhythm to the constitution of art forms and see aesthetic forms as temporal.[3]

From the perspective of pragmatist philosophy, ritual may be regarded as a large collective piece of art in the sense of what Dewey ([1934] 1958) sees as important to the experience of aesthetic forms, namely, the rhythmic principle. The experience of art happens when there is rhythm, that is, when the structure of the object interacts with the energies of the subject's experience to generate a substance that develops cumulatively toward fulfillment of impulsions. From another angle, Langer (1953: 126–127) sees the rhythmic principle in music as significant in all art forms. It is a characteristic principle of vital activity whose essence is the setting up of new tensions by the resolution of former ones. Art thus has to do with rhythmic tension. Taking the ideas of rhythm as related to art out into a collective social field, rhythmic tension is indeed what constitutes the whole social process of ritual. As a 'work of art' characterized by its form, ritual is special in the sense that it is both collective and performative. Its essence lies in a common performative practice. There are no nodes for ritual, no prescription of its enactment—and if there sometimes is, as I saw once in a modernized form of a Candomblé performance that made use of transcribed songs and nodes, the ritual takes on a whole different character with much more distance between audience and performers. I see the sense of authenticity as being closely related to the sociality performed (Sjørslev 2012), and the art of ritual as a collective and performative rhythm lies precisely in the social ability to synchronize, in brief, in the rhythm of the social. Rhythm is an aspect of temporality that is fundamental to aesthetic and social form.

Social Rhythm across Spaces: Coming and Going

After this detour into ritual, I want to look at the temporalities lived by my Candomblé sisters in relation to the temporality lived by myself or, in other words, my recurring presence in their lives. Two temporalities have been identified so far—that is, the temporality of the field and the temporality of specific events within the field, such as ritual—but there is also a temporality of the relation between fieldworker and field. Informed by my comings and goings, I am tempted to speak of 'our' time. Our time is a time of 30 years, of short and sometimes a little bit longer meetings within years of absence.

The incentive on the part of the Candomblé sisters to want me to return is a mixture of a sense of obligation regarding the gods, a concern for my well-being (since it is not healthy to go for too long without sacrificing to the Orixás), and a wish to preserve the coherence of the Candomblé house, which implies efforts toward a continuous inclusion of all initiates. However, it is also a reflection of their hope and expectation: the hope that I will contribute (financially and with food offerings) to the continuation of this particular house with its particular history and prestige, and the expectation that their progress in life may be linked to mine. My own incentive is a personal sense of obligation that goes beyond professional curiosity and my attempts to understand more of Candomblé.

A good part of the reason for my continued contact with Candomblé and the people involved in it lies in the character of Candomblé itself and its time-geography, as I have indicated. This is inseparable from the sociality surrounding this religion and its link to the cosmological foundation. One role of time in ritual is to establish and maintain the kind of organic sociality that comes about when people synchronize their actions. Ritual is a way of focusing collectively on time and thus, through the possibility of synchronic action, a celebration of sociality, a choreography of social interaction. However, in addition to these classical aspects of ritual, in Candomblé there is also a clear idea of progression, and this is one of the ways in which it is very much a modern religion. To my ritual sisters, I believe that my presence has always been associated with the future—theirs as well as mine. I have no doubt that they have seen me as a resource from the start, but they have also, ever since I took the first *bori*, regarded me as a person embarking upon a spiritual and social journey. The ritual rules require that a major sacrifice be made every seven years and that smaller ones be made (preferably) every year. Each time a sacrifice is made, it marks a transformation to a higher step in the ritual hierarchy by way of a temporal opening up to the otherworld of the gods. High status in the ritual hierarchy is associated with spiritual protection and prominent social status, as well as concrete opportunities for making money as a ritual professional and a magician. The sisters see their participation in Candomblé very much in a future-oriented light, which encourages them to hope for a better life. They probably look on it as being more or less the same for me. Whatever I am doing there gives me the promise of a better future, a career—if not in Candomblé, then in some other occupation (as indeed it has, somehow). The temporal and gradual initiation that they themselves undergo over the years would of course be the same for me. In this long-term perspective, ritual time—and, in a wider sense, social time—is then *our* time. It is not theirs and not mine, but a time of a social field that is much less limited in time than in space.

Conclusion and Perspectives

Based on recurring fieldwork experiences in Candomblé rituals, I aimed first to look at the significance of unfocused presence as a background for events and for the figures that are used later on for analysis in the anthropological endeavor. I also wanted to point to the temporality of fieldwork as something that acquires meaning as a post-result. I am tempted to quote the Danish philosopher Søren Kierkegaard's famous dictum that life is lived forward, but understood backward. It is quite possible to organize fieldwork from a time perspective, and, in fact, this is done all the time, whether planning an old-school Malinowskian two-year stay or a project that will last a few weeks, implying neatly time-set appointments for interviews. An important component in ethnographic fieldwork is, however, the occurrence of the unexpected. The importance of the unintended, of the side effects, of the whole course of events that cannot be foreseen is an important aspect of the particularity and value of the ethnographic method that should not be overlooked (irrespective of current political requirements in terms of detailed research project planning). However, it implies that the significance of the temporality of fieldwork is to a large extent to be grasped in hindsight. The methodological impact of boredom and of deep hanging out should also be regarded in this light.

Studying rituals may imply boredom, and it may lead to social rhythm based on expectation, regularity, and exception. Its rhythmic aspects being significant, ritual is a kind of collective social artwork. If fieldwork does indeed have some resemblance to ritual, how far does this resemblance go? Without answering this question in any definitive manner, I will limit myself to saying that fieldwork may imply boredom, and it should also imply deep hanging out and, if possible, recurring visits in order to arrive at an understanding of social rhythm. Whether that makes it social artwork, I shall leave as an open question.

Acknowledgments

I appreciate the comments of discussants Marilyn Strathern and Martijn van Beek at the 2009 workshop "Time and the Field" where this chapter was first presented. The editors of this volume have made valuable comments, as have Martin Demant Frederiksen and the other participants in a seminar held in Copenhagen in April 2012. The comments of the two anonymous reviewers were highly appreciated. Finally, I am grateful to my spiritual sisters in Candomblé and their Orixás for insisting that I come back again and again.

Inger Sjørslev is a Senior Lecturer in the Department of Anthropology, University of Copenhagen. She did long-term fieldwork on the Candomblé religion in Brazil in the 1980s and has gone back for shorter visits many times since then, often in connection with other kinds of research. She has done museum and exhibition work with the National Museum in Denmark and has been involved with indigenous politics and human rights issues. Lately, she has conducted fieldwork on materiality and sociality in Denmark, and she is currently working on performance and materiality in the context of religious and political manifestations in public space.

Notes

1. Candomblé is divided into *naçoes*, nations that relate to the African origin of the different ethnic groups that brought the religion to Brazil. Ketu is a Yoruba nation that traces its origin to the town of Ketu in what is today the People's Republic of Benin in West Africa (Bastide 1978: 58–62; Carneiro 1986: 50–59).
2. The philosophical background for the concept 'time of action' would be Alfred Schutz's (1971) distinction between acts, which he sees as having their meaning attributed reflectively, and actions, which are in the present and directed toward the future. Temporal strategies are bounded by the socially constituted common stock of knowledge (Adam 2004: 67–68).
3. For a discussion of parallels between Dewey's and Langer's ideas about rhythm and aesthetics, see Kruse (2007).

References

Adam, Barbara. 2004. *Time*. Cambridge: Polity Press.
Barbalet, J. M. 1999. "Boredom and Social Meaning." *British Journal of Sociology* 50, no. 4: 631–646.
Bastide, Roger. 1978. *The African Religions of Brazil: Toward a Sociology of the Interpretation of Civilizations*. Baltimore: Johns Hopkins University Press.
Bastide, Roger. 1983. *Estudos Afro-Brasileiros*. São Paulo: Editora Perspectiva.
Carneiro, Edison. 1986. *Candomblés da Bahia*. Rio de Janeiro: Editora Civiliação Brasileira.
Clastres, Pierre. 1998. *Chronicle of the Guayaki Indians*. Trans. Paul Auster. New York: Zone Books.
Clifford, James. 1997. *Routes: Travel and Translation in the Late Twentieth Century*. Cambridge, MA: Harvard University Press.
Csikszentmihalyi, Mihaly. [1975] 2000. *Beyond Boredom and Anxiety: Experiencing Flow in Work and Play*. San Francisco: Jossey-Bass.
Deleuze, Gilles. 2006. *The Fold: Leibnitz and the Baroque*. Trans. Tom Conley. London: Continuum.
Derrida, Jacques. [1982] 2007. "Signature Event Context." Pp. 110–134 in *Jacques Derrida: Basic Writings*, ed. Barry Stocker; trans. Alan Bass. Abingdon: Routledge.
Dewey, John. [1934] 1958. *Art as Experience*. New York: Capricorn Books.
Dion, Michel. 1998. *Omindarewa: Uma Francesa no Candomblé—a Busca de uma outra Verdade*. Higienópolis: Pallas Editora.

Dos Santo, Juana Elbein. 1977. *Os Nago e a Morte*. Petrópolis: Vozes.

Frederiksen, Martin D. 2011. "Haunted by Time: Brotherhood and Temporal Margins in the Republic of Georgia." PhD diss., University of Aarhus.

Geertz, Clifford. 1972. "Deep Play: Notes on the Balinese Cockfight." *Daedalus* 101, no. 1: 1–37.

Geertz, Clifford. 1998. "Deep Hanging Out." *New York Review of Books*, 22 October, 69–72.

Gell, Alfred. 1996. *The Anthropology of Time*. Oxford: Berg.

Goldman, Marcio. 2007. "How to Learn in an Afro-Brazilian Spirit Possession Religion: Ontology and Multiplicity in Candomblé." Pp. 103–119 in *Learning Religion: Anthropological Approaches*, ed. David Berliner and Ramon Sarró. New York: Berghahn Books.

Jackson, Michael. 2010. "From Anxiety to Method in Anthropological Fieldwork: An Appraisal of George Devereux's Enduring Ideas." Pp. 35–54 in *Emotions in the Field: The Psychology and Anthropology of Fieldwork Experience*, ed. James Davies and Dimitrina Spencer. Stanford, CA: Stanford University Press.

Jeffrey, Craig. 2008. "Waiting." *Environment and Planning D: Society and Space* 26, no. 6: 954–958.

Johansen, Anders. 1989. "Handlingens tid." Pp. 87–116 in *Hvor Mange Hvite Elefanter? Kulturdimensjonen i Bistandsarbeidet*, ed. Thomas H. Eriksen. Oslo: Ad Notam Forlag.

Kruse, Felicia E. 2007. "Vital Rhythm and Temporal Form in Langer and Dewey." *Journal of Speculative Philosophy* (n.s.) 21, no. 1: 16–26.

Langer, Susanne K. 1953. *Feeling and Form: A Theory of Art Developed from Philosophy in a New Key*. London: Routledge & Kegan Paul.

Leach, Edmund R. 1961. "Two Essays Concerning the Symbolic Representation of Time." Pp. 221–249 in *Reader in Comparative Religion: An Anthropological Approach*, ed. William A. Lessa and Evon Z. Vogt. New York: Harper & Row.

Musharbash, Yasmine. 2007. "Boredom, Time, and Modernity: An Example from Aboriginal Australia." *American Anthropologist* 109, no. 2: 307–317.

Nisbet, Robert. 1982. *Prejudice: A Philosophical Dictionary*. Cambridge, MA: Harvard University Press.

Schieffelin, Edward L. 1985. "Performance and the Cultural Construction of Reality." *American Ethnologist* 12, no. 4: 707–724.

Schutz, Alfred. 1971. "The Problem of Social Reality." Pp. 172–173 in *Collected Papers*, vol. 1: *The Problem of Social Reality*, ed. Maurice Natanson. The Hague: Martinus Nijhoff.

Serra, Ordep. 1995. *Águas do Rei*. Petrópolis: Editora Vozes.

Sjørslev, Inger. 1995. *Gudernes rum: En beretning om ritualer og tro i Brasilien*. Copenhagen: Gyldendal. Published in German in 1999 as *Glaube und Besessenheit: Ein Bericht über die Candomblé-Religion in Brasilien*. Gifkendorf: Merlin Verlag.

Sjørslev, Inger. 2006. "On Leaving the Field: Closure and Continuity as Seen through the Lens of the Candomblé Axexé Ritual." *FOLK: Journal of the Danish Ethnographic Society* 46/47: 11–41.

Sjørslev, Inger. 2012. "Is Form Really Primary or, What Makes Things Authentic? Sociality and Materiality in Afro-Brazilian Ritual and Performance." Pp. 111–127 in *Debating Authenticity: Concepts of Modernity in Anthropological Perspective*, ed. Thomas Filliz and A. Jaime Saris. New York: Berghahn Books.

Strathern, Marilyn. 2004. "On Space and Depth." Pp. 88–116 in *Complexities: Social Studies of Knowledge Practices*, ed. John Law and Annemarie Mol. Durham, NC: Duke University Press.

Svendsen, Lars Fr. H. 2001. *Kedsomhedens filosofi*. Copenhagen: Klim.

Chapter 7

EPISODIC FIELDWORK, UPDATING, AND SOCIABILITY

Michael Whyte

Many of us have experienced the social (and emotional) effects of returning to the field. It is always an exciting time, whether the absence has been weeks or years. Yet the practice of returning—and especially the process of being brought up to date—is more significant than at first it would seem. A close look at returning to the field is one way of learning more about what anthropologists do, about participation and positioning and the relationship of both to history and to the data we collect.

To be brought up to date, one must have been, at one point in the past, up to date. There is always a presumption of social familiarity, of local competence, perhaps a warm feeling of being welcomed back into a social world, a familiar social position. This sense of re-belonging may be fleeting, but its significance is beyond doubt. Just think of the occasions when it falters or fails, for example, when an apparent stranger greets me by name. Can I access the Michael she

References for this chapter are located on page 121.

knew, the Michael who remembers, before my silly smile gives the game away? And what is the game, anyway?

The small panic is not about a memory lapse but rather the social lapse that threatens. It foreshadows a point that I will be developing: being updated is more than receiving information. It is the condition of being part of a social group or network where stories, histories, carry meaning. However, no one can be socially active/online all the time. Social participation is inevitably a matter of comings and goings, a matter of updates.

Drawing inspiration from Simmel, I am suggesting that sociability is at stake here. For Simmel (1949: 254), sociability is "association for its own sake." He argues that this form of interaction, while not instrumental or goal directed in its 'pure form', is nonetheless a condition or framework for social existence. Sociability is play and necessity; it is "the play-form of association … related to the content-determined concreteness of association as art is related to reality" (ibid.: 255). As examples of sociability, Simmel offers conversation (as an end in itself), coquetry, tact, and "good form" (ibid.). In this conception, the art of interaction is paramount, and time is banished together with tactics. However, sociability is not simply what happens when nothing else is happening. Rather, it is a social mode that in some sense enables individual and collective actions. For Simmel, both sociability and play risk becoming "entangled with real life" (ibid.: 258), a possibility that disturbs his idealized schema. But for me it is precisely these margins where timeless sociability merges with calculation, and thus with time, that are interesting. Here, the forms and conventions of 'pure' sociability intersect with social calculation, with history and memory. Sociability, it seems to me, is both play and purpose, timeless and episodic. From my perspective, sociability is usefully seen as a condition that is achieved, again and again. Like play, it is dependent on knowing forms and rules, on historical experience. But because sociability is social, it also rests on an appreciation of social positions and events. The achieving of sociability, socially and temporally specific, is a process in time and in society. It is about maintaining a certain continuity, a practice of updating an existing social field and the positions of its players. Correspondingly, sociability in this sense is an irrelevance when dealing with those who are 'here today, gone tomorrow'. One does not update a stranger (Simmel 1950).

Returning to the field sets in motion sociability in the process of reconnecting—and it is a process that may well fail, even when memory does not. Old friends may now simply be irritating; have they changed or have I? Acquaintances may suddenly become friends, or at least more distinct persons, because I am now older, or because they have married, become established, and recognized, or because life events have transformed their social situation. "He is no longer married," they tell me. "His wife and the child have died, and he stays with his parents. Is it this new disease of ours?" Any update will be a painful review, a life heading in unexpected directions, with social consequences.

Finally, returning to the field is also about being brought up to date in the world, about re-establishing (or finding) Fabian's coevalness when political, economic, and ecological circumstances have changed. Fabian (1983) first discusses coevalness in *Time and the Other*. A quarter-century later, in *Memory against Culture*, he returns to the original argument. Anthropology, Fabian (2007: 22) notes, is based in "communicative interaction … [t]he sharing of time that such interaction requires demands that ethnographers recognize the people whom they study as their coevals. However … when the same ethnographers represent their knowledge in teaching and writing they do this in terms of a discourse that consistently places those who are talked about in a time other than that of the one who talks." Fabian's original essay was, at least in part, a political statement, written against models of development that ignored the links between First World wealth and Third World poverty. The danger of a 'denial of coevalness' in ethnographic writing and debate may be more recognized today, but it remains a fraught issue and a challenge to the interpretation of fieldwork data. Here I want to explore some consequences of the practical and analytical task of maintaining coevalness in interaction over many years.

Susan Whyte and I began research in eastern Uganda in 1969, a professional and 'communicative' association that has continued to the present. In the decades since this first fieldwork, the Pearl of Africa has survived and been transformed under the 'regimes' of Amin, Obote, and the Okellos, and then transformed again by the current president, Yoweri Museveni, the National Resistance Movement (NRM), and the donor community. The colonial economy, structured by export crops and subsistence cultivation, was still viable in 1969. Forty plus years later, the free internal market, where anything is for sale and people complain that that they have no cash crops, dominates. Donors and their programs are omnipresent, education is nearly universal—and jobs are still scarce.

In what follows, I draw on case material that stresses the shifting positions implied by long-term fieldwork. My goal, however, is not to glorify long-term fieldwork. Returning and updating are—or can be—a part of any fieldwork. In drawing attention to them, my purpose is to explore some more general links between fieldwork experience and different appreciations of time as they present themselves in what I call here 'episodic fieldwork'. I use 'episodic' because I want to emphasize the significance of absence and return for fieldwork relationships and the ethnographies that rest on these relationships. More generally, I suggest that social life itself is episodic. Communicative interaction—with or without the ethnographer's participation—plays out in space and time and is thus necessarily a discontinuous practice. We engage each other through social episodes, and we create a sense of time, change, and coherence by integrating and reintegrating our episodic interactions.

Fieldwork Competences: Facts and Relationships

Since I began doing anthropology, I have maintained a continuing association with one particular place, one particular group of people. The place is Bunyole, in eastern Uganda. It is a field to which Susan Whyte and I have returned, again and again, over many years and from many positions. It all began with a lengthy fieldwork, from January 1969 through April 1971. Our focus—admittedly fuzzy at times—was on gathering material for our dissertations. We explained this rather bizarre activity to the Banyole people with our first Lunyole sentence: "We have come to learn the things that are being done in Bunyole." It was a lovely sentence for novice linguists, including three verbal forms and several pronominal concordances. With a bit of practice, it rolled off our tongues, boosting our self-confidence and, we thought, our credibility. Fieldwork was all about learning things as they were done—about achieving competence, as we might say today.

Competence was a means to our academic ends, but it was also a goal in itself. As I look back through my journal from the period, I see two kinds of competences—scholastic and social or performative—under development. At that early point, scholastic or academic competence was what counted, and we deployed the methodologies that we had been taught to document, measure, and (above all) record. Initially, it was a matter of 'facts' and field notes. I remember the satisfaction of establishing basic categories and topics. We kept our notes and forms in a metal file, in folders arranged by topics. At first, each folder contained copies of field notes clipped from duplicate notebooks, amended and classified and ordered in terms of our total ethnographic project and our specific interests, with some considerable updating as we began to understand more. As our fieldwork progressed, other forms for data were developed. We carried out household surveys and weekly market price surveys, made extracts from magistrate's cases and other registries, and compiled lists of many cultural things (clans, words, and proverbs; trees and color terms; modern farmers, rainmakers, and diviners; even bus schedules). This system for organizing ethnographic data in the field, taken from John Beattie's (1965) admirable study of Bunyoro, created provisional categories, while at the same time preserving the ability to reorganize and cross-file information in new ways as our knowledge increased. Files grew as new material was added, but also as existing data were corrected, annotated with new experiences, and/or reclassified.

We also filled our notebooks and our files with another, more relational kind of data: extended cases. As we learned more Lunyole, it became possible to follow social life as a series of connected events. Such cases, we knew, were important (Manchester anthropology still being modern in 1970), and we recorded ongoing narratives of activities such as land disputes, funeral rituals, domestic quarrels, therapeutic journeys. We also followed continuing micro-sagas of friends and neighbors, and many of these narratives ended up as extended cases in their own right. Such 'case stories' required a degree of contextual knowledge, but once it was clear that we were interested, there were always interlocutors willing to help us interpret them. Collecting cases involved us in new kinds of collaboration with our field assistants and our friends and neighbors—and helped us to move beyond our initial focus on facts and lists, names and categories. Case material was continuous, socially mediated, and socially demanding. Hearing the latest about M's father-in-law (a new episode in a continuing story) was not simply data; it was information imparted to me because I was a friend or an honorary relative. It confirmed that I was—literally—in a position to know, part of a social network (if only as a game). Knowing what M had said, what B had done, and what S believed allowed us to become more nearly a part of Nyole social life on Nyole terms. We came to be able to ask about past events—and to receive updates.

Updating: The Dynamics of Fieldwork

From my journal, I can see (to my surprise) that there was a lot of coming and going during this initial fieldwork—and a lot of updating. We left the field for conferences and periods of writing, spent in Kampala, as well as holidays and an unplanned month in Nairobi due to illness. Returning after this absence with gifts of clothing bought at Kariokor Market made for a narrative that was locally more interesting/dramatic than a simple trip to Mbale or Tororo. Telling about where we had been induced narratives from our friends—about places they had reached and, of course, about what had happened in our absence. Being updated was both information—entered in field notes and added to cases—and, as I see now, a sign of our success at achieving a social place in our communities.

Our last months of fieldwork in 1971, after the Amin coup, were increasingly stressful. Whenever we left our Bunyole backwater for a trip to Mbale or Kampala, we drove past roadblocks and fear: young soldiers from the north were sweating even in the shade, trying to come to terms with their new power and its possibilities and pitfalls. Each return became another story, a contribution to the developing narrative about the danger of journeys and the parlous state of affairs 'outside'.

Today, 40 years later, when we come and go, there is still always someone who needs a ride, someone who relates the events of home in the expectation that we will understand. And there are still people in Kampala—or even in Denmark—who need to be greeted and, if possible, told the news of home. "Amang'uliro-hi?" (What news?) is a key part of the Banyole's standard greeting. However, unlike the typical reply to the English "How's it going?" Banyole still expect an elaborated response—an update.

The Nature of Episodic Fieldwork

Updating implies a sociability that is not continuous, one in which absence and return are normal. But what happens when the absences lengthen, lapping over major historical change? In such cases, returns may best be seen as episodes that reconnect the now of the fieldworker and the now of the field. Coevalness is reimposed with each visit. However, as we shall see, this is not simply a matter of learning the latest gossip. Communicative interaction involves reinterpretation of past understandings and also of one's understanding of the past.

According to my online dictionary, the word 'episode' comes from the Greek *epeisodios*, meaning 'coming in besides'. There are two primary definitions. The first states that an episode is "an event or a group of events occurring as part of a larger sequence; an incident or period considered in isolation: *the latest episode in the feud."* The alternative definition is perhaps more familiar—the episode as an installment in an ongoing story.

An episode is thus both part of a sequence and the part itself. Episodic fieldwork involves both senses of the term, reflecting different challenges and opportunities for reflection and understanding.

Historical Drift and the Power of Events

Our first fieldwork seemed at the time to be very nearly total immersion. Bunyole was both workplace and home; in fact, it was our longest time together in one place up to that point. However, our own lives went on, first back in the US and then in Denmark. The one-year job I had been given turned out to be permanent. Our children arrived, our dissertations were written, Susan too was offered a permanent job, and the intensity of our Nyole home began to fade.

The news from Uganda, when we could find any in those pre-Internet times, was increasingly disturbing. When it came our turn for sabbaticals, we chose to go to Marachi in western Kenya, only some 50 kilometers from the chaos of Amin's final days in Uganda. Amin invaded Tanzania, Nyerere refused to be cowed, and the Tanzanian army began the slow process of removing the first of Uganda's regimes.

I was in Busia, the border town that was also our district headquarters, when Tanzania's troops arrived there in 1979. Crowds surged back and forth across the normally closed and guarded border, and soldiers traveling on commandeered Jinja buses celebrated by shooting into the air. There was dancing and great excitement. Soon we would be able to return to Bunyole.

A few weeks later we did just that, making a quick trip over a border only casually manned, through thoroughly looted Tororo and Mbale, and on to a secondary boarding school in Bunyole where our oldest friend and one-time neighbor was teaching. This was an impromptu visit, a chance to test the water and plan for a lengthier stay in a month or so. Finally, after eight years, we were back, speaking Lunyole and hearing all about the things that were 'being done' and the things that had been done.

It was our first experience of being brought up to date after a significant temporal absence, the first of many episodic field trips. To our joy, the worst of the depredations of the Amin regime and of liberation had bypassed Bunyole, which was still very rural and now even poorer. What we heard were stories of survival in a country that had very nearly ceased to function. No cotton was being bought, so there was little cash and few commodities. Salaries were many months overdue and, paid in inflated shillings, almost valueless. We were welcomed for ourselves surely, but also as harbingers of a return to better times. Our host and his teacher colleagues told us with great pride that they were keeping standards alive, that students were still taught and exams were passed—and, most wonderfully, that in 1978 Uganda, with unpaid teachers and few books and resources, had produced more A-level graduates with distinction than Kenya.

Our Uganda, if not our Bunyole, had changed almost beyond recognition in those eight years, but our friends were convinced that now things would be better—that Nyerere would help them and that the country's former glory and stability would return. But that was not to be. The conditions that we witnessed on our return persisted, and Uganda had to wait many more years before rural life even began to improve. The episodic sequence that our friends had deployed during this first return visit was almost circular—the future as the past. It has stayed in circulation to this day—now an increasingly counterfactual trope, a vision of a 'golden age' when the government will (again) function and peasants will (again) be paid well for cash crops and eat their own food.

Over the next 10 years, Uganda endured far more state violence and a protracted civil war/war of liberation that ultimately led to victory for Museveni and his NRM in 1986. The second Obote period (1980–1985) had seen the further collapse of the rural cash crop economy amid a pervasive failure of governance. In rural Uganda, hyperinflation and the absence of management and resources transformed the position of the salariat, the educated government employees in public administration, teaching, health services, and other technical fields. These representatives of modernity were struggling to survive, let alone reproduce themselves, on their remuneration. Indeed, as I was to discover in Bunyole, a day laborer earned more than a graduate teacher, a nurse, or a clinical officer (Whyte 1990: 133).

After 1986, and certainly by the early 1990s, a slow recovery was reaching the countryside. With recovery came the first of many donor initiatives and, of course, HIV/AIDS programs. Not unreasonably, many continued to look back rather than forward. The golden age of Uganda was still in the past.

AIDS—Invisible, Visible, Hyper-visible

I was back in Bunyole for a brief field study just after the NRM victory in 1986, and from 1988 through to today I have been a far more regular visitor, mixing fieldwork in Bunyole with other activities. In 1992, Susan and I returned for another six months of research, followed by more or less regular short periods of fieldwork over the next decade.

Although AIDS was not a primary research focus for us at the time, it was quite impossible not to be involved in the pandemic. With each visit we were updated on "this new disease of ours." People we knew of—and later people whom we knew well—became infected. Every return meant a new visit to a graveside. AIDS education was the order of the day, and program replaced program while people continued to fall ill and die.

Looking back on our fieldwork visits to Bunyole in the early 1990s, a patterned chronology began to emerge through successive updates, marking a change in the way in which HIV/AIDS was conceived locally (Whyte 1996). Initially, we were told that AIDS was something of the cities, a disease of rich people and Westerners. AIDS was at this point invisible, and Banyole were suspicious of strangers—traders in rice and workers from the cities. Who could tell if they were infected? On subsequent visits, we were updated about the illnesses and deaths that were becoming more frequent. This visibility was helped by education campaigns, but it also marked a change in the discourse in Bunyole. People began to see—and to talk about—AIDS in homes and neighborhoods.

By 1994, AIDS perceptions had shifted once more. Now when I asked for updates, for accounts of the things being done in Bunyole, I was told of illness everywhere. Indeed, any death was now assumed to be caused by AIDS. Nurses explained that it was possible to see HIV infection on the faces and bodies of people attending the clinic; it was not necessary to wait for symptoms to appear. Men drinking beer in the evening told about a recent death and, with gallows humor, speculated about who was "in the line-up" (was thought to have been a partner to the deceased).

In the course of four years of returns, the larger sequence—the historical narrative into which AIDS events were being placed—had shifted. The older, invisible AIDS seemed linked to eastern Uganda's remoteness, that spatial distance from power, wealth, and cities that had in fact protected much of rural Uganda during the regimes and even in the earlier colonial period. Increasingly visible, AIDS was certainly a fact, but it was also part of a new narrative that was more global, although hardly more encouraging. AIDS, like everything else, was flowing: there was no longer safety in being unconnected in the countryside.

Long-Term Fieldworking: Change, Sociability, and Position

The times have changed, from a pre-Amin Uganda, only just post-colonial, to today's sophisticated, globalized, and conflicted state of affairs. Episodic fieldworking (the updating of fieldworks by returning social beings) brought out the ways in which Banyole link local and domestic events to wider—and emerging—social fields. Recognizing such changes as ongoing local reflections provides a framework for accessing new historical interpretations of the world and the direction that it is taking. Returning periodically was, however, not simply a matter of capturing events in new sequences. The very social relationships that define episodic fieldwork and continuing participation are, by virtue of their dependence on intersubjectivity and sociability, also malleable and contingent.

This is no doubt a complex way of stating the obvious: people and ethnographers change. My positions, my actual and possible relationships with others, have been transformed over the years—as have theirs. In some cases, we have simply grown up, and differences in age and experience that were great in 1970 or 1990 have become less so. The young boy who lived across the road from us in 1970 is now a parent and an academic, a fellow scientist with whom we discuss Uganda's ecological crises. His father, a headmaster in 1970, was our local mentor as well as our friend; today we are both grandparents in friendly competition over progeny. In other cases, our lives have taken different courses, and gaps have come into being that are difficult to bridge. In 1970, we had friends among the many small farmers in Bunyole, who were making what was considered a good living from subsistence production and a cash crop. Gifts of crops, animals, and food were commonplace, material expressions of sociability. Now their children and grandchildren are absolutely and relatively impoverished. They no longer have the capacity to be generous in the way they would wish to be.

I, too, have changed—again absolutely and relatively. I made my first friends in Bunyole as a young man, newly married and, by local standards, almost a youth. I was a PhD student sent by Makerere University to learn the things that are done in Bunyole; everyone was more competent. Over the years, I have developed and discovered different competences. I found a full-time university job, an elite job also in Uganda. I became known to district and national civil servants, and I have Ugandan colleagues and friends who are part of—or at least close to—the country's economic and political elite. I also have 'my family' in Bugombe, where we have built a house, supported children from school to university, and provided cash for family-related business projects and family emergencies. Genealogically, I am now counted with the most senior men in our lineage and am called in as a 'father' to solve problems. For any anthropology that takes participation and intersubjectivity seriously, these changes shape the nature of successive fieldwork episodes. Let me conclude with some brief examples.

In the course of the 1990s, I was often in Kampala and in other parts of Uganda, working as a consultant for international donors. While in Kampala, I kept in touch with my Banyole family and developed a close relationship with my 'brother', who worked as a freight forwarder. On quick visits to our 'home', his father (our father) made much of having two sons in Kampala and began to insist that I build a proper, iron-roofed house in our family compound. This was playing at kinship with a vengeance. The house-building project stretched over three years (although it felt like 10) and drew both Susan and me ever closer into new dimensions of Nyole kinship. This was not always—still is not always—a comfortable set of social relationships. We were taught, socialized, into a new set of roles as urban elites with family responsibilities.

The house project thrust us into new kinds of sociability. Our house was finished in the mid-1990s. It is shared with my Nyole brother (when he is home), his first wife, and their children (when they are home). It involves us—as participants as well as observers—in the domestic politics of a large family and in the tragedies and crises that come and must be endured. It also has forced us to be parents, watching children emerge into adolescence and young adulthood, and to be siblings, watching as generations age and replace each other.

Having a house in Bunyole also identified us in new ways for Banyole from other parts of the county. Where we had been seen before simply as Europeans who kept returning, we now began to be placed more specifically. We were from Mulagi, our village of residence, and Bugombe, our local clan settlement.

House building turned out to have a quite unanticipated resonance for my work in Uganda. As a consultant (and later as part of a Kampala-based research project) working with development issues and with Ugandans who were also concerned with development and modern agendas, I spent a lot of time with elite Ugandans in government offices, at the university, and when working with NGOs. Here my experience with the golden age of Uganda was a point of reference that created a presumption of sociability and common experience. It made it less likely that I would simply be offered program slogans when what I needed was insight. Having built a house signaled something more: a practical familiarity with the overlapping social networks that mark the worlds of elite Ugandans.

Building a house on a limited budget is an experience shared by many urban Ugandans. This kind of project is above all a job of management, a test of social maturity that my brother and I were at times close to failing. Builders—and relatives living nearby—removed essential components for their own projects. The local archdeacon came by while we were absent and 'borrowed' all our carefully acquired door latches. And there were never enough small stones. Necessary 'things' had to come from Kampala or Tororo, and all too often the required item was gone by the time the *fundi* (artisan) needed it. In addition, when it was finally found, or replaced, the *fundi* had disappeared.

This albeit limited engagement with house building served me well in much the same way that academic competence—facts and details, language and kinship and agricultural patterns—was a first step toward the social competences that enabled and underpinned participation. In the office of a commissioner in the Ministry of Women and Development, I was able to chat about the merits and prices of Bamburi cement from Kenya and the Tororo product. We did not go on to become special friends, but we did enjoy our meetings and our common problems—with a good bit of irony, no doubt. We had, for the moment, created a space where our several identities and experiences could meet in a very specific Ugandan now. This sort of play is what Simmel (1949) sees as the essence of sociability. However, when Simmel takes 'pure' sociability as an end in itself, distinct from both "individual intimacy" (ibid.: 259) and associations marked by purpose, the temporality of this sort of play may be lost. The commissioner and I were not simply playing at sociability; we were also placing each other through a specific conversation that, in this case, certainly had implications for what could be said about donor policy and Ugandan reality. Playing with house building was also a way of achieving a certain coevalness— we literally shared a 'concrete' world—that allowed the interview to probe practices and contradictions of some importance.

In our continuing relationship with our Banyole family, house building became house ownership, and house sharing became house maintenance. Play and reality intermingled. Some years after the house was built, there was a party. Bunyole is characterized by virilocality and exogamous, patrilineal clans. Susan's Nyole family came with the gifts that a wife brings to her marital home, and members of my clan came to eat and to drink. A group of my clanswomen toured the house with Susan and made a point of reminding her that this was their house, not hers. While they were daughters of the clan, she was a mere wife, with a birthright elsewhere. This is play, of course, but significant play, focused on a place and its meanings. Certainly, over the last decades, being increasingly placed has transformed our position in Bunyole—and our insights into Ugandan life. We entered a period of more intense, more specific participation. We were now providing real resources. The house led to other engagements appropriate to our increasingly well-defined role as elite kin. We paid school fees and helped with agricultural inputs and tools and medical expenses. And because kinship relationships are extended and extensive, and because neighborliness is also a kinship responsibility, we became increasingly drawn into the kind of network of demands, deference, and intimacy that Ugandan elites must also navigate.

Updating is not a simple linear process: more stories, more events, more money, and greater insight. It is more than continually capturing the latest installment in an ongoing story. By returning again and again, we are not simply being *brought* up to date. We participate in a temporal process that is also transformative: we are *ourselves* updated. The two processes are linked. By returning again and again, we learn more—and we become capable of understanding more. Becoming more involved, more placed, we take on positions that are about sociability (playing at being a brother, an uncle, an elite relative) and about obligations: children are educated, and medicine is made available. And networks based on research relationships in Uganda and beyond are shared with the 'objects' of research, sometimes with surprisingly complex outcomes.

Returning can emphasize progressive difference and lead to Fabian's "discourse that … places those who are talked about in a time other than that of the one who talks." Updating pushes us to retain a sense of coevalness; we continue to be a part of each other's now, even as that now changes. We get jobs and raise a family, learn to use computers and mobile phones and to surf the Net. Our Ugandan friends are also growing up, growing older, coping more or less successfully with the exigencies of life in the countryside or, increasingly, in town. They, too, use mobile phones and sometimes the Internet. Updating continues to connect us even as we change—and to remind all of us that the sharing of time has not diminished inequality. Europeans and Ugandans are still systematically and structurally separated—not by time, but certainly by degree of access to resources of all sorts.

Acknowledgments

Earlier versions of this chapter were presented at the 2009 Megaseminar of the Danish Research School of Anthropology and Ethnography and at a departmental seminar at the University of Copenhagen. I am grateful for very useful discussions in both places. I especially wish to thank Morten Nielsen, Susan Whyte, and Zachary Whyte for their close reading and comments.

Michael Whyte is an Associate Professor Emeritus with the Department of Anthropology, University of Copenhagen. He has carried out long-term field research in eastern Uganda and has worked in western Kenya and Lesotho on issues including kinship, food security, HIV/AIDS, and agricultural and economic change.

References

Beattie, John. 1965. *Understanding an African Kingdom: Bunyoro*. New York: Holt, Rinehart & Winston.

Fabian, Johannes. 1983. *Time and the Other: How Anthropology Makes Its Object*. New York: Columbia University Press.

Fabian, Johannes. 2007. *Memory against Culture: Arguments and Reminders*. Durham, NC: Duke University Press.

Simmel, Georg. 1949. "The Sociology of Sociability." Ed. Everett Hughes. *American Journal of Sociology* 55, no. 3: 254–261.

Simmel, Georg. 1950. "The Stranger." Pp. 402–408 in *The Sociology of Georg Simmel*, trans. and ed. Kurt Wolff. New York: Free Press.

Whyte, Michael. 1990. "The Process of Survival in South-Eastern Uganda." Pp. 121–145 in *Adaptive Strategies in African Arid Lands*, ed. Mette Bovin and Leif Manger. Uppsala: Scandinavian Institute of African Studies (SIAS).

Whyte, Michael. 1996. "Talking about AIDS: The Biography of a Local AIDS Organization within the Church of Uganda." Pp. 221–230 in *AIDS Education: Interventions in Multi-cultural Societies*, ed. Inon Schenker, Galia Sabar-Friedman and Francisco S. Sy. New York: Plenum.

Chapter 8

TRANS-TEMPORAL HINGES
Reflections on a Comparative Ethnographic Study of Chinese Infrastructural Projects in Mozambique and Mongolia

Morten Axel Pedersen and Morten Nielsen

According to Mark Hodges (2008: 402), a severe blind spot may be identified in much so-called practical-theoretical anthropological work, namely, what he describes as "a tacit unspecified temporal ontology that is evoked through a common root vocabulary of process, flow or flux—itself implying, and facilitating in an unspecified way the notion that time involves 'change'." Thus, Hodges argues, many anthropologists operate with a "spatialized conception of linear time" (ibid.: 405), that is to say, a more or less implicit model or theory of human temporality, according to which two events either precede or supersede one another like beads on an endless string suspended in abstract, empty space (see also Gell 1992). But perhaps it is possible to theorize socio-cultural practice

Notes for this chapter are located on page 140.

in more *sui generis* temporal terms. Doing so would imply constructing a model of anthropological knowledge production—and therefore of ethnographic field-work and ethnographic method more generally—that retains the open-ended holism and empirical sensibility of classic ethnographic fieldwork, but which rests on a much more explicit and coherent temporal ontology. This is what we shall attempt to accomplish in this chapter by introducing the concept of the 'trans-temporal hinge' as an apt methodological device for studying the effects of various ongoing Chinese infrastructure projects in Mozambique and Mongolia.[1]

In recent years, there has been growing academic interest in China's rising political-economic clout abroad, especially in Africa but also in Central Asia and Latin America (Alden et al. 2008; Brautigam 2009; Kleveman 2003; Swanström 2005; Taylor 2006), and it is fair say that China's influence beyond its borders is now truly global. Reminiscent of the modernization theory that inspired Western development assistance after World War II, Chinese aid projects and private investments focus on the construction of infrastructure such as roads, power plants, dams, factories, and government buildings. Designed, built, and often managed by Chinese professionals and workers with mostly limited levels of consideration for local needs and participation, these infrastructural projects have emerged as "zones of awkward engagement" (Tsing 2005: xi) in which Chinese and local worlds meet, mix, and clash in the co-construction of socio-material entities. These entities are ripe for anthropological analysis but also seem to call for new ethnographic and analytical methods.

The present chapter is an attempt to grapple with some of the methodological opportunities and challenges that have arisen in the process of carrying out a collaborative research program, titled "Imperial Potentialities." In it, the two of us, along with Mikkel Bunkenborg (University of Copenhagen), seek to compare Chinese development projects and resource extraction in Inner Asia and sub-Saharan Africa by conducting three closely interlinked ethnographic field-works on Chinese interventions in infrastructure projects and natural resource extraction in Mongolia and Mozambique. Our objective in what follows is simultaneously ethnographic and theoretical, that is, to identity socio-economic junctures in which Chinese infrastructural activities studied by us in Mongolia and Mozambique may be simultaneously analyzed in their present and future forms. Put differently, it is our ambition to locate certain ethnographic phenomena and practices that may be 'extracted' by us in order to frame analytically and to compare disparate cases that are otherwise distributed across space and time. Our challenge is consequently to forge heuristic methodological concepts that, at one level, bring together local temporalities in an 'emically' meaningful way and, at a more 'etic' level, may be used to theorize our data in new ways. In order to accomplish this, we wish to introduce the notion of 'trans-temporal hinge', which we will subsequently use as our guiding theoretical concept in a comparative exploration of two ethnographic cases involving Chinese infra-structural interventions: a Chinese-built football (soccer) stadium in Maputo, Mozambique, and two Chinese oil fields in southeastern Mongolia.

By trans-temporal hinge, we understand any configuration of socio-cultural life that is imbued with the capacity for bringing together phenomena that are otherwise distributed across disparate moments in time. Based on a Bergsonian conceptualization of durational time (Bergson 1965; Deleuze 1988), we take time to be a co-existence of different temporalities that emerge as overlapping tendencies in the present, such as when a momentary orientation toward the future is enveloped by an only partially actualized memory of a past occurrence. Here, it makes little sense to conceive of time in terms of binary oppositions, such as 'more or less' or 'before and after' (Ansell Pearson 2002: 13; Deleuze 1988: 20). Instead, we may think of time as a heterogeneous simultaneity of disparate temporalities, whose mutual relationship is neither linear nor cyclical but rather transversal, multi-temporal, or (as we call it here) trans-temporal. Phrased in the vocabulary used by the editors of this volume, we advocate for a particular theorization of 'time of the field', namely, a temporal ontology that is not so much 'extensive' and 'quantitative' in the progressively linear manner of most current anthropological paradigms (including the practical-theoretical paradigm discussed above), but 'intensive' and 'qualitative'. In this view, time emerges not so much as a relationship between discrete temporal moments characterized by mutual exteriority (e.g., moment B succeeding and therefore being different from moment A), but rather as an ever-unfolding virtual (i.e., interior and intensive) whole that expands and contracts in gradually actualized forms. The key anthropological question here becomes how to operationalize such a seemingly intangible notion of time that brackets clear-cut distinctions between different temporal moments, such as before and after. What needs to be clarified is how to study the ways in which multiple temporalities in various contracted forms intersect and actualize in ethnographically significant phenomena and events. It is precisely for this purpose that we have devised the concept of a trans-temporal hinge.

The trans-temporal hinge may be described as a durational middle point that connects the multiple temporalities of our research project and its equally multiple field sites. Similar to an ordinary physical hinge between, say, a door and its frame, the trans-temporal hinge holds together otherwise disparate elements (certain past, present, and future events) in a manner that serves to maintain an optimal balance of distance and proximity between them, so that a certain technical operation (like the mechanics of opening and closing a door, or the logic of generating ethnographic knowledge) can occur in a smooth and subtle way. For is that not what a hinge basically is—a point of symmetry defined by its capacity to be always in the middle without constituting a center, instead demarcating the shared margin of two entities each of which define opposing centers? Consider figure 1, which is our attempt to depict the formal properties of the trans-temporal hinge and the new temporalization of the ethnographic field that it opens up.

As a particular kind of durational object that exists solely on a virtual plane (Deleuze 2004), the trans-temporal hinge is conductive of two simultaneous processes that, within the realm of the actual, move along opposing temporal trajectories, one from the present to the future, and the other from the future to the present. On the one hand, there is an anticipatory or protensive (in Husserl's sense) temporal vector, which, as Bourdieu (1977, 2000) and other

FIGURE 1 Trans-temporal Hinge

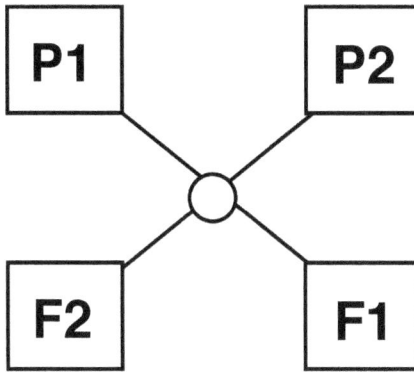

Note: F = future; P = present

phenomenologically inclined anthropologists have accounted for (e.g., Vigh 2006), involves the stipulation of a possible future scenario from the perspective of the present. In figure 1, the transversal line from the top left corner (P1) to the corner in the bottom right (F1) represents this well-known temporal conjecture. The other, simultaneous but reverse temporal process—depicted by the other transversal line in the diagram that points from the corner in the left bottom (F2) to the top right corner (P2)—is more novel in terms of anthropological knowledge making of time and temporality, although we would maintain that it constitutes an intrinsic but hitherto largely unrecognized element of it (da Col 2007; Miyazaki 2004, 2006; Nielsen 2008, 2011; Pedersen 2012). This reverse temporal movement involves a seemingly speculative intuiting of the inherently unknowable contours of a certain future scenario and then 'protospectively' (i.e., retrospectively from a future moment that is fundamentally unknown) tracing its dynamics and ramifications to the present moment at hand. However counter-intuitive this colonization or obviation of the present by the future may seem, it is, we insist, just as intrinsic to the ethnographic knowledge process as the more commonly accepted and seemingly more intuitive temporal vector of anticipatory protension in Bourdieu's Husserlian sense.[2] Taken together, these two knowledge processes constitute an 'ethnographic moment' (Strathern 1999): an intensive version of the 'ethnographic present', which is both the product of an imagined, unknown future and the context for an anticipated and known one (cf. Holbraad and Pedersen 2009).

In what remains of this chapter, we draw on recent field experiences from Mozambique and Mongolia to demonstrate that the ethnographic knowledge process rendered possible by the trans-temporal hinge allows for continuous shifts of temporal perspective so that multiple ethnographic fields are made simultaneously visible. More precisely, as we wish to show in the following case studies, two productive trans-temporal hinges derived from our respective ethnographic fieldworks enable us to move simultaneously and symmetrically backward and forward between actual (present) and virtual (future) case studies at our respective field sites in Mozambique and Mongolia.

Case 1: Temporal Envelopings of Chinese Infrastructure Projects in Mozambique

"It won't be a happy ending, you know!" Jan de Moor, an environmental specialist working in the fertile Zambezi valley in the middle region of Mozambique, took a sip of his beer before continuing. "When the Chinese arrive in the Zambezi valley, they are going to mess everything up. How are the farmers [*camponêses*] going to survive? With 10,000 Chinese there, the situation is going to be very difficult." Sitting in the shade outside a small liquor stall in the center of Maputo, de Moor had vividly described to Nielsen the consequences of the expected invasion of Chinese small-scale farmers that was most likely going to occur within the next few years. To be sure, the future scenario outlined by the portly NGO worker was anything but rose-colored. State officials had recently confirmed that a Chinese construction consortium had won the project of constructing 200 kilometers of tarred road in the middle of the Zambezi valley. "It's in the middle of nowhere!" de Moor wryly noted. "Now, why would a Chinese company want to throw cement in an area without any civilization?" His answer was straightforward: it is in the same area that a $50 million agricultural production facility—also funded by Chinese investors—is expected to be built. To make matters worse, the agricultural produce to be processed at the facility would be cultivated by a group of Chinese small-scale farmers who would be allocated plots of land in the area.[3] According to de Moor and several other NGO workers and municipal officials, the future realization of these projects will undoubtedly create tensions among local farmers, community leaders, and the Chinese workers coming to the area, with disputes arising over land use rights, salary policies, transactions involving construction materials, and so forth.

The interview with de Moor took place during the initial phase of Nielsen's field trip to Mozambique in 2009 when the primary case studies to be carried out as part of this African arm of "Imperial Potentialities" had not yet been defined. Hence, at the moment when the conversation took place, the information gathered about the potential conflicts in the Zambezi valley seemed only to constitute a necessary contextual canvas upon which the central cases would subsequently figure. Indeed, only a few days after the nightly visit to the liquor stall with de Moor, Nielsen found what seemed like the appropriate case for studying the socio-economic effects of Chinese infrastructure projects in Mozambique.

Already before commencing the field trip in February 2009, Nielsen had heard about the ambitious project of building a football stadium on the northern outskirts of Maputo. In 2005, the Chinese government had agreed to donate a national football stadium to Mozambique, and in accordance with the initially defined time schedule, the construction process commenced on 22 April 2008. Ten months later, 273 Chinese and 331 Mozambican workers were involved in the process of building what was to become the biggest sports arena in the country since independence from the Portuguese colonizers was achieved in 1975. It was this project that Nielsen assumed would constitute a central case study, and, despite being refused entry on numerous occasions, he continued to make daily trips to the construction site. After an exhausting trip around the massive walls that fenced off the construction site from the nearby sprawling market, Nielsen went into a small food stall (*baraca*). While waiting to order, he spotted a young man, eating a plate of rice and beans (*feijão nhembe*), who was wearing a light-blue boiler suit, and that easily distinguished him as a worker on the football stadium. Nielsen approached the young man, named Ramón, and after a hesitant beginning, he agreed to talk about his work on the construction site.

Ramón was part of a group of Mozambican welders hired by the Chinese building consortium to work on the massive iron framework that was to constitute the stadium's foundation. When Nielsen met him, he was having a quick lunch before returning to the construction site for the afternoon shift. Only minutes into their conversation, it was obvious that Ramón was far from enthusiastic about his Asian employers, the wage policy being the most salient point of critique. "The thing is," Ramón said, holding Nielsen's arm as if to focus his attention on his words, "they [the Chinese employers] don't tell us how they calculate our monthly pay. You just go there at payday, and they give you what they think is sufficient … As employers, they ought to say, 'Hey, your daily pay is this, and after eight hours of work, your salary goes up to this'. But that's not how it works. None of us knows what we make from 30 days of work." To make matters worse, Ramón told Nielsen, salaries were paid out of a movable stall placed in the middle of the construction site. At payday, all the Mozambican workers would line up and receive their salaries from a Chinese accountant handing out bundles of notes through an open window. "No one likes that!" Ramón thumped his index finger on the bar counter several times. "They really ought to put the money in an envelope, you know. In this situation, that would be the proper way to do it."

To many Mozambican workers involved in the impressive construction project, quotidian interactions with the Chinese were fraught with uncertainty. As Nielsen was constantly being told, it was completely impossible to decipher the actions of the Chinese co-workers, something that served to buttress the already widespread feeling of being radically different from the latter. Elísio, a young man from a nearby neighborhood, worked as a bricklayer at the construction site. A few days after Nielsen's initial meeting with Ramón, Elísio elaborated on how the Chinese were perceived by Mozambican workers. "We don't speak to them," he said with conviction, "because their way of doing things [*a maneira deles*] doesn't even seem human. I don't know … The Chinese … they aren't human. They aren't persons to whom you can actually talk … They don't respect you … They are really racists, you know. They don't consider the Negro as a human being."

Placed in an unknown environment governed by what seemed to be radically different and potentially malevolent others, who, paradoxically, were also crucial to one's continued socio-economic existence, the key issue for Elísio and his peers was therefore how to establish stable and (relatively) predictable forms of social interaction. As Elísio and many of his Mozambican colleagues saw it, the envelope would have produced just that. This was made clear when Elísio explained to Nielsen the importance of the envelope by outlining the consequences of its absence. "Anyone can see that they are handing out money," Elísio argued. "It's like taking money off the street." Without the concealment of the envelope, Elísio and his Mozambican co-workers felt an increasing exposure as they were fundamentally prevented from acquiring a well-defined social identity. In the southern part of Mozambique, people are essentially what their relations to others make them be (Nielsen 2009; Paulo et al. 2007: 4). Without the envelope, the recipient is thrown into anonymity, which invariably minimizes the ability to act as a social persona as there is nothing to define the parameters of discrete relationships. Any transaction covers a multiplicity of potentially enhancing forces, and in order for these to benefit the interacting parties, it is crucial that only they know about the particularities of the implicit agreement. Simply put, to Elísio and his colleagues, the degree of exposure is inversely proportional to one's possibilities for social agency: the more people know about you, the more restricted is your room for maneuver, as others will probably try to appropriate what is momentarily revealed.

As a consequence of the missing envelopment, as it were, of the relationship with their foreign superiors, it was impossible for people like Elísio to make functional prospective assumptions regarding interactions with the Chinese. This was made vividly clear when Ramón responded to Nielsen's question as to why he and his co-workers refused to teach the Chinese workers some basic Mozambican words. "No, no, no!" Ramón shook his head energetically. "Why should you teach them any words at all? In the future, they'll use those same words against you; they'll use them to insult you [*começa ti insultar com ela*]." In other words, social interactions with the Chinese were ipso facto defined as being potentially dangerous and thus requiring a productive distance in order for co-existence to occur. And as Elísio, Ramón, and their peers saw it, the envelope would have established a necessary separation while simultaneously creating a restricted space for social interaction. Without completely eliminating the widespread sense of uncertainty, it would compartmentalize, so to speak, the dangers always lurking at the construction site so that they became a question of clearly defined relations rather than coincidental occurrences. This kind of stability was considered as being completely absent in the present situation.

If we take an ethnographic scale to constitute a perspective on a given phenomenon emerging through a framing activity that correlates the phenomenon in question with the dimensions of the scale (Latour 2005: 186; Strathern 1991: xiv), then we may argue that the envelope constitutes a unique temporal scale. Crucially, time is not here to be understood as linearity where moments follow each other in a chronological and thus exterior form (i.e., where each moment is defined by its distance to all others). As a temporal scale, the envelope operates by gradually investing its (equally temporal) surroundings with its own characteristics. Rather than outlining a linear timeline composed by a series of differentiated moments, the envelope essentially distributes its own dimensions into a broader temporal assemblage that stretches both forward and backward in time. In a nutshell, had the envelope been used at the construction site as a temporal scale, it would have constituted an essential relational component that, like a seam, could have allowed for the different heterogeneous components interacting to co-function in a flexible temporal assemblage.

To take one example, to Mozambican workers at the construction site, the envelope constituted an imaginary (or speculative) future moment that structured the present in accordance with its virtual dimensions. When interacting with the Chinese, each occurrence was consequently infused with its logic by making explicit what was missing. Thus, it was by positioning himself at the imaginary moment of receiving money in an envelope that Ramón realized the potential danger of teaching his Chinese co-workers some basic Mozambican words. As such, the envelope constituted a unique temporal scale that brought together events that were otherwise distributed across different moments in time. Within the specific setting of the stadium construction site, the envelope (or more precisely its absence) structured social life by indicating how appropriate distances to radically different others might be established and acted upon. This implied a series of immediate temporal shifts between the present and an imagined future moment (i.e., when receiving money in an envelope). Crucially, it is this process of figure-ground reversals that we define as an oscillation between protensive and protospective figurations and that is made possible by the envelope functioning as a unique trans-temporal hinge. Returning again to the model presented in figure 1, the envelope may consequently be considered as the motile middle point holding together occurrences that are otherwise distributed across time. Within the relatively secluded social universe emerging at the construction site, it is conductive to two simultaneous temporal processes: firstly, a leap from the present toward the imagined future moment when payments will be delivered in sealed envelopes and, secondly, a parallel temporal displacement from the future moment toward the insecurities of the present day.

While doing ethnographic research at the half-built football stadium, Nielsen also continued exploring the alleged future invasion of Chinese farmers in the Zambezi valley mentioned by de Moor. Gradually, as it became apparent to Nielsen that social life among the Mozambican construction workers was imbued with a lack of mechanisms for apportioning relations with the unknown others, it became clear that the (etic and emic) significance of the Zambezi valley case changed accordingly. Rather than being a question of merely adding more context to his knowledge about administrative structures and their lack, the situation seemed to call for—if not require—an 'envelope-like' reading, as it were. Not unlike the processes of temporal displacement related by Ramón and Elísio, the present situation in the Zambezi valley, as described by people like de Moor, was couched in a vocabulary defined by the properties of events that had not yet occurred. These events fundamentally reflected an 'economy of distance' privileging the need for reciprocal encounters with capricious others to be balanced, for example, by socio-temporal media such as the envelope. In order to push this line of thinking about his material further, Nielsen met up with Lourenço Duvane from ORAM, a local NGO that focuses on property rights and land conflicts in rural areas, including the Zambezi valley. For several years, Duvane had worked with farmers in the area to ensure that their land claims would be heard. In ORAM's packed Maputo office, Duvane described the current situation: "Basically, they [the Mozambican farmers] will be kicked out. The government will probably make the regional leaders try to persuade people to move, perhaps by arguing that the local infrastructure needs to be improved … Then, while they are away, the Chinese will take their lands." Still, as Duvane also emphasized, people in the area did not reject the Chinese presence since the expected improval of the agricultural production facility might also strengthen the possibilities for disposing of their produce.

What is interesting, however, is that the projects might never actually be realized. As an effect of the global financial crisis, several international investors, including Chinese construction consortia, are becoming increasingly cautious about implementing large-scale development projects. According to sources in the Ministério da Planificação e Desenvolvimento (Ministry of Planning and Development), although projected infrastructure plans are not currently being withdrawn, they are frequently stalled or downsized. As Duvane told Nielsen, however, whether this pertains to the two Chinese projects in the Zambezi valley is still an open question. Notwithstanding any uncertainty, the development projections have already had a considerable effect by shedding light on, and thus adding fuel to, heated debates over the weaknesses of land management mechanisms in the area. Similar to many other rural areas of Mozambique, access to arable land in the Zambezi valley is hampered by inefficient governance structures and an increasing number of illegal appropriations by local and national elites. According to Duvane, the coming 'invasion' of the Chinese thus served to locate with an uncomfortable degree of precision the problems regarding insufficient capacities for operationalizing existing land laws. "To the farmers and their families, the problem is one of security," Duvane concluded with a series of nods. Confronted by unknown strangers, such as the Chinese, no administrative technology or juridical framework was currently capable of functioning as a 'buffer' (*intermediária*), which would allow for the amiable co-presence of both groups. Without the necessary means of negotiating with a potentially malignant other, many Mozambican farmers currently living in the Zambezi valley were therefore convinced that eviction from their lands was both unavoidable and imminent. Similar to the situation at the construction site in Maputo, it would seem that the situation in the Zambezi valley reflects a peculiar interdependent relationship between an unstable present and an imagined future in which each may be seen as unfolding from the other. In both cases, current practices are couched in the vocabulary of future events that, as emphasized by Duvane (and documented by state officials), may never occur.

And at the same time, the imagined future moment fundamentally emerges through a temporal displacement from the insecurities of the present.

Our point is that this ongoing process of figure-ground reversals was made analytically visible to Nielsen by aligning both cases using the envelope as an ethnographic scale. The ethnographic case in the Zambezi valley was consequently opened up by the economy of social distance that the 'envelope scale' from Maputo instantiated. Moreover, by approaching the particular events associated with the projected Chinese infrastructure initiatives in an envelope-like way, an (intensive) ethnographic time that cuts across analysis and events was and still continues to be unearthed. Thus, analyzing the situation in the Zambezi valley though a temporal trajectory laid out by an envelope scale extracted from Maputo, the key methodological question of Nielsen's (and Bunkenborg's) later fieldwork in Mozambique (in late 2010) became to identify which social practices in the local terrain could be said to operate through an economy of distance. Methodologically, this implies not simply an interpretive deciphering of an indigenous concept (say, the envelope), but, more radically, using such concepts as heuristic devices for connecting temporally disparate cases.

Case 2: Trans-temporal Events around Two Chinese Oil Fields in Mongolia

"We don't know anything about those Chinese over there, and we don't have any interest in them." These were the words of an old Mongolian nomad at whose yurt Pedersen and Bunkenborg stopped in 2009 on one of their trips in search of Chinese companies engaged in resource extraction in rural Mongolia. Outside, they had caught a glimpse of an oil rig looming in the desert horizon to the south, perhaps 10 kilometers away. The nomad's lack of interest came as a surprise to Pedersen and Bunkenborg. Surely, they thought to themselves as they waved goodbye from their jeep, although relations between Mongolians and Chinese have been fraught for centuries (Billé 2008; Bulag 1998), one would expect a remotely located household like this to be interested in finding out more about what is happening at a new oil field. Might there not be money to be made from the Chinese, either as hired hands or via informal trade?

The next morning, a battered pickup truck loaded with goats passed by their camp site in the desert close to the oil field. Much to Pedersen and Bunkenborg's surprise, it turned out to be the head of the nomadic household, along with two of his sons. "Where are you going?" they quizzed. "Over there, to the oil field," he replied. And so it transpired that his family was a regular supplier of meat to the Chinese, who purchased a few goats every fortnight, delivered and paid for in cash at the gates of the oil production compound via the mediation of the single Mongolian person present there (who was employed as a security guard and described himself as the loneliest person in the world). Naturally, Pedersen and Bunkenborg wanted to ask the old man how this new information might square with what he had told them the day before. Alas, the possibility never arose, because in the same breath as he finished his curt answer, the nomad stepped on the gas pedal and the pickup disappeared in a cloud of Gobi dust.

Many anthropologists would undoubtedly interpret the above anecdote as a good illustration of the old Malinowskian lesson about always distinguishing between what people say and what they do. Indeed, as all culturally sensitive but at the same time critically inclined ethnographers are supposed to do in such situations, Pedersen and Bunkenborg had already anticipated the existence of this kind of discrepancy by asking themselves—in an act of prospective stipulation in which a possible future scenario was extensively imagined from the perspective of the present—whether there might not be a hidden reason behind the man's answer during their first meeting. Probably there were economic and/or political interests that accounted for the old man's evasive response during that initial encounter, such as the possibility that he did not wish to disclose what was evidently a good business arrangement, or that he felt ashamed and certainly did not want others to know of his ongoing liaison with the hated Chinese.

Yet something did not add up. Heading toward their next destination—a bigger Chinese oil field located in far eastern Mongolia about 1,000 kilometers away from the lone oil rig in the Gobi Desert—Pedersen and Bunkenborg had a nagging sensation that they had missed something crucial in their brief but obviously important encounter with the old nomad, and that an alternative interpretation of this ethnographic moment might be possible. It is this sensation—which may be described as 'ethnographic intuition', and which arguably constitutes an irreducible feature of all anthropological analysis—that we wish to explore in the present case study.[4] Basically, we suggest that Pedersen and Bunkenborg's doubt might be described as a protospective effect of an unknown future acting on the present as its 'cause'. In this capacity, it represents a reversal of the temporal movement from the present moment into the future, which is characteristic of conventional prospective acts of critical ethnographic suspicion. In that sense, as we shall see, the 'ethnographic intuition' to which Pedersen and Bunkenborg were subject may be explained as a 'trans-temporal event' through which 'something of the future' installed itself in their minds without them being able to pinpoint why, for 'it' did not yet (and might never) exist other than in a virtual realm of potential actualizations. Over the coming days, as we shall also now recount, a new train of ethnographic events unfolded by means of which a locally significant scale became transformed into an analytical scale, which in turn rendered explicit to Pedersen and Bunkenborg what they had first intuited.

"The relationship between the Chinese company and the local community is flawless." Such was the not-to-be-questioned assessment provided by a high-ranking Mongolian government representative, whom Pedersen and Bunkenborg met on a windswept hill near the production headquarters of PetroChina Daqing Tamsag, a Mongolian subsidiary of China's state-owned energy giant PetroChina, which, since 2005, has operated an oil field in the Dornod Province of eastern Mongolia.[5] In presenting in these positive terms the relations between the predominantly Chinese employees of this company and the mostly nomadic Mongolian population of the local Matad district, the senior official was echoing the rosy narrative offered by all company representatives and many state officials in the capital of Ulaanbaatar (although local officials were more divided on the matter). In the words of Mr. Chimegtseren, a former mayor of the Matad district who was in charge of the interactions and negotiations between the Matad community and PetroChina Daqing Tamsag from 2005 to 2008, "This company plays by the book. The last thing they want is to have bad relationships with the local people. Remember, this is not a small private firm polluting the desert and underpaying their workers like many foreign mines in the Gobi. This is the Chinese state, and they are doing everything they can to leave a favorable impression on the Mongols."

The Chinese companies in Mongolia certainly seem to be in need of improved impression management. As anthropologist Franck Billé (2008: 1) has observed in an article about Sino-Mongolian relations in contemporary Mongolia, "China is not merely portrayed negatively: a belief that the country harbours sinister intents and is plotting to destroy the Mongols' very existence is prevalent and expresses itself in a wide range of stories and rumours." Against this background, Pedersen and Bunkenborg were hardly surprised to learn that, among the nomads, villagers, local officials, and environmental NGOs with whom they met in the Matad district, as well as in the provincial capital of Choibalsan, the large majority of people expressed deep skepticism about, if not downright hostility toward, the presence of a Chinese oil company in what they considered to be their homeland (*nutag*). Seen in this light, the striking thing about the present case study is not the Chinese companies' unpopularity in the rural community at hand, but the lack of visible conflict surrounding the presence of a large, foreign-owned and polluting oil field with thousands of Chinese workers in the midst of Mongolia's sparsely populated and most cherished wildernesses (*heer*).

Consider how the relations between Chinese oil workers and Mongolian nomads have developed over the years. During the first period after PetroChina's purchase of the oil field in 2005, a number of incidents took place in which Chinese workers approached local nomads with the intention of purchasing meat and other produce from them. Since the two sides did not speak each other's language, the Chinese workers had to use gestures to communicate their needs. Presumably, this could have worked out, but that was not how Mr. Chimegtseren and several other Matad residents saw it, as they explained to Pedersen and Bunkenborg. "It was a total mess [*zambaraagüi*]," Mr. Chimegtseren recalled, slowly shaking his head disapprovingly. "Groups of Chinese workers tried to express their wish to buy meat by holding their hands to their heads and grunting, as if were they cows. But the nomads could not understand what these people wanted, and now and then, when the men had gone hunting, the women and children would become so afraid that they ran from their homes. Such chaos!"

Soon rumors also began to circulate that local women were engaged in illegitimate sexual relations with Chinese men, and that 'bastard' (*erliiz*) children were being born in the district—a common fear all over Mongolia, which is exasperated by the fact that people find it impossible to distinguish *erliiz* from so-called genuine Mongolians. Eventually, a meeting was set up between managers from the company, the regional police chief from Choibalsan, and Mr. Chimegtseren, in his capacity as governor. From this point onward, no Chinese worker would be allowed to leave the oil field unless authorized to so. Chinese drivers, who would sometimes visit nomadic households on route to the border, were instructed to stick to the roads, and locals were banned from carrying out trade with anyone from the company. Instead, a central trading company was set up by the district administration through which all trade had to be conducted at a fixed price. "Soon after," Mr. Chimegtseren proudly concluded, "all strife and conflict disappeared, and disorder was replaced by order."

Note that for Mr. Chimegtseren, as well as several other (Mongolian as well as Chinese) officials and managers, 'order' here seems to mean that a complex multiplicity of relations is somehow reduced to a more homogeneous set of manageable connections. Indeed, what is characteristic of PetroChina Daqing Tamsag and the other Chinese resource extraction outfits in southeastern Mongolia investigated by Pedersen and Bunkenborg is the seemingly deliberate if not systematic manner in which the relationship between Chinese workers and managers, on the one hand, and the local communities and Mongolian workers, on the other, has deliberately been 'hollowed out' over time. For that was what many leaders and officials, including Mr. Chimegtseren, took pride in: the forging of an optimal distance between two worlds that are mutually dependent but must be kept separate at all costs (see also Willerslev and Pedersen 2010).

Pedersen and Bunkenborg's visits to the Tamsag production headquarters from 2009 to 2011 confirmed this observation. Unlike the arrangements with many smaller Chinese (and other) companies in Mongolia's natural resource sector, the Mongolian staff at this oil field received stable and relatively high salaries (around $500 per month in 2009), plus a proper pension scheme and health insurance. The food and the accommodations at the headquarters were of equally high standard when compared to many other Mongolian and foreign-owned mining companies: the living quarters and bathroom facilities (both consisting of air-conditioned special-purpose containers of the same type that many Chinese companies use in Mozambique) were clean, spacious, and functional, just as the food was plentiful and geared toward different tastes by cooks belonging to the respective nationalities. And while minimal informal interaction took place between the Chinese and the Mongolians workers—who were eating different food in different cafeterias, and who never formed the same groups of friends smoking and chatting or playing sports outside—there was little evidence of conflict between the two groups. Instead, the limited interactions that took place between them, whether they were part of the same drilling team at one of the wells or were waiting at the showers before dinner, seemed perfectly amiable—to the point of being so polite and so mutually tolerant that the two sides could be suspected of striving to remain indifferent to each other.

What all this points to, we argue, is the workings of a distinct economy of distance by which the interactions between the two sides in a given social relationship are kept to an absolute, functional minimum. It is, we submit, the succesful instantiation of this peculiar hollowed-out sociality that has ensured, ever since PetroChina Daqing Tamsag began producing oil in 2006, that the trend has been one of moving toward less and less—as opposed to (as one would tend to expect from social relations over time) more and more—contact between Chinese nationals and Mongolians. It is this carefully forged hollowing out of Sino-Mongolian relations in eastern Mongolia that we think is of wider methodological significance for our comparative research agenda in Inner Asia and sub-Saharan Africa. It is also an insight that, as we are about to learn, speaks directly to the earlier anecdote from Pedersen and Bunkenborg's research trip to the Gobi in 2009.

Precisely how is this hollowing out done? Elsewhere, Pedersen and Bunkenborg (2012) have accounted in some detail for the network of roads and tracks built between the company headquarters and the different oil wells and exploration sites, as well as between the oil field as a whole and the local communities in the Matad district and the Dornod region, including the recently upgraded highway running eastward toward China from Tamsag. One of the things that this road ethnography shows is that the construction and use of roads between the Chinese and the Mongolians seem to indicate a desire for disconnection rather than any yearning for contact with which most roads are associated. Nowhere was this more apparent than in the aforementioned example of the trading monopoly set up between PetroChina Daqing Tamsag and the Matad community. As Mr. Chimegtseren emphasized, it was thus only after a "proper road" was made between the company headquarters and the local district center, along with various legal, economic, and political arrangements between managers from the oil company and local leaders, that the "chaotic" and "conflict-ridden" relations between the two sides were transformed into an "orderly arrangement." As Pedersen and Bunkenborg (ibid.) conclude in their study, roads between Mongols and Chinese in Mongolia thus serve as a 'technology of distanciation' by which the two sides can be maximally separate while engaging in a mutually beneficial trade arrangement.

Returning to the earlier story of the old nomad from the Gobi Desert who was caught red-handed selling goats to the Chinese oil workers he was not supposed to know anything about, the question now is whether the road, as a particular scale of social life in eastern Mongolia, can be transposed to this particular fieldwork encounter as well and perhaps elicit an alternative and more novel interpretation of it. We suggest that it can and in a way that is imbued with peculiar methodological implications for the temporal ontology of ethnographic knowledge production more generally. The moment that roads are conceived not so much as interfaces by which entities are connected but as technologies through which latent relationships are truncated—which is precisely how Pedersen and Bunkenborg came to think of roads, but only after their visit to the Tamsag oil field—it becomes possible to scale the old man's words in what could be considered a more satisfactory (and less skeptical) manner. If we try to 'road' Pedersen and Bunkenborg's ethnographic moment in the same way as some of Nielsen's fieldwork material from Mozambique was earlier 'enveloped', Pedersen and Bunkenborg's vague intuition concerning their encounter with the old Mongolian nomad is materialized exactly in the form of the road. What had previously showed itself only as an intuitive 'sign from the future', a nagging sensation that something was missing (or had been overlooked) in their interpretation of this event, now became explicit when elicited by the locally important socio-material configuration of the road. In that sense, the road came to serve as an ethnographically derived analytical scale for Pedersen and Bunkenborg by which the man's seemingly contradictory (or untruthful) remark—that he and the rest of his nomadic household did not know anything about the Chinese—may be taken more seriously (literally) as a genuine (earnest) indigenous description of the particular Sino-Mongolian relationship at hand. In this non-skeptical interpretation of the encounter, then, the nomad *did* 'mean' what he said, for the road reduced a latently multi-faceted relationship into the single and hollowed-out one that Mr. Chimegtseren called 'pure business'.

What, then, is 'the time' of Pedersen and Bunkenborg's field? In some ways, the answer is surprisingly obvious and not as metaphysical as one might expect. It is now apparent that the road, as a distinct trans-temporal hinge, was already available for them in their encounter with the old nomad in the Gobi, but that this analytical scale only became actualized through their subsequent visit to Tamsag in eastern Mongolia. Because of the virtual nature of Pedersen and Bunkenborg's nagging sensation that something was missing in their understanding of the encounter with the old nomad, things could easily have developed in such a way that their lingering doubts were forgotten, relegated, along with countless other signs from the future that constantly impinge on the ethnographic fieldworker and feeds his intuition, to the churchyard of forgotten hunches and half-baked interpretations. Not so in this case, however. Pedersen and Bunkenborg were, in a rather literal sense, exposed to their primary scale of analysis all along the way, as their route between the two field sites eventually turned out also to be their analytical concern in the form of the road. Unbeknown to them, they had been driving on what was soon to become their key concept.

Temporalized Scales of Ethnographic Analysis

To sum up out argument so far, if, in our first case study from Mozambique, the locally significant configuration of Sino-African social life that turned out to work as a trans-temporal hinge was the envelope, then, in our second case study from rural Mongolia, the ethnographically salient scale that emerged as our second trans-temporal hinge was the desert road. In the first case, exchanges between Chinese and Mozambicans were guided by an economy of distance where productive transactions were predicated on a mutual effort to avoid exposing the 'content' of the relation. In the latter case, it was also a capacity for separation—as opposed to connection—that was appreciated by Mongolians and Chinese alike. Similar to the Sino-Mozambican scale of the envelope, the road as a scaling of the Sino-Mongolian relationship thus rendered possible the ongoing reproduction of an optimal distance in the awkward encounter between the two sides through its capacity as a technology of distantiation for stretching out and hollowing relations.

But this still leaves the question of the relationship between 'their scale' of social life and 'our scale' of analysis. Before closing, we would therefore like to elaborate further on what we mean by 'scale' and how our use of this crucial concept compares with that of Marilyn Strathern and with other 'post-plural' understandings of it (see Holbraad and Pedersen 2009). In a study of concepts of land and value among Hageners in Papua New Guinea, Strathern (2000: 51) observes that "culture lies in the value which people give to things and the concepts through which they express it. It involves the facility for imagining one's own conditions of life. Scales, whoever constructs them, are thus cultural artefacts. At the same time, the observer would not give any scale to the facility itself." Here, for something to operate as a scale, it is necessary that the effects of social processes are imagined as phenomena in their own right (scalable, as it were), while the imaginary capacity for doing so remains beyond any scalar extension or dimensioning. And indeed, when analyzing indigenous conceptualizations of wealth in Papua New Guinea, it does seem very relevant to distinguish between a general facility for imagining one's conditions of life and the specific scaling process by which, say, land is made culturally significant. By so doing, it becomes possible to examine the systemic effects of switching scales, such as when changing from measuring in terms of population density to measuring in terms of different production regimes. The result, as Strathern (1991: xv) explains, is that "relations between phenomena appear 'complex'. Complexity is culturally indicated in the ordering or composition of elements that can also be apprehended from the perspective of other orders." For, as long the distinction between scale and facility is assumed always to remain intact, then the ethnographer is continuously reminded that any interpretation is invariably partial since the "capacity for conceptualization ... outruns the concepts it produces" (ibid.; cf. Strathern 2006: 96–97).

Yet the question is whether our concept of trans-temporal hinges actually observes this distinction between a single, general (human?) capacity for scaling and multiple culture-specific scalings. As we have tried to make clear in both of our case studies above, one of the defining characteristics of temporalized scales, such as the Mozambican payment envelope and the Mongolian oil road, is their capacity to operate as dynamic middle points that hold together otherwise disparate occurrences and events. As ethnographic scales that serve a particular role in concrete Sino-Xeno encounters in Africa and Inner Asia, they do not indicate a set of invariable principles by which to generalize and compare particular social configurations; rather, as inherently temporalized articulating joints, they connect and disconnect at the same time and thereby expose the continual flow of relations through which various forms of social life emerge and disappear. In both of the above case studies, the trans-temporal hinges facilitated not just exterior temporal scalings of the social contexts under investigation, but also an interior differentiation that allowed our analysis to differ *from itself* in the course of making it. Thus, while the anthropological scalings discussed by Strathern require that the capacity for scaling is held stable across different scales, the trans-temporal hinges explored by us here seem to allow for a more dynamic form of analysis, whereby the facility for imagining and comparing people's condition of life becomes an effect of the ethnographic scale identified and explored rather than the other way around.

Consider again the envelope by which the Mozambican workers sought to apportion the proper distance to their Chinese superiors. This economy of distance was made emically and etically visible through a series of immediate temporal leaps between the present and an imagined future moment when paid-out salaries would be received in the appropriate, concealed manner. By imaginatively probing the effects of holding together an untenable present with a potential but unlikely future, the envelope came to function as a viable temporal scale by which to measure certain domains of social life. Similarly, in the case of the Mongolian road, Pedersen and Bunkenborg's analytical capacity for scaling was not separate from the ethnographic scaling they ended up extracting from—or rather bumping into in—the field. Quite the contrary, their 'roading' of certain fieldwork events from two Chinese oil fields in rural Mongolia was to a large extent an effect of an initial inability to imagine an appropriate scale for making sense of their data.

In both of the case studies explored in this chapter, it therefore makes little sense to distinguish between a scale-insensitive facility for differentiation and a proportioning of social activities instantiated by the former. Trans-temporal hinges fundamentally proceed from, or we could say 'envelop', the facility for imagining how people's conditions of life might be measured and acted upon. As such, they serve as the ethnographic ground upon which to figure the proportional capacity that might subsequently activate other social environments, such as when the problematic situation in the Zambezi valley was imagined in an envelope-like way, and when the mutual propensity for hollowing out the Sino-Mongolian relationship was conceptually 'roaded'. in Central and Eastern Mongolia's deserts In both cases, the facility for differentiation was contained by ethnographic scales that initially emerged as an effect of the awkward relationship between local workers and their Chinese superiors in the two contexts. Rather than having the facility for differentiation held in proportion across different scales, the envelope and the road suggest a kind of 'transformation from within' whereby people's life conditions seem to be predicated on how different temporal moments are briefly held together. Put somewhat differently, the envelope and the road emerge as ethnographic scales-cum-heuristic anthropological concepts through the optimal distances that they afford between particular presents and futures rather than vice versa.

Conclusion

We hope to have shown that trans-temporal hinges of the kind discussed in this chapter may allow for a better understanding of the inherent unpredictabilities of certain ongoing Mozambican-Chinese and Sino-Mongolian relationships, as well as the ethnographic knowledge process involved in studying and comparing them. Trans-temporal hinges, we have argued, are heuristic methodological tools devised for studying volatile social relations that allow ethnographers to take the future seriously as an object of analysis and methodological reflection. Because all ethnographic phenomena can, in principle, be 'scaled' in the manner suggested by us in this piece, any given practice, concept, or event from our respective project sites in Mozambique and Mongolia can be said to contain the time of our field as a whole. Still, certain ethnographic phenomena, events, or scales seem better equipped to serve as trans-temporal hinges than others. Apart from the fact that that such scales should be socially significant in the ethnographic contexts from which they derive, the key criteria behind the selection of the scales that are to act as trans-temporal hinges must be that they remain temporally equidistant from the different cases studied, for only by keeping the same distance from actual and potential events witnessed by the ethnographer will these scales be able to hold together present and future events in non-linear, trans-temporal 'hingings' of the sort outlined above.

As noted at the outset of this chapter, trans-temporal hinges must always be derived from socially significant phenomena in their respective ethnographic contexts. But precisely because trans-temporal hinges in their etic role as scales of anthropological analysis are fundamentally inseparable from their emic role as important scales of indigenous social life, such scalings cannot serve as frames for generalizations on a 'higher' epistemological order than the phenomena that they compare. Whereas such quantitative scales order social domains in terms of fixed and hierarchical dimensions (e.g., if a certain phenomenon is found to be more local, then it is, in a proportionally inverse manner, also less global), trans-temporal hinges are rather a form of qualitative scales that contain within themselves the facility for differentiation and dimensioning. To this it may be objected that any analytical attempt to uproot or to extract a scale that cannot keep its proportions stable even in its local context is doomed to fail due to its obvious inability to map symmetrically onto the 'bigger' dimensions of other cases. This is, however, precisely the point that we have been trying to make here: it is *because* trans-temporal hinges, such as the payment envelope and the oil road, are so glaringly incapable of maintaining fixity and thus are so obviously unable to allow for generalizations between ideally self-identical cases that they are so apt as anthropological concepts.

Acknowledgments

We thank the two anonymous reviewers and Hans Steinmüller for their challenging critiques and insightful comments, which have greatly improved our argument. A first version of this chapter was presented at the Megaseminar of the Danish Research School of Anthropology and Ethnography at Sandbjerg in August 2009, and we thank the participants in the panel "Time and the Field," in particular Steffen Dalsgaard and Antonia Walford, for their comments. Finally, we thank the Danish Research Board of the Social Sciences (FSE) for generously funding the three-year project (2009–2012) "Imperial Potentialities: Chinese Infrastructure Investments and Socio-economic Networks in Mozambique and Mongolia," of which the present chapter represents one among several outputs, with others to follow.

Morten Axel Pedersen is a Professor of Social Anthropology at the University of Copenhagen. Based on fieldwork in Mongolia, Siberia, and western China, he has published numerous articles on shamanism, cosmology, materiality, post-socialism, violence, security, imagination, and hope. He recently published a monograph, *Not Quite Shamans: Spirit Worlds and Political Lives in Northern Mongolia* (2011), and is co-editor of *Times of Security* (2013), *Comparative Relativism* (2010, a special issue of *Common Knowledge*), *Technologies of the Imagination* (2009, a special issue of *Ethnos*), and *Inner Asian Perspectivism* (2007, a special issue of *Inner Asia*). He is the principal investigator of several large research programs, including the comparative investigation of Chinese infrastructural interventions in Mozambique and Mongolia on which the present chapter is based.

Morten Nielsen is an Associate Professor in the Department of Anthropology at Aarhus University and coordinator of the interdisciplinary research network Urban Orders (URO). Based on his fieldwork in Brazil, Mozambique, and, most recently, Scotland, he has published on issues such as urban aesthetics, time and temporality, materiality, relational ontologies, infrastructure, and political cosmologies. Recent publications include articles in the *Journal of the Royal Anthropological Institute*, *HAU: Journal of Ethnographic Theory*, *Social Analysis*, and *Social Anthropology*.

Notes

1. Both authors have contributed equally to this chapter.
2. While both operations are linear in that they involve a unidirectional connection of one event with another along a spatialized temporal vector (a progressive present-future vector and a regressive future-present one), their irreducible simultaneity—the fact that they are folded into one other as each other's grounds—ensures that they cancel each other's unidirectionality out, delineating a non-linear temporal plane. Thus, as shown by Nielsen (2011) in his work on house building and inverse temporality in Mozambique, temporal obviation revolves around a series of inverse cause-effect relationships in which, say, occurrence A is rendered possible by occurrence B, even though the latter chronologically follows the former.
3. Rumors have it that up to 10,000 Chinese small-scale farmers will cultivate the land. This figure has, however, never been confirmed by official agencies.
4. A differently focused and lengthier account of the present case can be found in Pedersen and Bunkenborg (2012).
5. With a $511 million investment in 2009 and an annual payment of $19 million following the product-sharing agreement between PetroChina and the Mongolian government, the oil field is tiny by international standards. Nevertheless, PetroChina Daqing Tamsag represents the biggest foreign direct investment in Mongolia's Dornod Province, and it involves one of the highest concentrations of foreign workers in the country. In 2008, the number of Chinese nationals working at the oil field surpassed the local population of 3,000 inhabitants in the district of Matad. Since then, the number of Chinese workers has hovered between 3,500 and 6,000.

References

Alden, Chris, Daniel Large, and Ricardo Soares de Oliveira. 2008. *China Returns to Africa: A Rising Power and a Continent Embrace.* London: Hurst.

Ansell Pearson, Keith. 2002. *Philosophy and the Adventure of the Virtual: Bergson and the Time of Life.* London: Routledge.

Bergson, Henri. 1965. *Duration and Simultaneity.* Trans. Leon Jacobson. Indianapolis, IN: Bobbs-Merrill.

Billé, Franck. 2008. "Faced with Extinction: Myths and Urban Legends in Contemporary Mongolia." *Cambridge Anthropology* 28, no. 1: 1–26.

Bourdieu, Pierre. 1977. *Outline of a Theory of Practice.* Trans. Richard Nice. Cambridge: Cambridge University Press.

Bourdieu, Pierre. 2000. *Pascalian Meditations.* Trans. Richard Nice. Oxford: Polity Press.

Brautigam, Deborah. 2009. *The Dragon's Gift: The Real Story of China in Africa.* Oxford: Oxford University Press.

Bulag, Uradyn E. 1998. *Nationalism and Hybridity in Mongolia.* Oxford: Oxford University Press.

da Col, Giovanni. 2007. "The View from *Somewhen*: Events, Bodies and the Perspective of Fortune around Khawa Karpo, a Tibetan Sacred Mountain in Yunnan Province." *Inner Asia* 9, no. 2: 215–235.

Deleuze, Gilles. 1988. *Bergsonism.* Trans. Hugh Tomlinson and Barbara Habberjam. New York: Zone Books.

Deleuze, Gilles. 2004. *Difference and Repetition.* Trans. Paul Patton. London: Continuum.

Gell, Alfred. 1992. *The Anthropology of Time: Cultural Constructions of Temporal Maps and Images.* Oxford: Berg.

Hodges, Matt. 2008. "Rethinking Time's Arrow: Bergson, Deleuze and the Anthropology of Time." *Anthropological Theory* 8, no. 4: 399–429.

Holbraad, Martin, and Morten Axel Pedersen. 2009. "Planet M: The Intense Abstraction of Marilyn Strathern." *Anthropological Theory* 9, no. 4: 371–394.

Kleveman, Lutz. 2003. *The New Great Game: Blood and Oil in Central Asia.* New York: Atlantic Monthly Press.

Latour, Bruno. 2005. *Reassembling the Social: An Introduction to Actor-Network-Theory.* Oxford: Oxford University Press.

Miyazaki, Hirokazu. 2004. *The Method of Hope: Anthropology, Philosophy, and Fijian Knowledge.* Stanford, CA: Stanford University Press.

Miyazaki, Hirokazu. 2006. "Economy of Dreams: Hope in Global Capitalism and Its Critiques." *Cultural Anthropology* 21, no. 2: 147–172.

Nielsen, Morten. 2008. "In the Vicinity of the State: House Construction, Personhood, and the State in Maputo, Mozambique." PhD diss., University of Copenhagen.

Nielsen, Morten. 2009. "Contrapuntal Cosmopolitanism: Distantiation as Social Relatedness among House-Builders in Maputo, Mozambique." *Social Anthropology* 18, no. 4: 396–402.

Nielsen, Morten. 2011. "Futures Within: Reversible Time and House-Building in Maputo, Mozambique." *Anthropological Theory* 11, no. 4: 397–423.

Paulo, Margarida, Carmeliza Rosário, and Inge Tvedten. 2007. *"Xiculungo": Social Relations of Urban Poverty in Maputo, Mozambique.* Bergen: Chr. Michelsen Institute.

Pedersen, Morten Axel. 2011. *Not Quite Shamans: Spirit Worlds and Political Lives in Northern Mongolia.* Ithaca, NY: Cornell University Press.

Pedersen, Morten Axel. 2012. "A Day in the Cadillac: The Work of Hope in Urban Mongolia." *Social Analysis* 56, no. 2: 136–151.

Pedersen, Morten Axel, and Mikkel Bunkenborg. 2012. "Roads that Separate: Sino-Mongolian Relations in the Inner Asian Desert." *Mobilities* 7, no. 4: 555–569.

Strathern, Marilyn. 1991. *Partial Connections.* Totowa, NJ: Rowman and Littlefield.

Strathern, Marilyn. 1999. *Property, Substance and Effect: Anthropological Essays on Persons and Things.* London: Athlone Press.

Strathern, Marilyn. 2000. "Environments Within: An Ethnographic Commentary on Scale." Pp. 44–71 in *Culture, Landscape, and the Environment: The Linacre Lectures, 1997,* ed. Kate Flint and Howard Morphy. Oxford: Oxford University Press.

Strathern, Marilyn. 2006. "On Space and Depth." Pp. 88–115 in *Complexities: Social Studies of Knowledge Practices,* ed. John Law and Annemarie Mol. Durham, NC: Duke University Press.

Swanström, Niklas. 2005. "China and Central Asia: A New Great Game or Traditional Vassal Relations?" *Journal of Contemporary China* 14, no. 45: 569–584.

Taylor, Ian. 2006. *China and Africa: Engagement and Compromise.* London: Routledge.

Tsing, Anna L. 2005. *Friction: An Ethnography of Global Connection.* Princeton, NJ: Princeton University Press.

Vigh, Henrik. 2006. *Navigating Terrains of War: Youth and Soldiering in Guinea-Bissau.* New York: Berghahn Books.

Willerslev, Rane, and Morten Axel Pederson. 2010. "Proportional Holism: Joking the Cosmos into the Right Shape in North Asia." Pp. 262–278 in *Experiments in Holism: Theory and Practice in Contemporary Anthropology,* ed. Ton Otto and Nils Bubandt. London: Wiley-Blackwell.

AFTERWORD
Ethnography between the Virtue of Patience and the
Anxiety of Belatedness Once Coevalness Is Embraced

George Marcus

> If we follow [Crapanzano's] distinction between a social-cum-ontological produc-
> tion of time and an analytical-cum-methodological vocabulary through which the
> former emerges as a distinct object of study, the contributions to this volume are
> occupied precisely with exploring the interrelations between the two ... As such,
> several of the contributors ... show that different fields contain social perspectives
> as moments in time that can merge temporalities and thus equally erupt from time.
>
> — Steffen Dalsgaard and Morten Nielsen, introduction to this volume

> In contradistinction to Plato's ... lawyer, or Cicourel's ... physician, we have all the
> time in the world, all our time, and this freedom from urgency, from necessity—
> which often takes the form of economic necessity, due to the convertibility of
> time into money—is made possible by an ensemble of social and economic
> conditions, by the existence of these supplies of free time that accumulated
> economic resources represent.
>
> — Pierre Bourdieu, "The Scholastic Point of View"

Notes for this section are located on page 155.

From the many acute angles drawn in this volume's chapters on how time and temporalities are integrated into ethnographic representations from fieldwork experiences, I want to focus my discussion on a distinctive problem of how an 'analytical-cum-methodological' solution to the narration of ethnography's time (in producing representations or accounts) as the contemporary (see Rabinow et al. 2008) merges with subjects' 'social-cum-ontological' production of temporalities. For me, the essence of ethnographic interpretation arises from concept work progressively and politically done in fieldwork (a variation on the classic and durable trope of translation) between anthropologist and others who increasingly and self-consciously collaborate, and from the modulation of differing tempos and temporalities that both grossly and subtly affect the analytic terms of ethnography. From start to finish, the authoritative language of analysis that is forged from the scripts of fieldwork is modulated by the clash or negotiation of time budgeting and invested tempos deeply embedded in the act of thinking together and in the evolution of key interpretive ideas of fieldwork. The interest of the anthropologist and the differential interest of the subject in increasingly shared analytic thinking in concepts are starkly expressed by modulated investments in focusing attention and literally spending time in articulating certain ideas and concepts instead of others.

As every anthropologist knows, 'good' ethnography takes all of the time in the (Western) world. This norm of patience and cumulative achievement in ethnography has held as long as what Johannes Fabian (1983) termed 'the denial of coevalness' has remained a powerful fiction of professional ideology, shaping the practice and object of both fieldwork and ethnographic writing. That is, as long as the subjects of ethnography existed in their own time-space, outside the contemporaneity of the ethnography, anthropology could confidently insist on standards of research performance that valued deliberation, patience, and a stable scene and subject of study. The extent of the dependence of these standards by which anthropologists have judged each other as ethnographers on a certain regime of temporality cannot be underestimated. Control of another language, the effect of demonstrating depth of knowledge of another culture, the writing of ethnographies as if the author is telling less than he or she could—in short, all of the performative elements of demonstrating ethnographic authority have depended on the valorization of a temporality of patience. There have been a few anthropologists admired for what they could produce from short periods of fieldwork in diverse places (e.g., famously, Fredrik Barth), but very few indeed. Even the historicization of the ethnographic subject, which is now a commonplace, has been easily accommodated to this valorized temporality of research.[1] Yet while the norms of a temporality of patience are still formally in place, several factors and tendencies have conspired in recent years to undermine any semblance of conforming in practice to this temporality, creating a veritable symptom of anxiety in the way much ethnography is produced today.

The anthropology of contemporary change in both new topical arenas of research and older domains of area-based studies has indeed become pervasive. Still, in the name of long-standing ideals in the practice of fieldwork and ethnographic writing, research is changing both dramatically and circumstantially.[2] And nothing is changing more than the temporality holding the deeply embedded conception of ethnographic research in place. Here I want briefly to examine the conditions and sources of the anxiety arising from, on the one hand, the time pressures on the deliberate and patient production of ethnography and, on the other, the sense of belatedness that can affect ethnographers when trying to produce knowledge of the contemporary. These ruptures of the traditional ideals of temporality in anthropological research, in turn, go to the heart of the circumstances that are transforming the work of ethnography, for which anthropologists do not have as yet an alternative set of norms of professional practice.

There are two factors operating in the contemporary mode of the production and reception of ethnographic research within the community of anthropologists (at least, in the United States) that are critically responsible for defining the conditions that are affecting the ideal temporality on which the authority of traditional ethnographic research has depended. First, there are generally much increased time pressures in the university to complete graduate degrees more quickly. In my own generation of graduate training (the early 1970s), for example, there was no administrative limit on the time one could take with dissertation research, and there were reasonable resources to be found to extend fieldwork or writing-up periods. These liberal conditions for taking one's time could be devastating to a student's progress in some cases, but it was a crucial resource for producing the norm of patience in the case of the best and subsequently most influential career-defining projects of dissertation ethnography. In the current trend of the corporate university toward efficiency in graduate training, along with fewer funding sources (as well as a decline in their monetary level) for ethnographic research from fieldwork to write-up, the norm of temporality is challenged as a professional standard of ethnography at the very beginning of careers, when anthropologists most crucially define their 'capital' and reputation as ethnographic researchers.

Second, the most engaged reception that many projects of ethnographic research receive has shifted from the professional community of anthropologists to various other constituencies and readerships. To me, this move in the relative significance of the reception of anthropological ethnography from its professional community of standards to constituencies external to this community, created by the course and relations of fieldwork itself, is perhaps the most fascinating development in the current evolution of social/cultural anthropology—a development that needs explicit discussion in rethinking the norms of the long-standing ethos of anthropological research. But this move is also the crucial condition that has challenged the temporality of ethnography and given rise to an anxiety about the belatedness of producing ethnography at a deliberate pace, now exposed to other constituencies of both reception and competing, overlapping forms of representation from which anthropologists were formerly isolated by the priority of professional standards that valorized patience in producing ethnography. The 'scholastic point of view' that Pierre Bourdieu (1990) defends in the epigraph at the outset of this afterword—especially against the tendency to move the conceptual work of researchers closer to those of sub-jects, as suggested in the 'writing culture' critique of the 1980s (see Clifford and Marcus 1986)—is challenged in contemporary anthropological research, even as it persists as the privilege of professionalism. Indeed, the scholastic point of view hangs on a particular temporality, and its privileges, which eth-nography, among other scholarly practices, has favored. It has heretofore been expressed in primarily spatial terms that mask coevalness and differences in attention to and time investments in particular concepts, as many of the chap-ters in this collection point out.

In the remainder of this afterword I want to examine elements of the expo-sure of ethnography to other agendas, receptions, and ecologies with regard to its constitution (in this sense, its authority is more 'found' in fieldwork than given), and how this gives rise to a certain anxiety about relevance and belat-edness that inhibits an ethnography that strives to take its time. But first, I offer brief characterizations of two examples among others of how ethnographic research that tries to take its time, in conforming to the norm of temporal-ity in anthropological research practice, is oriented to contemporary change and pushed into quicker tempos of producing descriptions and interpretations of shifting realities amid many forms of competing representations, including those that are themselves objects of ethnographic analysis.

In *French DNA: Trouble in Purgatory*, Paul Rabinow (2001) has acutely observed the French achievement and success in mapping the genome before the Americans and what this means distinctively in a French context. Yet his fieldwork for this study is belated. It takes place among the team of scientists in the period following this achievement and reports in detail on the 'forms' that are emerging around genomics in France. What endures in Rabinow's book is perhaps the least developed, that is, the French cultural context for DNA, while what receives detailed treatment is what is belated and ephemeral. Rabinow struggles to conceive of a new conception of ethnography (in which the explicit concept of ethnography itself plays no part) that justifies the moment and the 'singularity' that he opportunistically assimilates by having 'been there' in fieldwork. What is 'thick description' in Rabinow's work (the politics of science, corporations, and funding in the aftermath of the success) is not as dramatic as mapping the genome, but as perhaps Rabinow would like to argue, it is more consequential than what is ethnographically 'thin' or undeveloped in his account (the peculiarly French context of the effort to map the genome).

Then there is the work *Advocacy after Bhopal: Environmentalism, Disaster, New Global Orders* by Kim Fortun (2001), which is a rich text on the issue of generating enduringly relevant ethnography from a project that is belated at the outset. The Bhopal disaster occurred in 1984. Fortun spent two years at the Bhopal site in 1988–1989, during the period of the settlement. Her time was spent among activists in the aftermath of this disaster, and she pro-duced accounts of the meanings of this event in multiple contexts through an ethnography of advocacy itself. Following her dissertation, she did not pub-lish a full work until 2001, as the memory of the Bhopal event receded even more among readerships she might want to reach. Fortun's responses both in fieldwork and writing to the anxieties of working with the traditional norm of slowness in producing ethnography were thoughtful and innovative, to which I will return at the end of this piece.

The trajectory of Fortun's post-dissertation work—on constantly moving ground, so to speak, and in the face of complex regimes of representations of differing embedded temporalities that overlapped and sometimes contrasted with those she was creating—was to keep on doing fieldwork, which in her case meant to continue to write for different constituencies and occasions. The ongoing problem of Fortun's research, and the central problematic of her field-work, was to find new forms and styles of writing to sustain the relevance of her work in constantly changing space-time contexts. It was, perhaps, only the requirement of submitting work for tenure evaluation that made her produce a long work—the equivalent of a published ethnography that anthropologists usually submit for academic promotion. The pattern in which she produced her work and the relative standing of major published work for conventional professional review, in relation to the manner of producing anthropology on this topic amid multiple constituencies and regimes of reception, are sugges-tive of the changing forms and valences that much anthropological research on contemporary problems seems to be manifesting. As we will see, strategies of temporalizing work in order to offer conceptually stable knowledge of a subject in the realm of the scholastic point of view, at least in the report to the academy (which her book is), play a major role in giving new patterns and forms of research authority within the older reigning norms for such research.

These two examples show the job of ethnography neither to be the tradi-tional task of describing a process that is more or less stabilized or structural nor to explain what is culturally distinctive in the changes addressed—for instance, to determine what is French about DNA or what is Indian about the Bhopal environmental disaster—although in each case, and especially in Rabinow's, this sort of expected anthropological expertise plays an important role in consti-tuting the subject of study. To demonstrate cultural difference and distinction is part of the scenery of analysis, to be sure, but it is not the point of analysis in either of these cases. Rather, there is a set of events that are localized but are of global significance and must be described by an assemblage constituted by and argued for in the design of ethnography and its movements that bring certain sites and actors into analytic relation to one another. What takes time in describ-ing objects such as these is not the kind of descriptive thickness that Clifford Geertz made famous as the special contribution and virtue of ethnography, but rather attention to extra dimensions of situations and sites brought into analytic relation so as to demonstrate the symbolic, real, and imaginary relations exist-ing among them, justifying the particular assemblages of objects, subjects, and situations that the ethnography describes. These relations are not at all obvious, and demonstrating them requires meticulous fieldwork and a probing of the actors' own capacities for critical reflexivity. To get at this multiplicity of per-spectives and critical sensibilities embedded in social life and expertises stud-ied indeed takes all the time in the world, and it may be precisely the kind of knowledge that actors and makers of representations competing or overlapping with the anthropologists' own may be less interested in, less conscious of, or less valuing of. This would not be of such consequence if anthropologists were not so exposed to the politics of knowledge and the reception of subjects to their own work in ways that matter more than ever, as I have argued that they are.

Taking the time to provide thickly descriptive/analytic ethnography in this sense, then, is what is at stake in such projects. The anthropologist is often engaged in overlapping discourse and purposes with participants for whom the pace of ethnographic insight may seem slow, and the anthropologist is anxiously dependent on this judgment once she is operating outside or only partially in relation to the privileges of the scholastic point of view. In each of the above examples, the production of a distinctive ethnographic knowledge, if that is possible, is as significantly subject to constituencies within the boundaries of fieldwork as to the disciplinary community that may admire itself for moving into these arenas of contemporary change but may not be able to grasp, critique, or engage in as sustained a way with the products of such research as are the constituencies of this research themselves. Anthropology is finally on the verge of fulfilling its dream of receiving direct and meaningful response from its 'natives' (a prominent ideal in the professional lore of classic fieldwork), but the natives in this case are not the classically conceived, or at least represented, subjects. They are more often counterparts from whom the tempos and modes of anthropological practice cannot be authoritatively separated.

The Sources of Anxiety about the Slowness of Ethnography Exposed to Other Representations and Other Temporalities in Producing Knowledge

Anthropologists today seem to want their ethnography to be relevant to others, to a generalized public, to other communities of experts, to subjects themselves, perhaps as much as it is relevant to their own disciplinary projects and problems. Furthermore, in many arenas, to do good ethnography today requires placing the practices and cultures of other kinds of experts, whom the anthropologist might otherwise treat collegially, within the bounds of fieldwork itself, as subjects like any other. This requires that anthropologists ally with or take seriously in the production of their own knowledge the expert or practical knowledge of others. In the resulting collaborations that define the field of ethnographic research, there must thus be an explicit negotiation of authority that might involve a clash of norms for producing knowledge, in which a sense of the tempo at which ideas are produced and elaborated and things become known with more or less certainty is a key factor. And, finally, to do good ethnography today is to be critically self-aware that ethnographic findings and knowledge are offered in a complex zone of representations from which they cannot be absolutely distinguished. How to insert ethnography within zones of anticipated reception, debate, and overlapping modes of similar knowledge production is increasingly becoming part of what constitutes good ethnography, as well as of the conception of what is to be included and done within the 'field' bounded as fieldwork. Here, too, the timing and pacing of ethnography in relation to the often quicker studies characteristic of alternative modes of representation of what is happening in the realm of a common object of interest are crucial factors in affecting the self-confidence and authority of ethnography as it massively enters into the study of the contemporary. The following are three related sources from which temporal challenges to the norm of patience in the enterprise of anthropological ethnography arise.

The Desire to Be Relevant

During the 1980s and 1990s, anthropology, among other disciplines, was strongly influenced in topics, concepts, and styles of research by the waves of critical interdisciplinary fashion, focused on the study of culture, that first explored the idea of the postmodern and then settled into projects of scholarship under the label of 'cultural studies'. Cultural studies, in particular (perhaps in atonement for the apparent apolitical sins of postmodernism), constructed a distinct persona for the academic scholar and a rhetoric for inquiry that emphasized relevance and the activist voice and potential of research. The idea that such a movement could and should generate public intellectuals out of academic careers—at least in the United States, and certainly in a world that is increasingly transnational—has been avidly debated, giving a sense of purpose to all varieties of left-liberal scholarship that have been supported by the interdisciplinary movements of recent years.

Anthropology always had this sort of liberal commitment and spirit in its professional culture, even though it was only marginally expressed in its conformity to the scientist rhetorics in the heyday of positivist social science. The influence of cultural studies, then, only released into the designs of fieldwork and ethnographic writing, and the way that they were evaluated, what was already deeply embedded in the professional culture of anthropology.

The anthropology of the contemporary became driven by the same issues that defined NGOs, social movements, journalism, and left-liberal commentaries on the unfolding of distinctive events in the United States and elsewhere, in a world that was conceived to be globalizing. In the absence of a defined past or project for this activist-inflected research within anthropology itself, the desire for a publicly relevant anthropology has become even stronger. Yet, after all the years of critical thinking about the nature of public spheres, it is perhaps naive to think that anthropologists could still hope to inform a general public, the symbolic capital of which is the op-ed piece on the editorial pages of leading papers or catching the attention of major policy makers. More realistically, anthropology is increasingly accountable to, and defines its forms of knowledge in relation to, the specific publics for its work that are created by the activity of ethnographic research itself. These are often extended and far-reaching publics, but they are at least defined specifically by how a project of ethnographic research touches them. These are the sorts of publics to which anthropological research could aspire to be relevant, by the reactions it receives in the forms by which it produces and circulates its knowledge.

It is not that ethnography does not have unique things to say to the constituencies defined by the sites of its research. The problem rather is in the belated forms in which it produces its results, still oriented authoritatively to a professional readership. And in this, the pacing and tempo by which ethnography is produced still conforms to the traditional norm of taking one's (almost unlimited) time. While the resulting anxiety in the production of ethnography is not as apparent as in the frenzy of activist cultural studies writing to keep up with the events it would like to comment relevantly upon (events that are almost always preceded or surrounded by lucid and penetrating treatments in other media), the same current desire for relevance pressures the temporality of patience prominent in the identity of being an ethnographer. Perhaps the saving grace in this conceit and ambition to matter more now is that anthropologists at least keep in close touch with the more realistic specific publics for their work as defined by the ethnographic research process. They listen to them first as subjects, informants, and collaborators in order to produce their own knowledge. Thus, ethnographers experience the anxiety of belatedness strictly within the bounds of spaces defined by the research process itself. At least this makes such an anxiety manageable and perhaps even productive within the specific pattern of relations defined by contemporary ethnographic research itself.

Anthropological Ethnography and Expert Modes of Knowledge

These days, an ethnographer is most pointedly aware of the slowness of her work when she encounters someone in the field to whose ideas and perspectives she attaches great importance for her own (a veritable collaborative relationship), but whose use and valuing of such perspectives and ideas is of a very different, and quicker, temporal order than hers. The dependence on relationships with such de facto counterparts, I would argue, is ever more common in ethnographic projects that move among an assemblage of sites and persons in an anthropology of the contemporary. It is not that ethnographers make such experts or specialists involved with their research the object of study (as in some ethnography of the culture of expertise-scientists, consultants, lawyers, activists, corporate executives, etc.), or else consider them colleagues collateral to their research, out of bounds of the field. Rather, they actually seek permissions, authority, overviews, and eventually engaged critiques for their research through and from them. Often, it is through relations with such persons and their cooperation that the ethnographer enters the field and defines her own project of inquiry within it. Such approximate counterparts in the field are subjects of the research, but ultimately not its object. At various times they serve differentially as its patrons, partners, and subjects. We have as yet few descriptions in memoirs and published discussions of recent fieldwork dependent on such figures (but see Rabinow 1999). However, they define the collaborations that make good ethnography of the present feasible. Inside these relationships occurs the mesh, and often clash, of temporalities that define the valorization of certain kinds of interpretations and reflections and their expression. For example, the consultant or lawyer counterpart of the ethnographer may retail or dispose of a shared good idea, an interesting insight, or a useful concept far more quickly than would the ethnographer who might want to hold onto it, make it endure, give it a more central thematic place in the developing research than would her counterparts. These conflicts of temporalities are worked out in many ways in fieldwork and are often covered up in ethnographic writing, but there are as yet no strategies that anthropologists have discussed for dealing with this aspect of these key collaborative relationships of ethnographic work. The noticeable residue of this predicament of fieldwork is one telling dimension of the ethnographer's anxiety about being slow to which I am drawing attention.

Ethnography within Complex Zones of Overlapping Representations

Recently, a Chicana graduate student of mine who was seeking a subject for her dissertation fieldwork that addressed life on and across the border of Mexico aånd the United States discovered the complexity of the used clothes business as a transnational, transcultural activity with many actors, sites, and diverse cultural codings, unified in a single frame and rationale of business. She was excited about this activity as the focus of her dissertation fieldwork. Then she found a brilliant piece featured in a Sunday edition of the *New York Times* that provided a virtuoso treatment of this subject in a few pages. An ethnographic study on the topic could only be an elaboration of what this inspired journalism had already accomplished, with the aid of considerable resources (what I call a writing/research machine), much more concisely and more timely than ethnography is capable of. Placing a high value on originality in her work and considering carefully whether such a duplicate study over a much longer period of time would contribute significantly in the context of media and scholarship that treat the US-Mexican border as well as Chicano culture itself as a kind of social movement, the student decided to abandon her interest in developing dissertation research on this subject, with the idea of perhaps reprising it later as a component of a broader study of objects and symbols that flow across the border.

In any case, the situation of this student is typical of many anthropologists in formulating their research today, in particular scholars who are beginning their careers in the present professional culture for the production of ethnography that I have outlined—a professional culture that highly values recognition and response from outside its own disciplinary community and that has been deeply affected by the desire for relevance that I have described. Rarely does an anthropologist take up a topic or interest that has not already been more prominently and more promptly treated by other media, journalism being only the most common example. Nor can this field of already existing representations be bracketed and ignored in the name of disciplinary purpose, as might have been the case in the past. The challenge is to devise normal strategies to incorporate such zones or fields of representations and their modes of production within the boundaries of the 'field' of fieldwork, or at least ethnographers should have a clear and explicit understanding of how the work that they produce in its changing forms fits into the zones of representation that pre-exist and surround it.

And in this rethinking of the zones of reception of ethnography, or rather the incorporation of this kind of consideration into the explicit norms and forms of the doing of ethnography, the question of the relative slowness of ethnography—its tempo and pacing, and finally its belatedness—is foremost. How are ethnographers to become comfortable with their inevitable belatedness compared to the tempos and values involved in the rapid turnover of knowledge, concepts, and interpretations in the ecology of overlapping discourses in which any ethnographer of the contemporary finds herself today, during fieldwork and after producing writing from it?

Responses

Resisting the pressures to speed things up in the pursuit of ethnographic research is probably a good thing, or at least I think so. Even as ethnography changes its modus operandi and its identity, there is nothing to suggest that the valuing of a patient, deliberate norm of temporality will not continue to be necessary, although it might require a different sense of fulfillment as ethnography revises its accountabilities, ethics, and relevance amid diverse constituencies in any single project of research.

The bold and confident response would be to argue unequivocally that slowing things down and the benefits thereof are actually a contribution to domains of discussion and representation that need it. In itself, slowing things down would provide a strategy of mundane subversion that critical social science has always hoped for. This is precisely what subjects and discourses that are the object of ethnography need, and the strategy of critical anthropology is not so much to preach a particular counter-message, which is already likely to be expressed in some ambivalent form by subjects themselves within the scenes of fieldwork, but to explore patiently a cogent argument in ways that are probably not produced in the spaces and sites of fieldwork. Resolute slowness thus might create an effective and critical politics of knowledge by introducing what the distanced scholastic point of view otherwise allows outside the realms of practical consciousness. This is an attractive and self-confident response to an anxiety concerning the belatedness of ethnography, but it is also unrealistic about the extent to which the contrasting tempos of representation among the subjects and constituencies of ethnography challenge the authority and privilege of being slow. The critical virtues of being slow are a fine rationale for their work that members of the professional community of anthropologists may tell each other, but in the end does being slow have demonstrable critical effect and power among the constituencies of fieldwork?

A more defensive but equally attractive rationale for ethnography that is always slightly belated is that it works in historical time. This equally naive and hopeful view is that the ethnography is a historical document in the making whose true relevance lies in the future as part of an emerging archive. Suggesting this rationale grasps for the historian's freedom from the anxiety of belatedness by escaping the judgment of present relevance through deferral, even though many historians produce their accounts of the past with the present in mind (a motivation that is also unmentionable, at least in the routine rhetorics offered for historical research located in its own past time-space). In any case, dissolving a circumstantial belatedness—the result of the norms of practicing ethnography—into an alibi of historical perspective ignores the powerful motivation of a growing anthropology of the contemporary to be engaged with present and emergent processes unfolding and to be recognized as such.

Still, the way that an anthropology of the contemporary reflexively temporalizes itself—in both situating fieldwork and, more crucially, the writing that comes from it—does address the anxiety about belatedness and is a key to offering an appropriate authority for a deliberate, patient ethnography that is slower than a rapidly changing present or other kinds of modes of representing it. As Rabinow (2004) temporally characterizes the work of studying the coming of something new through contingent apparatuses and assemblages, the anthropologist is operating in fieldwork and writing in a time that encompasses the tripartite 'the recent past, the emergent, and the near future'. This suggests the usefulness of a device or strategy for conceptually creating the frame for a deliberate ethnographic process that 'buys time' at least and lessens the anxiety of belatedness of an ethnography of the present amid other kinds of overlapping representations that get there faster, so to speak, or keep up better with changes in the objects of study.

In his ethnography of the work of foreign correspondents, Ulf Hannerz (2003) subtly considers the technologies of investigation and writing of this kind of journalism in the frame of the related issues that have been raised about the craft of ethnography in recent decades. At one point, he also deals with the appropriate temporality for the more enduring accounts of the journalist working in an otherwise supremely ephemeral genre. Hannerz evokes Fernand Braudel's distinction of three time spans in the writing of history: there is event history, history of the long perspective (Braudel's own specialty), and, in between them, conjunctural history, or what Hannerz calls 'medium-term history', which covers a decade, a quarter-century, or a half-century. When figured in the recent past, this last distinction is the sort of history that allows the historian to approach the present while still retaining the privilege of distance, deliberateness, and patience that is accorded to the scholarly time-space of doing historical research. However, when this medium-term temporality is evoked within the ethnography of the contemporary, challenged by the need to reconceive the traditional norm of an unbounded slowness in producing classic ethnography in order to relieve the anxiety of belatedness, it becomes the sort of 'past-present-future' suggested by Rabinow. The historian's medium-term history still in the past is shifted a bit and mapped on to the 'becoming' time-space of the ethnography of the contemporary. It is this kind of conceptual resituating of ethnography that needs explicit treatment and experimentation in the design of fieldwork and ethnographic writing.

To return briefly to *Advocacy after Bhopal,* Fortun offers a skillful temporal architecture for her account that effectively defines the medium-term frame that negotiates the necessary slowness of ethnographic research with the threat of ethnography's permanent belatedness in relation to its object. Fortun powerfully stimulates the memory of the reader for her purposes. She opens with a striking reminder of what happened in 1984, the year of the Bhopal disaster, describing a diverse and carefully orchestrated list of events. The reader's fading memory of that year is restimulated and oriented to the past-present-emergent time-space in which Fortun's account operates. For her purposes, and effectively for the reader's, the contemporary *is* this conceptually created time-space, and in my view this invention works effectively to create time for ethnography without the anxiety or judgment of belatedness. In Fortun's text, both as an event and as a textual object, Bhopal is as relevant as it was in 1984. Fortun's sustained device is partly a circumstance of her continually deferring the moment of genre ethnographic writing until the time of tenure consideration that I described, but it nonetheless defines one effective strategy as a response to the bind of producing an ethnography of the contemporary that I have focused upon in this afterword.

In sum, then, it appears that the complex of rhetorical strategies around the condition of 'being there' in classic ethnographic research that were so thoroughly exposed and critiqued as the sources of authority for ethnography as a knowledge form by the writing culture critique of the 1980s is being supplanted at present by strategies for dealing with the temporal challenges of doing ethnography with a necessary deliberateness in changing time-spaces of fieldwork and writing. Thus, 'being there' is perhaps no longer as important as 'taking one's time' in sustaining an authority for ethnography as a knowledge form among its complex constituencies in fieldwork and zones of overlapping representation in its reception.

Acknowledgments

This afterword continues themes first explored in an essay titled "The Unbearable Slowness of Being an Anthropologist Now: Notes on a Contemporary Anxiety in the Making of Ethnography," published in 2003 by the journal *Xcp: Cross-Cultural Poetics*.

George Marcus is Chancellor's Professor in the Department of Anthropology at the University of California Irvine and the founder of the university's Center for Ethnography. He has conducted ethnographic studies of elites and elite cultures in a variety of settings. Since the mid-1990s, he has been working with the idea of 'multi-sited ethnography' and experiments with the classic form of anthropology's method of inquiry and its teaching to meet the challenge of new topics and contexts of research.

Notes

1. The recent, favored post-colonial framework for historicizing mainstream ethnographic research has accommodated a deliberate, patient ethnography of the present by providing a meaningful long view to understanding the present in the traditional regions of anthropological expertise.
2. The volume *Global Assemblages* by Aihwa Ong and Stephen Collier (2005) is representative of this trend in research.

References

Bourdieu, Pierre. 1990. "The Scholastic Point of View." *Cultural Anthropology* 5, no. 4: 380–391.

Clifford, James, and George E. Marcus. 1986. *Writing Culture: The Poetics and Politics of Ethnography*. Berkeley: University of California Press.

Fabian, Johannes. 1983. *Time and the Other: How Anthropology Makes Its Object*. New York: Columbia University Press.

Fortun, Kim. 2001. *Advocacy after Bhopal: Environmentalism, Disaster, New Global Orders*. Chicago: University of Chicago Press.

Hannerz, Ulf. 2003. *Foreign News: Exploring the World of Foreign Correspondents*. Chicago: University of Chicago Press.

Ong, Aihwa, and Stephen J. Collier, eds. 2005. *Global Assemblages: Technology, Politics, and Ethics as Anthropological Problems*. Oxford: Blackwell.

Rabinow, Paul. 1999. "American Moderns: On Sciences and Scientists." Pp. 305–333 in *Critical Anthropology Now: Unexpected Contexts, Shifting Constituencies, Changing Agendas*, ed. George E. Marcus. Santa Fe: School of American Research Press.

Rabinow, Paul. 2001. *French DNA: Trouble in Purgatory*. Chicago: University of Chicago Press.

Rabinow, Paul. 2004. *Anthropos Today: Reflections on Modern Equipment*. Princeton, NJ: Princeton University Press.

Rabinow, Paul, and George E. Marcus with James D. Faubion and Tobias Rees. 2008. *Designs for an Anthropology of the Contemporary*. Durham, NC: Duke University Press.

INDEX

Gell, Alfred, 82, 96
Georgia, the Republic of, 50–63
gestalt, temporal, 101
gift, 36, 38, 39, 40, 41, 45, 56
Gobi Desert, 131–133, 135, 136
gossip, 87, 100, 114
Gregorian calendar, 98
Gupta, Akhil, 5

habitus, 67, 96
Hannerz, Ulf, 153
health care management, 80, 81, 83, 89
    new public management (NPM) of, 81
    and time management, 80
    See also planning
Hedman, Nils, 91n1
historicity, 7, 71
Hodges, Mark, 122, 137
hollowing out, 134–138
home (as opposed to 'field'), 2, 3, 5
hope, 50–63
    against life, 52
    method of, 53
    as the 'not yet', 57
    as praxis, 56
    as subject of description, 59
Husserl, Edmund, 124, 125

India, 15n1
individuality, 56
    individual as projectile, 56
    individual intimacy, 119
    individual life, 60
infrastructure, 123, 126
Ingold, Tim, 82, 91n4
initiation, 98, 104
    temporal and gradual, 106
institutionalization, 35, 36, 42
interaction, 82, 106, 111–114
    social, 8, 34, 42, 44, 45, 106, 128
intuition, 132, 136
    ethnographic, 132
invisibility, 82–87, 89

James, Wendy, 16n3
James, William, 10
Jensen, Casper Bruun, 92n12

kalsa, 73
Kapferer, Bruce, 8
kastam, 35, 36, 69, 73–75

knowledge, 80, 85, 87
    ethnographic, 82, 125
    politics of, 148, 152
    tradition, 71

Langer, Susanne, 105, 108n3
Latour, Bruno, 81–90, 91n6, 92n12
Law, John, 92n12
Leach, Edmund, 100
liminal phase, 97, 98, 100
Lipan, 40, 41, 47n4
location, 2, 5, 6, 9, 35, 44, 46
    political, 5
Lorengau, 40, 42

Malinowski, Bronisław, 64
Manchester School, the, 7
Manus Province, 35, 45, 72, 73
Manus Provincial Administration, 42
Maputo, 126–127
Marcus, George, 5, 65
Matad, 132–135
materiality, 7, 34, 36, 39, 44
materialization. *See* materiality
Mead, George Herbert, 66–67, 77n1
Mead, Margaret, 3
meaning, 67, 103
    lack of, 97, 103
    making, 22, 58
    of a story, 58, 111
memory, 11, 15n1, 22, 41, 68, 80, 101, 111, 124, 146, 154
mess, 82, 84–85, 90. *See also* clutter
method. *See* ethnographic analysis; ethnographic method; ethnography; fieldwork
micrometeorology, 24–25
Mills, David, 16n3
Miyazaki, Hiro, 53, 56, 57, 59
mobility, 44, 87
Mongolia, 131–139
montage, 57
Mozambique, 126–131
multiplicity, 82, 84, 85, 87–89
Mumford, Lewis, 91n4
Munn, Nancy, 16n4

NGOs, 119, 133, 149
nomads, 131–133

oil extraction, 131–135
open-endedness, 60